THE PRACTICAL
WRITER

FIFTH EDITION

THE PRACTICAL WRITER
Paragraph to Theme

Edward P. Bailey, Jr.
Philip A. Powell

Harcourt Brace Jovanovich College Publishers

Fort Worth   Philadelphia   San Diego   New York
Orlando   Austin   San Antonio
Toronto   Montreal   London   Sydney   Tokyo

Publisher	Ted Buchholz
Acquisitions Editor	Michael Rosenberg
Developmental Editor	Stacy Schoolfield
Project Editor	Vicki Young
Production Manager	Ken Dunaway
Art & Design Supervisor	Vicki McAlindon Horton
Text Designer	Rita Naughton
Cover Designer	Brenda Chambers

Library of Congress Cataloging-in-Publication Data
Bailey, Edward P.
    The practical writer : paragraph to theme / Edward P. Bailey, Jr.,
Philip A. Powell. — 5th ed.
      p.   cm.
    Includes index.
    ISBN 0-03-055544-2
    1. English language—Rhetoric.   I. Powell, Philip A.   II. Title.
PE1408.B226   1991b
808′.042—dc20   91-17937
                                               CIP

ISBN: 0-03-055544-2

Requests for permission to make copies of any part of the work should be mailed to: Permissions Department, Harcourt Brace Jovanovich, Publishers, 8th Floor, Orlando, FL 32887

Address editorial correspondence to: 301 Commerce Street, Suite 3700, Fort Worth, TX 76102

Address orders to: 6277 Sea Harbor Drive, Orlando, FL 32887
1-800-782-4479, or 1-800-433-0001 (in Florida)

Printed in the Unirted States of America

3 4 016 9 8 7 6 5 4 3

Acknowledgments

P. 202   *Readers' Guide to Periodical Literature*, 1989, p. 368. Copyright © 1989 by The H.W. Wilson Company. Material reproduced with permission of the editor.

P. 203   *Social Sciences Index*, Vol. 15, 1989, p. 227. Copyright © 1989 by The H.W. Wilson Company. Material reproduced by permission of the publisher.

P. 204   From *Psychological Abstracts*, Vol. 76, No. 3 (1989), p. 831.

P. 206   PAIS—Public Affairs Information Service, Inc.

Preface to
The Practical Writer,
5th Edition

We've made some significant changes in this edition—all the while remaining true to the original concept of the book.

First, we've shown connections *The Practical Writer* has to the writing students will be called upon to do once they finish freshman English. So we've added a section called "Practical Writing" to many chapters in the book. In other words, we point out that *The Practical Writer* does, in fact, have many practical applications. The end of Chapter 1 gives you a good idea of what we mean.

Next we've added three chapters:

- *Chapter 6, "Tips on the Writing Process."* This chapter helps students understand a good writing process. There's also a section on the value of computers in that process.

- *Chapter 10, "Techniques of Layout."* This chapter shows the value of headings, indented lists, and short paragraphs. We then show how students can apply these techniques to the five-paragraph essay. This chapter dramatically changes the appearance (for the better) of five-paragraph essays. It also establishes some practical ties with the world of writing outside freshman English.

- *Chapter 22, "Organizing Your Thoughts and Support."* This chapter helps students move through these key steps in the process of writing their research papers.

We've also revised many exercises in the book, especially in Part Seven, "Expression."

We'd like to express our appreciation to our editors at Harcourt Brace Jovanovich, Publishers: Stacy Schoolfield, Michael Rosenberg, and Vicki Young. They've helped us develop the new edition and offered good advice along the way.

We'd also like to express our thanks to our reviewers: Julie Bertch, Rio Salado Community College; Paul Devlin, Ferris State University; Beatrice Egle, Pan American University; Valerie Faith, University of Maryland; Kelly Hoxmier, University of Dubuque; Kathleen Tickner, Brevard Community College.

February 1991

Edward P. Bailey, Jr.   Marymount University
Philip A. Powell   Burke, Virginia

Contents

SECTION TWO

Beyond the Model Essay   **117**

SECTION THREE

Improving Your Punctuation and Expression   **279**

PART SEVEN
Expression   **321**

How This Book Works

The Practical Writer is intended for typical first-year college students, who perhaps lack knowledge but don't lack intelligence. We assume that these students can learn quickly and well from a step-by-step approach to the fundamentals, good examples to follow, and carefully designed exercises.

We begin by presenting the fundamentals (organization, support, unity, coherence)—one at a time—in a tightly structured one-paragraph essay. The paragraph, we've found, is a unit large enough for students to demonstrate their understanding of the fundamentals and small enough for them to work toward mastery. At this point, we don't overwhelm them while they're learning the fundamentals by making them struggle to find support; instead, we ask them to write about personal experiences and the people and things they know well. We encourage them to be colorful, interesting, and—above all—specific.

We then move through several longer stages of writing to a 1000-to-2000-word research paper. By the time students complete the research block, they can write a serious paper—the kind they will have to write in other college courses and beyond them—with a less mechanical structure than we required earlier. We still offer a model, of course, but it becomes a guide rather than a goal.

The last two topics of our book, punctuation and expression, are not part of the step-by-step approach. These chapters can be studied any time, whenever your students are ready for them. They are not typical handbook material, though, because we've been careful to select only what first-year students need to learn, leaving out the skills they probably know and those they're not yet ready to apply.

Finally, we try to avoid the "scholarly" style of writing and speak personally to the students, as though we're talking to them in class.

A Model for Writing

Part One

The One-Paragraph Essay (Stage I)

This part of the book shows you how to write a good one-paragraph essay.

Although you rarely see one-paragraph essays in publications, you'll find them remarkably handy for improving your writing:

- One obvious advantage is that they are short—so you can spend your study time writing a really good one.

- At the same time, they're long enough for you to practice some fundamentals of writing.

- Finally, what you'll learn about one-paragraph essays transfers nicely to larger themes and even research papers.

In Part One, you'll learn about the simplest one-paragraph essay, which we call Stage I. Later, in Part Two, you'll study the organization for a slightly more sophisticated one-paragraph essay, which we'll call Stage II.

Part One presents a very tightly structured model for a paragraph. You may wonder if all good writers follow such a structure for persuasive writing. No, of course not. This structure is not *the* good way to write a paragraph, but it is *one* good way. And this way has a very real advantage: it automatically gives your paper organization so that you have one less thing to worry about. You then can concentrate on learning the other fundamentals that experienced writers already know.

3

And by working constantly with this model paragraph, you will learn organization too, the easy way.

Support for the paragraph's main idea is also easy. Right now we don't care if you know how to find facts in the library. We're much more concerned that you can recognize and use good support once you find it. So we make finding it simple. You don't need to go any further than your own mind: you can use either your experiences or your imagination for support. As a result, you can have fun with your one-paragraph essays. They can be intriguing and perhaps humorous.

Writing doesn't have to be dull!

Chapter 1

Overview of the One-Paragraph Essay (Stage I)

You may already be familiar with a common organization for good writing:

- Tell the readers what you're going to tell them.
- Tell it to them.
- Then tell them what you just told them.

This chapter shows you how to apply that organization to the one-paragraph essay. The one-paragraph essay has three main parts:

- The first sentence states the idea you want your readers to accept. We call this a *topic sentence.*
- All middle sentences present specific support for that idea.
- The last sentence rewords the topic sentence—to remind your readers of the point you've just made.

Let's look at those three points another way—as a model.

THE MODEL FOR THE ONE-PARAGRAPH ESSAY (STAGE I)

The model looks like this:

Topic Sentence

    Specific Support
    Specific Support
    Specific Support

Reworded Topic Sentence

Now let's look at a "real" paragraph—one that follows the model we've just shown you:

Topic Sentence —— The Boundary Waters Canoe Area, a wilderness park in northern Minnesota, is a refreshing change from the city. Away from the din of civilization, I have canoed silently across its waters for an entire afternoon and not heard a *Specific Support* —— single noise except for an occasional birdcall and the sound of waves beating against the shore. Also, my *Specific Support* —— partner and I were able to navigate our way through a string of five lakes by following a campfire's scent *Specific Support* —— drifting through the pure air. Most refreshing, the park is so magnificently beautiful that even the voyageurs of old *Reworded Topic Sentence* —— were willing to endure its hardships in order to settle there. The Boundary Waters Canoe Area is thus an ideal place to clear your head of the congestion of urban life.

Here's an outline of that paragraph:

Topic Sentence The Boundary Waters Canoe Area is a refreshing change.
Specific Support quietness
Specific Support purity of the air
Specific Support beauty
Reworded Topic Sentence It's an ideal place to clear your head of the congestion of urban life.

The structure of the paragraph is absolutely clear, unmistakable, obvious. For some writing (fiction, personal essays), an obvious organization is not necessarily an asset. But for writing that takes care of the day-to-day business of the world, an obvious organization is an asset.

In fact, for most of the daily reading we do, the content is challenging enough. Who needs an organization that's hard to follow?

As writers, then, we should take into account what works best for our readers. Getting right to the point with a topic sentence and then providing the support is a very good way to keep our readers on track.

ANOTHER EXAMPLE

Here's another sample one-paragraph essay. Notice it, too, follows the model perfectly:

Topic Sentence ——— { Even though I have never really lived there, going to my grandmother's farm always seems like coming home.

Specific Support ——— { The feeling begins as soon as I cross the threshold of that quaint, little house and tumble into the arms of waiting aunts and cousins. The sense of welcome overwhelms me.

Specific Support ——— { Then there are the cozy rooms—the ceilings don't seem higher than six feet—with their crackling fireplaces that make me want to snuggle down into the feather-stuffed chairs.

Specific Support ——— { But the memory that always lasts the longest is the smell of Grandma's biscuits and pastries cooking in her coke-fed stove.

Reworded Topic Sentence ——————— { Yes, only in Grandma's house do I feel the warmth and welcome that always seem like coming home.

Again, let's outline it:

> *Topic Sentence*   Going to my grandmother's farm seems like com-
> ing home.
> *Specific Support*   greeting by relatives
> *Specific Support*   coziness of house
> *Specific Support*   smell of home-cooked food
> *Reworded Topic Sentence*   Visiting Grandma's seems like coming
> home.

Notice that each of these sample paragraphs has three items of specific support. Sometimes five or six items are necessary to be persuasive; other times, one long example will do.

Although the sample paragraphs in the first two or three chapters of this book are good, they are intentionally fairly simple so you can easily see their basic organization. But if you don't fully understand the one-paragraph essay yet, don't worry. The other chapters in Part One explain further.

Also, you can find a checklist for the one-paragraph essay immediately following Chapter 8.

PRACTICAL WRITING

The one-paragraph essay, simple as it is, has significant value in school—and beyond.

So far, the one-paragraph essay may seem like only a teaching tool. However, since we wrote the first edition of this book, we've done a great deal of work with business and government writers—lawyers, accountants, auditors, doctors, bankers, military officers, government analysts, computer experts, political scientists, scientific researchers, and others of similar skill. Our main task has been to help these people—usually bright, educated, and successful professionals—express their ideas clearly.

One consistent message we tell them is this: readers in the busy world of work strongly prefer to have the main point up front for almost everything they read. In fact, if they don't find it there—right away—they often skip to the back and start hunting for it.

When you're reading a report from your doctor, don't you want the diagnosis up front instead of three pages later, after all the lab results and all the possible illnesses you might have, but don't?

Suppose you work in an office and have a five-page report to read and comment on for your boss. Where do you, as the reader, want the main point? Do you want it at the end? Or at the beginning?

If you're like most readers, you prefer the main point at the beginning. Otherwise, all the facts and supporting logic will only confuse you.

And just as the main point comes at the beginning of good business writing, the topic sentence (or *main point*) comes at the beginning of our model paragraph.

Let's look at an example of poor business writing—a memo that delays the main point (a recommendation) until the end. Notice how confused you get trying to struggle with all the details without a main point to guide you.

Memo With the Recommendation Last

```
From: Alex Tynel
To:   Maribeth Wyvill
Date: July 7

The copying machine was broken for three days this
month--June 2, 5, and 9. During that time, nobody was
able to do any of the photocopying crucial to our
work. Also, it had routine maintenance two other days
this month--June 15 and 30. Then, too, nobody could
use the machine. Finally, Neal and Sharon had a large
photocopying project that kept others from using the
machine for three other days--June 1, 3, and 4. I
recommend, therefore, that we buy a second copying
machine because the one we have can't meet our needs.
```

It's easy to get lost in the facts of that paragraph, isn't it? If you were the boss—the one deciding whether to spend the money—you'd certainly have to read that memo *twice:* The first time you'd be hunting for the recommendation. The second time, with the recommendation in mind, you'd read to see if the facts served as effective justification.

Writers can't expect their readers to re-read. And few bosses like re-reading, either.

So wouldn't the memo be better with the recommendation up front, like this?

```
          Memo With the Recommendation First

From: Alex Tynel
To:   Maribeth Wyvill
Date: July 7

I recommend we buy a second copying machine because
the one we have can't meet our needs. It was broken
for three days this month--June 2, 5, and 9. During
that time, nobody was able to do any of the
photocopying crucial to our work. Also, it had routine
maintenance two other days this month--June 15 and 30.
Then, too, nobody could use the machine. Finally, Neal
and Sharon had a large photocopying project that kept
others from using the machine for three other
days--June 1, 3, and 4. For these reasons, I strongly
urge that we buy a second copier.
```

As you can see, the memo now takes the shape of the model we gave you at the beginning of this chapter.

Practical Writing

Throughout the book, we'll point to the connections between our models and good business writing. The connections are strong and important.

What you learn here can be useful not just in college, but also on the job.

There's another place the model for a one-paragraph essay has value: for key paragraphs *within* longer pieces of complex writing. Reports, memos, and letters in "the real world" are almost always longer than a single paragraph. But there are often places within those documents where you can use the model.

So the one-paragraph essay is a valuable little tool.

You may have gotten the impression so far that this is a book on business writing. Not at all—the emphasis throughout is on writing traditional to freshman English.

But we do think of this as a *practical* book—one that can help you many times, in one way or another, throughout your life. That's why we try to show connections beyond freshman English. And that's also why we've named the book *The Practical Writer.*

EXERCISES

A. Outline the following paragraph the same way we outlined the two paragraphs in the chapter:

Three common electric distractions on my desk waste my precious study time at night. The worst distraction is my clock, constantly humming to remind me how little time I actually have. Another interruption is the "high-quality" fluorescent desk lamp that sometimes buzzes, flickers—and then goes out. And, finally, consider that fascinating little invention, the computer, that not only does all kinds of complicated math problems, but also challenges me to games and helps me write letters home. After stopping to worry about the time, fix my lamp, and play with the computer, I am too tired to study, so I just go to bed.

Topic Sentence _____

   Specific Support _____

   Specific Support _____

   Specific Support _____

Reworded Topic Sentence _____

B. Outline this paragraph:

Old, stiff, and weathered, by grandfather's hands show the strenuous way of life he has known as a working man. Many hot summer days tilling the stubborn soil of West Texas have left their lasting mark in the form of a deep and permanent tan. Grandpa's hands are also covered with calluses—begun, perhaps, when he split cordwood for two dollars a day in an effort to pull his family through the Great Depression. Most striking, though, are the carpenter's scars he has collected from the days of building his house, barn, and fence and from the unending repair jobs that still occupy his every day. Although small and battered, Grandpa's hands bring back images of a time when men and women worked from dawn to dusk just to survive, a difficult but respected way of life.

Topic Sentence _____

   Specific Support _____

   Specific Support _____

   Specific Support _____

Reworded Topic Sentence _____

C. Outline this paragraph:

The East Wing of the National Art Gallery in Washington, DC, is a showplace of modern art. Inside, it houses collections of such artists as Picasso and Matisse, artists well known for their nonrepresentational works. Hanging from the ceiling is a mobile, normally thought of as a dangling toy parents hang above their infant's crib. This one, however, is several stories high and much more impressive to the parents (and children, too). Even the building is in keeping with its contents: it has lots of glass, open spaces, and strange angles and corners. For modern art, this wing of the gallery is an excellent place to visit.

Topic Sentence _____

   Specific Support _____

   Specific Support _____

   Specific Support _____

Reworded Topic Sentence _____

D. Now outline the business memo you saw earlier in the chapter.

I recommend we buy a second copying machine because the one we have can't meet our needs. It was broken for three days this month—June 2, 5, and 9. During that time, nobody was able to do any of the photocopying crucial to our work. Also, it had routine maintenance two other days this month—June 15 and 30. Then, too, nobody could use the machine. Finally, Neal and Sharon had a large photocopying project that kept others from using the machine for three other days—June 1, 3, and 4. For these reasons, I strongly urge that we buy a second copier.

Topic Sentence _____

   Specific Support _____

   Specific Support _____

   Specific Support _____

Reworded Topic Sentence _____

Chapter 2

Support: Examples, Statistics, Statements by Authorities

The first sentence in our model paragraph is the topic sentence, but let's save that for the next chapter. Instead, we'll start with support. Once you understand support—and how specific it must be—you'll understand much more easily how to write a good topic sentence.

This chapter talks about three different kinds of support:

- examples
- statistics
- statements by authorities

EXAMPLES

"The secret to good writing—the real secret," many professional writers would tell you, "is using examples."

"The biggest problem with undergraduate writing—the one that almost all students have," many teachers would tell you, "is that they don't know how to use examples."

Here's a chance to solve a problem by learning a secret. Let's begin by talking about two different kinds of examples: *quick examples* and *narrative examples.*

Quick Examples

You already know from your everyday experience what a quick example is: *a quick example is one instance, one occurrence of whatever you're talking about.*

If you're talking about the meals available at fast-food restaurants, a hamburger is one example—one of several possibilities. You could have named fried chicken, tacos, roast beef sandwiches, or (at the waterfront in San Francisco) even sourdough bread and crabs.

For a quick example to be effective, it must be very specific. If you want to show that Constance Dilettante can't stick with anything, don't say, "She changes her mind a lot." Don't even just say, "She changed her major frequently in college." Be still more specific: "She changed her major from philosophy to computer science to animal husbandry—all in one semester."

Do quick examples really make any difference? We think so. Consider the following:

Sentences Without Quick Examples

There were many expensive cars in the school's parking lot during the football game.

*   *   *

You could tell spring was here because of all the flowers in bloom.

*   *   *

Why do lawyers use words that mean one thing to them and something entirely different in ordinary English?

Sentences With Quick Examples

There were many expensive cars in the school's parking lot during the football game—Mercedes convertibles, low-slung Porsches, red Ferraris.

*   *   *

You could tell spring was here because of all the flowers in bloom: tulips of all colors, yellow daffodils, and (if you want to call them flowers) even a few early dandelions.

*   *   *

Why do lawyers use words that mean one thing to them and something entirely different in ordinary English (words like *party* and *action* and *motion*)?

See the difference that quick examples make? They take something rather abstract—cars, flowers, legal words—and make them much more concrete. It's almost as though the abstract words don't really communicate, don't really find a place to lodge in the brain cells. But the more concrete words—Mercedes, tulip, party—do.

Using Quick Examples

When should you use quick examples? How often do you like to have such examples when you're a reader? Pretty often, right? And that's how often you should use them when you're a writer.

Quick examples, of course, don't have to come at the ends of sentences. You could have a paragraph, probably one that's very short, that depended entirely on quick examples:

A Paragraph Depending on Quick Examples

Chairs come in many different designs. Easy chairs—designed for people who like to lounge back—usually have lots of padding, perhaps a curved back, and comfortable armrests. Straight chairs usually have minimal padding, a vertical back, and sometimes no armrests. Some contemporary computer chairs, kneelers, have padding for the knees and seat, but no back at all and no armrests. So, depending on their purposes, chairs differ quite a bit.

The topic of that paragraph may not be exciting, but the quick examples—easy chair, straight chair, kneeler—certainly communicate much more than the abstract beginning: *Chairs come in many different designs.*

Narrative Examples

A quick example is just one instance, one occurrence. But a *narrative example* is a brief story. A narrative example can provide effective support, so we really emphasize it in this book.

Sometimes you really want to emphasize an idea to help your readers understand what you mean. So you decide to run a little 'motion picture'; that is, you decide to tell a story that will help your readers visualize what you are saying—as though they are watching a short motion picture rather than simply reading words.

For example, if you want to show that shark hunting is dangerous, you can give a quick example by saying, "A friend of mine was once maimed while hunting sharks." Or you could really make your point by telling the story:

With a Narrative Example

I still have nightmares about the time last June when Rocky and I were scuba diving off the coast of Baja California. Rocky spotted a great white

> shark and tried to shoot it with his spear gun. As he fired, the shark spun suddenly toward him. Before I knew what happened. . . . [Then—poor Rocky—finish the story.]

Can you see how a narrative example really drives the point home?

A narrative example, then, is a specific incident (usually with names, dates, other details). It is not the *kind* of thing that can happen (not "sometimes people get hurt when they try to shoot sharks with spear guns"). It is the story of something that *did* happen (June, Rocky, Baja California, great white shark).

Let's examine another narrative example. You might find a paragraph like this in a magazine like *Time* or *Newsweek:*

Another Narrative Example

Alison Marks, a twenty-three-year-old graduate student in architecture at the University of Colorado, had a blood pressure of 180/120 in February. Her doctor prescribed Elavil, which Alison took for three months until she became so busy with exams that she found taking medicine too much trouble. After exams, she still neglected her medicine. As a result, her blood pressure rose so sharply that in September she was rushed to the hospital with a stroke.

Do we care that this patient was an architecture student, or that she was twenty-three, or that she was named Alison Marks? Yes, somehow we do. Alison becomes more real to us, someone we can sympathize with. And, because Alison's case becomes believable and typical, we begin to be convinced that people with high blood pressure should take their medicine. The narrative example has helped convince us.

Now let's apply what we've learned about narrative examples to the one-paragraph essay. Suppose you are sitting in your room trying to write your first college English paper—the one for this course. You remember your professor's words: "I want to see examples—*specific* examples—whatever else you do on this paper." She's told you to write about something that distracts you.

You look aimlessly around the room, your eyes suddenly brighten, and you slap down this sentence:

■   My roommate distracts me when I try to study.

Now you need some examples. Let's see: she has that record player going again, she's smacking her gum again, and you remember all those dumb questions she asks every few minutes. Here goes:

First Try

Although my roommate is a helpful companion at times, she is a distracting nuisance whenever I try to study. Throughout the evening, her stereo blares in my ears. Even worse, she insists on smacking her gum. She also interrupts me with questions that have nothing to do with homework. At any other time, my roommate is a friend, but while I'm studying, she's my greatest enemy.

"Pretty good," you say. "I think I'll show it to my roommate to see what she—on second thought. . . ."

Now, suppose you're sitting in your room a couple of days later, ego deflated by a bad grade, trying to rewrite that paper. Your examples seemed specific enough to you—record player, gum, questions—but they obviously weren't. You used quick examples when a narrative example might have been more effective.

Instead of presenting the *kinds* of things your roommate does to distract you, you could have used a narrative example—a story of something that actually did happen at a particular time and a particular place.

In other words, you could have talked about one specific study period; you could have told us not just that her stereo was going—you could have told us what record she was playing. You could have told us what kind of gum she was chewing. You even could have told us what specific "dumb" questions she asked you. In other words, you could have written this paragraph:

Better Version With a Narrative Example

Although my roommate is a helpful companion at times, she is a distracting nuisance whenever I try to study. Just last Wednesday night, Anna decided to spend the evening playing her "classic" Bob Dylan records. While I was trying desperately to integrate a math function, all I could hear was that the answer was somewhere "blowin' in the wind." Even worse, the entire time Dylan was rasping away, Anna accompanied him by smacking and popping her Bazooka bubble gum. I'd finally given up on math and started my struggle with chemistry when she abruptly asked (loudly, of course, so I could hear her over the music), "Do you think any Cokes are left in the Coke machine?" My stomach started rumbling and my throat suddenly felt dry—even drier than the chemistry text I was trying to read. As I dropped the change into the Coke machine, I realized that although Anna is usually a friend, while I'm studying she is my greatest enemy.

Now we can picture you, Anna, and all those distractions. You've told us the *story* (a narrative example) of your evening trying to study, helping us to see you and feel your frustration. That's communication.

Remember the secret that all professional writers know: *examples.*

STATISTICS

Examples are an important form of support. They help convince your readers and make the essay more interesting. Examples alone, though, may not be enough. We need something else; we need some *numbers.* Who doesn't love numbers, trust them, believe in them? Give us a statistic we don't suspect is phony, and we are probably convinced right there. Alison Marks and her trouble with high blood pressure may move us emotionally, but we will more likely be persuaded by a medical report like this:

With Statistics

Recent statistics show convincingly that jogging is saving the lives of many Americans. Of the 12.5 million who jog at least 10 miles a week, 78 percent have a pulse rate and blood pressure lower than nonjoggers the same age have. Estimates indicate that these joggers can expect to live to an average age of 77—more than three years longer than the average age of their contemporaries. The lesson seems clear, doesn't it?

To be convincing, statistics must be unambiguous. We are not necessarily alarmed, for example, to hear that 47 of 54 football players were injured in a practice session because we have no way of knowing how serious the injuries were. Perhaps 46 of the players were treated with Band-Aids. We would become alarmed, however, to hear that 47 of 54 football players were hospitalized for at least one night following a practice session. The second statistic defines *injury* more clearly, so it is more convincing than the first.

STATEMENTS BY AUTHORITIES

The last kind of support we will consider in this chapter is the statement by an authority, a person who is in a position to know about something. If someone we trust tells us something, we just might believe him. But we do so because we trust *him:* his character, his judgment, and his knowledge of the subject.

We would never believe Alison Marks, the architecture student who forgot to take her pills, if she tells us that shark hunting is one of the safest sports, but we might listen to her if she tells us that patients with high blood pressure should take their medicine. We also might believe the president of the American Medical Association or a research specialist in high blood pressure or our family doctor—people who know what they're talking about.

Who are some people whose unsupported opinions about high blood pressure would not be convincing? We would not trust someone whose character, judgment, or knowledge of the subject is questionable.

We would not trust the unsupported opinion of the druggist convicted of selling overpriced drugs to people who did not need them anyway; we would not trust the doctor being investigated for gross incompetence by the American Medical Association; and we would not trust our roommate, who thinks blood pressure is measured by a thermometer. The first has doubtful character; the second, doubtful judgment; and the third, doubtful knowledge.

By the way, the use of authority is particularly important when you are presenting statistics. Remember all those impressive figures about people who jog? Guess where the numbers came from. For all you know (and, in fact, for all those statistics are worth), they came from Miss Fisher's sixth-grade creative writing class. The point, of course, is that unless the writer tells you the source of the statistics, you don't know whether you should trust them.

Here's a revision of that paragraph showing the use of authorities, both with and without statistics:

Authority and Statistics

Recent statistics show convincingly that jogging is saving the lives of many Americans. According to the Congressional Subcommittee on Physical Fitness, 78 percent of the 12.5 million people who jog at least 10 miles per week have a pulse rate and blood pressure lower than nonjoggers the same age have. This committee estimates that these joggers can expect to live to an average age of 77—more than three years longer than the average age of their contemporaries. Dr. Hans Corpuscle, chief adviser to the committee, says that "joggers are the healthiest single group of people in America today." The lesson seems clear, doesn't it?

COMBINED TYPES OF SUPPORT

A paragraph that uses one type of support—examples, maybe—is often convincing, but many good paragraphs contain several types: a couple of examples and some statistics, or a statement by an authority and an example, and so on.

The following paragraph attempts to show that people attend yard sales for entertainment. Can you identify the types of support?

Combined Support

Although you might think that most people attend yard sales for the bargains, the main reason they attend is for the entertainment they find there. For example, consider what happened to my family last summer when we held a yard sale to get rid of some old things before moving to a new place. Many people came, but few bought. Each new carload of people disgorged a new group that would while away an hour or so on a Saturday by caressing the sun-faded curtains, thumbing through ancient *National Geographic* magazines, and carefully considering sweaters eight sizes too small for them or anyone else in their group. Then the group would gather around a folded section of the classified ads and pick the next sale they'd visit. My suspicions about why those people came to our sale were confirmed a few months later by a survey I read in *Psychology Monthly*. The survey showed that seven of ten people who attended yard sales admitted they did so "just for the fun of it." The psychologist who conducted the survey then reached a conclusion I could have told him last summer: "The real bargain that people seek at yard sales, if only subconsciously, is not another frying pan or partially burned plastic spatula, but just a little weekend entertainment."

Notice that the statement by the authority is an effective rewording of the topic sentence, so no separate concluding sentence is necessary for this paragraph.

The above paragraph uses all three kinds of support—all of it invented by the writer. When you are inventing support for exercises or when you find it in books or magazines, statistics and statements by authorities are no problem. If, however, you are writing paragraphs based on personal experiences (much like many samples in Section One), you will naturally rely heavily on examples. Fortunately, the example is one of the most colorful and convincing kinds of support.

INVENTED SUPPORT

Before you begin the exercises, let's discuss invented support. It greatly simplifies the learning process for you. You don't have to struggle to find real support at the same time you're trying to figure out just what good support is. You don't have to search any further than your own mind, and you can be as specific as you like.

But please remember, inventing evidence for a class is just an exercise, a convenience for you and your instructor.

Rules for Inventing Your Support

Please follow these rules when you invent your support:

- Never write invented support unless your readers know that is what they are reading.
- Never write invented support unless your instructor approves.

If you're careful, you can have fun with your writing. Most of the examples we used in this chapter were invented; you could easily tell that. So try to be imaginative.

At the same time, though, try to be realistic. Don't, for instance, try to convince us that the Grand Junction School of Cosmetology is noted for its scholarly excellence because it had thirteen Rhodes scholars last year. The school may be good, but such an exaggerated figure is bound to raise eyebrows.

PRACTICAL WRITING

Good support is important for any kind of writing. In fact, a common problem with business writing is that it leaves out the convincing support, relying instead on generalizations.

Suppose you've had some people inspecting your company—the one you're president of. A section of the inspection report has this generalization with only poor support:

Poor Start: Only a Generalization

We made many random observations of the work force. Much of the time, workers were not productive.

"That's interesting," you may say, "but I'm hardly convinced. Where's the proof?"

Now let's consider a rewrite, this time adding some statistics:

A Little Better: With Statistics

During June, we made 118 random observations of the work force. At least 78 times, the workers were not productive.

"Hmmm," you might say. "So what do you mean by 'not productive 78 times.' Can you tell me more?"

The inspector can tell more—and should have in the first place. Let's look now at what should have been the first version. This time, it has not only statistics but some quick examples, too:

Much Better: With Statistics and Quick Examples

During June, we made 118 random observations of the work force. At least 78 times, the workers were not productive. These are some of our observations:

- After clocking in, about 20 employees routinely left their workshops in company vehicles and went to the cafeteria. Some stayed more than an hour.
- During one five-day period, 9 of 19 employees didn't work a full shift. They arrived as much as 30 minutes late, left as much as 30 minutes early, or *both.*
- On June 19, about 40 employees returned to the shop area 30 to 60 minutes before the end of the work day.
- On June 20, some employees parked for over 40 minutes behind the library. Others drove company vehicles for long periods without stopping to do any work.

From our inspection, we believe these observations in June are typical of what goes on year round.

The inspectors seem much more convincing now, don't they?

So remember: detailed support is a key to communication at school and on the job.

EXERCISES

A. For each of the topic sentences below, invent (in other words, simply make up) a quick example (1 sentence), a narrative example (3-5 sentences), a statistic (1-2 sentences), and a statement by an authority (1-2 sentences), as required. Use the sample paragraph on yard sales, which has invented support, as a model.

1. Weather forecasting is definitely a science.

   a. narrative example _____

   _____

   _____

   _____

   _____

   b. statistic _____

   _____

   _____

   c. statement by an authority _____

   _____

_____

_____

2. Ceiling fans are effective.

   a. statistic _____

_____

_____

   b. narrative example _____

_____

_____

_____

   c. statement by an authority _____

_____

_____

3. Twentieth century medicine really works.

   a. quick example _____

_____

_____

   b. quick example _____

_____

_____

   c. narrative example _____

_____

_____

_____

_____

B. Follow the same instructions for these topic sentences:

   1. Weather forecasting is hardly a science.

      a. statement by an authority _____

_____

_____

b. statistic _____

_____

_____

c. narrative example _____

_____

_____

_____

_____

2. Ceiling fans aren't effective.

   a. narrative example _____

_____

_____

_____

_____

   b. statistic _____

_____

_____

   c. statement by an authority _____

_____

_____

3. Twentieth century medicine sometimes causes problems.

   a. quick example _____

_____

_____

   b. quick example _____

_____

_____

c. narrative example _____

_____

_____

_____

_____

C. Invent support for the same topic sentence four different ways:

1. Computers help people write.

   a. statistic _____

   _____

   _____

   b. statistic _____

   _____

   _____

   c. statistic _____

   _____

   _____

2. Computers help people write.

   a. statement by an authority _____

   _____

   _____

   b. statement by an authority _____

   _____

   _____

   c. statement by an authority _____

   _____

   _____

3. Computers help people write.

   a. quick example _____

   _____

   _____

b. quick example _____

_____

_____

c. quick example _____

_____

_____

4. Computers help people write.

a. narrative example _____

_____

_____

_____

_____

b. narrative example _____

_____

_____

_____

_____

D. Answer these questions about Exercise C:

1. Which form of support was most effective? Why?

_____

_____

_____

2. Which form of support was least effective? Why?

_____

_____

_____

3. For that topic sentence, what combination of support (statistics, statements by authorities, quick examples, narrative examples) would you recommend? Why?

_____

_____

_____

E. Look at the paragraph on yard sales at the end of the chapter. Now, intentionally destroy the effectiveness of the paragraph: rewrite the good example (the second through the fifth sentences) by making it too general.

_____

_____

_____

_____

F. Now let's reverse Exercise E. Here are some topic sentences followed by examples that are too general. Improve each italicized example by converting the dull generality into a narrative example. You'll need several sentences for each one.

1. Vacations to other states can be exciting. *Last summer, for example, I had quite an experience.*

_____

_____

_____

_____

2. Floods can cause tremendous damage. *Once the Mississippi River overflowed and many people lost everything.*

_____

_____

_____

_____

3. Television can help young people develop character. *There's one program that really does a lot.*

_____

_____

_____

_____

G. In Exercises A, B, and C you outlined several paragraphs. Choose the one that interests you the most and use the support you invented to write the paragraph. The appendix to this book gives you a suggested format.

Chapter 3

Topic Sentence

Now we move to the first sentence of the one-paragraph essay: the topic sentence.

Think of the topic sentence as the main idea of the paragraph—the point you're making, the generalization that the rest of your paragraph will support.

Writing texts try to define the topic-sentence idea with a number of terms: it is the writer's "viewpoint" of the topic, the writer's "judgment" about the topic, the writer's "conviction," the writer's "assertion." Those texts are right; the topic-sentence idea is all these things. However, we prefer the term *opinion:* the topic sentence is a precise statement of opinion you wish to persuade your readers to accept.

Why do we associate a topic sentence with the word *opinion?* An opinion is a judgment that seems true only for the person who believes it. Imagine for a moment that you're telling a friend something you believe—a viewpoint, a judgment, a conviction, an assertion you hold to be true. Your friend replies, "That's just your opinion."

He's not denying that you believe what you say, but he is letting you know that you'll have to persuade him to agree with you. He's placing the burden on you to support your belief so that he can accept the idea as you do.

A similar relationship exists between you (the writer) and your readers. Your topic sentence stands as a statement of your opinion *until* you persuade your audience to accept it fully. Recognizing that the topic sentence is a statement of opinion will help you remember your obligation to support your idea.

Why should the topic sentence be an opinion instead of a fact? If you state your idea and your readers respond with "Oh, yes, that's true" or "That's a fact," what more can you say? Suppose you write this topic sentence:

■ William Shakespeare wrote *Hamlet.*

In your paragraph you could discuss Shakespeare or his play, but you wouldn't be trying to convince a reader to accept the topic sentence itself; that Shakespeare wrote *Hamlet* is accepted as fact. And statements of fact (or at least what everyone accepts as fact) don't make good topic sentences because they leave the writer nothing important to say. On the other hand, suppose you try this topic sentence:

■   Francis Bacon wrote *Hamlet.*

Now you've stated an opinion. Unfortunately, hardly anyone believes it. You've crossed into such extreme controversy that you'll really have to work to convince readers to accept your topic-sentence idea.

Your topic-sentence opinion doesn't need to arouse instant doubt. You don't need to take outrageous stands like these:

■   Dogs are really man's greatest enemy.

■   A toupee is better than real hair.

In fact, most good topic sentences bring neither instant acceptance nor instant doubt. Usually readers have not formed their own judgments, and they're willing to accept yours if you persuade them. For example, consider this topic sentence:

■   Today's toupees are so well made that they look like a person's own hair.

The writer is stating what she believes to be fact. Although readers have no reason to doubt her, they are not obliged to believe her either. They probably will agree with what she says once she provides specific support for her opinion. And it *is* her opinion—until she persuades readers to accept it as fully as she does.

When you write a one-paragraph essay, you'll begin with a topic sentence and follow it with specific support (examples, statistics, or authoritative statements). If you structure the topic sentence well and support it well with specifics, you'll persuade your readers to accept your idea fully. The rest of this chapter shows you how to write a good topic sentence.

A Good Topic Sentence

A good topic sentence contains two parts: a *limited subject* and a *precise opinion* about that subject.

LIMITING THE SUBJECT

The first step in writing a good topic sentence is to choose a subject limited enough to support in a single paragraph. If you try to support a large subject in a one-paragraph essay, your argument is not likely to be convincing because the subject (which is too general) will demand more support than you can develop in one paragraph. Thus, limiting the subject is the first step toward writing a good topic sentence.

Let's examine a sample case. You begin with a general subject: advertising. Since the topic is obviously too large for a one-paragraph essay, you must limit it. Of the many types of advertisement (television, radio, newspaper, billboard, and the like), you choose one—for instance, magazine advertising.

As you glance at the advertisements in your favorite magazine, three attract your attention. In one advertisement, you see a scantily clad woman holding a tape recorder she wants you to buy. In another, a shapely blond is stroking a luxury automobile. And in a third ad, a couple embrace in delight as they hold cigarettes in their free hands. You see a common element in each sales pitch: the advertisers use sex appeal to make you want the things you see before you.

In this way you limit the subject from *advertising* to *magazine advertising* to *sex appeal in magazine advertising.*

Consider the process you just went through. You might have noticed the lack of color in the tape-recorder advertisement, the large amount of space wasted in the automobile ad, or the small print that obscures the Surgeon General's warning in the cigarette advertisement. Instead, you focused your attention on sex appeal in the ads, thereby limiting the subject.

STATING THE PRECISE OPINION

The second part of the topic sentence tells your opinion about the limited subject. Although limiting the subject is a step toward precision, an opinion about even a limited subject will remain vague unless you tell your readers what your idea is exactly.

The precise-opinion part of the topic sentence is a word or phrase that makes a judgment, such as *dangerous* or *exciting.* But a warning is necessary here, for not all judgment words will express precise opinions. Words like *interesting, nice, good* or *bad* start to take a stand but remain vague. What do you really mean when you say something is "interesting"? What have you said about a person you call "nice"? Such vague judgments make imprecise opinions. On the other hand, precise judgments combine with a subject to define your opinion about the subject.

Again, let's apply this theory to our sample case, sex appeal in magazine advertising. So what if advertisers support sales with sex appeal?

You look again at the ads that will support your argument only to find another common element: sex appeal isn't really related to the items for sale. The ads hold your attention because sex appeal was connected to nonsexual items. You are irritated because the advertisers are trying to manipulate your senses so that you will buy whatever they put in the advertisements. Thus, you are ready to state precisely your opinion about sex appeal in these three advertisements: it *irritates* you.

Again, consider the process you used. You had to make a judgment about sex appeal in the advertising; you had to establish your precise opinion about the subject. Because you didn't like the sex appeal in the ads, you might have said that the sex appeal was bad. But what would *bad* mean? Did the sex appeal disgust you? Did it appeal to your prurient interests in a manner not consistent with community standards (whatever that means)? Did the sex appeal in the ads merely irritate you? Just what was the *badness*?

When you made the precise judgment that sex appeal in some magazine advertisements is irritating, you established your exact stand on the subject.

WRITING THE TOPIC SENTENCE

Once you have limited the subject and have decided precisely your opinion about it, you have formed the two basic parts of the topic sentence—a *limited subject* and a *precise opinion* about that subject. You can easily structure a topic sentence by stating the precise opinion in some form after the sentence's subject, as in the following:

■   For me, dieting is futile.

Dieting, the subject of the sentence, is the limited subject, and *futile,* which follows, is the precise opinion about it.

Now we can write the topic sentence for the paragraph on sex appeal in magazine advertisements.

■   Magazine advertisements that try to use sex appeal to sell any product are irritating.

We can see, then, that the basic pattern for the topic sentence is *"limited subject is precise opinion."* Consider these examples:

■   Arcade video games are challenging.

■   Restoring old houses is rewarding.

In the first sentence, *arcade video games* is the limited subject and *challenging* is the precise opinion. In the second, you intend to persuade the readers that *restoring old houses* (the limited subject) is *rewarding* (the precise opinion).

REFINING THE TOPIC SENTENCE

Even though this pattern is basic for a topic sentence, you need not feel restricted to it. Perhaps the model seems too mechanical. You can easily convert the topic-sentence model to a more sophisticated form. Look at the following topic sentence in the basic pattern:

■   Overpackaging of supermarket items is seriously wasteful of natural resources.

Here is the same idea in another form:

■   Overpackaging of supermarket items seriously wastes natural resources.

Notice that the verb *is* and the precise opinion *wasteful* (the basic pattern) became the verb *wastes* in the second sentence form. Now look at a topic sentence from an earlier chapter:

■   Even though I have never really lived there, going to my grandmother's farm always seems like coming home.

Converted to the basic pattern, the idea of the sentence is as follows:

■ Going to my grandmother's farm is like coming home.

In another topic sentence we may say this:

■ Hitchhiking is dangerous.

But we may also state the sentence more imaginatively:

■ Hitchhiking has proved to be the last ride for many people.

The important point is that refined topic sentences, such as those above, always can be converted to the model: *"limited subject* is *precise opinion."* When you write a topic-sentence form beyond the model, take a moment to make sure that you still can convert it to the two basic parts.

Whatever the pattern of the topic sentences, the result is the same. When you have limited your subject and precisely defined your opinion about it, you have formed the necessary parts of the topic sentence. You have created an assertion that will guide both you and your readers through the supporting material of the paragraph.

PRACTICAL WRITING

As we discussed in Chapter 1, topic sentences are useful beyond college. Technical writing, reports, letters, memos—all usually benefit from getting to the point quickly, from putting the bottom line at the top.

In this book, we treat that main point as something persuasive:

Persuasive Main Points

Buying a second copying machine would make our office more efficient.

Hitchhiking is dangerous.

In business, however, that main point could simply be informative:

Informative Main Points

The copying machine will arrive on time. Here are the steps I've taken so far to order it. . . .

The policemen arrested the burglars. These are the details of the arrest. . . .

Whether writing aims to inform or to persuade, having the main point first is usually very helpful to readers.

EXERCISES

A. Place a check mark by the sentences that would not make good topic sentences because they do not state precise opinions.

_____ 1. Van Gogh painted *A Starry Night.*

_____ 2. Kerosene heaters are dangerous.

_____ 3. There are no rain forests in North Dakota.

_____ 4. Rain forests are crucial to our planet's health.

_____ 5. According to the U.S. Weather Service, eight inches of snow fell overnight.

_____ 6. The snowfall turned the city's streets into a nightmare for commuters.

_____ 7. Laser printers are faster than typewriters.

_____ 8. Laser printers waste paper.

_____ 9. Door-to-door salesmen didn't come here at all last month.

_____ 10. Mule deer must be hardy to survive Colorado winters.

B. For these topic sentences, underline the subject once and the opinion twice. Also, circle any subjects that aren't limited enough and any opinions that aren't precise enough.

1. Basketball teaches sportsmanship.

2. Basketball is fun.

3. The time machine was unreliable.

4. Associating with students from different backgrounds has made me more tolerant of other people's behavior.

5. Transportation is important.

6. Today's golfers are extraordinary athletes.

7. Summer vacations are wonderful.

8. Insecticides can be harmful to human beings.

9. Military jets can fly fast.

10. Soccer is great.

C. Limit the general subjects below and then state a precise opinion about each limited subject:

Example: General Subject   Traveling

_____Hitchhiking_____ is/are _____dangerous_____

(Limited Subject)   (Precise Opinion)

1. **General Subject**   The Sun

   _____ is/are _____
   (Limited Subject)   (Precise Opinion)

2. **General Subject**   Charity

   _____ is/are _____
   (Limited Subject)   (Precise Opinion)

3. **General Subject**   Animal Rights

   _____ is/are _____
   (Limited Subject)   (Precise Opinion)

4. **General Subject**   Meals

   _____ is/are _____
   (Limited Subject)   (Precise Opinion)

5. **General Subject**   Television Movies

   _____ is/are _____
   (Limited Subject)   (Precise Opinion)

6. **General Subject**   Political Matters

   _____ is/are _____
   (Limited Subject)   (Precise Opinion)

Chapter 4

Unity

You know a topic sentence presents a precise opinion about a limited subject. Now we can go to the next step in good writing: unity.

Think about the word *unity* for a moment. It means *oneness*, doesn't it? So for a paragraph to have unity, it must have *oneness*. More specifically, each idea in the paragraph should clearly support the "one main point," the topic sentence. Normally there shouldn't be any ideas that are irrelevant, that don't support the point of the paragraph.

If, for example, you're writing about the dullest class you ever took, you'd destroy the unity by talking about the fascinating lectures and exciting field trips. Or if you want to show that your mynah bird is an ideal pet, the friendliness of the boa constrictor is off the subject and, therefore, irrelevant. In other words, everything you say in a paragraph must support your paragraph.

Can you find the two places in this next paragraph where the writer loses her sense of unity?

Poor Unity

My most frustrating job was cooking for the dorm cafeteria during my freshman year. No matter how hard I tried, I never could cook what the menu said because the food company always delivered the wrong food or brought it late. I also was frustrated because I had trouble estimating how much food to cook—many times we ran short of hamburgers or had to throw away pounds and pounds of French fries. Sometimes we ate the extra French fries, though, and we'd sit around, joking and having a good time.

The worst thing, however, was the condition of my clothes after the meal was over. Even if I hadn't spilled anything (and I usually had spilled spaghetti or something worse), my clothes smelled awful. I'd want to go home to change before going anyplace else. Some of the other students who didn't work in the cafeteria also spilled food and had to change, too. No wonder, then, I thought cooking for the dorm cafeteria was frustrating.

Did you find the two sentences that violate the unity of the paragraph?

The first is about eating French fries and having a good time; the second is about other students spilling food on themselves and having to change clothes. Neither of those sentences has anything to do with the main topic of the paragraph: working in the cafeteria is a *frustrating job for you.*

Here's a diagram showing what we mean:

> **Topic Sentence**
>
> My job as cook was frustrating.

> **Support**
>
> Wrong food was delivered.

> **Support**
>
> I had trouble estimating amounts.

> **Support**
>
> Had fun eating extra food.

> **Support**
>
> My clothes were messy.

> **Support**
>
> Other students changed clothes, too.

Conclusion

My job as cook was frustrating.

Now let's fix the unity of that paragraph:

Good Unity

My most frustrating job was cooking for the dorm cafeteria during my freshman year. No matter how hard I tried, I never could cook what the menu said because the food company always delivered the wrong food or brought it late. I also was frustrated because I had trouble estimating how much food to cook—many times we ran short of hamburgers or had to throw away pounds and pounds of French fries. The worst thing, however, was the condition of my clothes after the meal was over. Even if I hadn't spilled anything (and I usually had spilled spaghetti or something worse), my clothes smelled awful. I'd want to go home to change before going anyplace else. No wonder, then, I thought cooking for the dorm cafeteria was frustrating.

Note the difference: the writer sticks to the subject. All the examples help show that being a cook for the dorm cafeteria was frustrating. A diagram of this paragraph looks unified, showing that all the blocks fit:

Topic Sentence

My job as cook was frustrating.

Support

Wrong food was delivered.

Support

I had trouble estimating amounts.

```
┌─────────────────────────────────────┐
│              Support                 │
│                                      │
│     My clothes were messy.           │
│                                      │
└─────────────────────────────────────┘


┌─────────────────────────────────────┐
│             Conclusion               │
│                                      │
│   My job as cook was frustrating.    │
│                                      │
└─────────────────────────────────────┘
```

As you can see, the idea of unity is really simple: stick to the point. Don't be led astray by a word or idea in one of your sentences the way the writer was in the first paragraph. Make sure everything in your paragraph belongs there. That way, your reader won't be distracted—or worse, confused.

EXERCISES

A. Read these paragraphs and underline the precise opinion in the topic sentence. Then identify those sentences that don't help support the precise opinion.

1. [1] Television comedy shows are undermining America's social values. [2] The most obvious way is that these shows usually portray the father or other male power figure as foolish, incompetent, or corrupt. [3] The shows also make women only sex objects, bouncy but brainless. [4] Likewise, people who are honest or hardworking sometimes appear stupid. [5] Some of the "one liners" in these shows are pretty good, though. [6] It's clear that sit-coms are harming America's values.

   The irrelevant sentence is _____ .

2. [1] Compared with the Earth, the moon is an unusual geological specimen. [2] Its surface, once turbulent, is now so tranquil that the astronauts' footprints probably still remain virtually unchanged. [3] Also, the surface of the moon is, of course, entirely barren and, except for its shape, almost dully consistent. [4] The view from there is spectacular, which makes me really want to visit it. [5] In summary, the moon has some important geological differences from Earth.

   The irrelevant sentence is _____ .

3. [1] Railroad trains can haul freight much more efficiently than trucks can. [2] For one thing, trains can have many cars—sometimes well over a hundred—and each railroad car can hold many times what a truck (or tractor-trailer) holds. [3] Therefore, a relatively short train carrying only a small crew can carry thousands of tons more than a truck can for each trip. [4] For another thing, trains use much, much less fuel per ton of freight than the trucks do. [5] Finally, trains are

breathtaking to watch, moving powerfully and smoothly across the country as they have for well over a century. [6] Let's not forget, the trains helped open the West. [7] So let's give trains their due: they are much more efficient than trucks at hauling freight.

The irrelevant sentences are _____ and _____ .

B. In the following examples, provide unified support for the topic sentence. If you need to, invent specific details for your support.

   1.

Topic Sentence Charity begins at home.
Support
Support
Support
Reworded Topic Sentence Therefore, charity begins at home.

   2.

Topic Sentence Fireplaces can be dangerous.
Support
Support
Support
Reworded Topic Sentence So fireplaces can be dangerous.

3.

Topic Sentence   Libraries contain fascinating facts.
Support
Support
Support
Reworded Topic Sentence   Libraries contain fascinating facts.

C. Write a paragraph on one of the topic sentences in Exercise B; use your invented support. Add two irrelevant sentences to destroy the paragraph's unity, and underline them.

Chapter 5

Coherence

A one-paragraph essay needs more than unity. It also must have coherence.

The best way to define *coherence* is to look at its opposite: *incoherence*. If a man runs into a room screaming "Fire! Dog! House!" we call him incoherent. Does he mean that a dog is on fire in the house? Or that the house is on fire with the dog inside? Or that a doghouse is on fire?

We don't know. Although the man apparently has some very important ideas he wishes desperately to communicate, he has left out the essential links of thought. Coherence requires including those links.

This chapter discusses three important ways to achieve coherence in the one-paragraph essay:

- explanation of the support
- reminders of the opinion in the topic sentence
- transitions

These important techniques will help your readers move smoothly from idea to idea within your paragraph. Then, when your doghouse catches on fire, you'll know exactly how to call for help.

EXPLANATION OF THE SUPPORT

Don't assume that your readers are specially gifted people able to read minds. You must not only present the support to the readers but also explain how it is related to the topic sentence. In other words, you must link your support—clearly and unambiguously—to the topic sentence. The author of the following paragraph does not try to explain his support at all, apparently hoping that his readers are clairvoyant:

First Try

In the early morning, I am easily annoyed by my roommate. I have to shut the ice-covered windows. A white tornado of dandruff swirls around the room. A mass of smoke from cigarettes hovers near the door. No wonder I find my roommate annoying.

No wonder, indeed! The paragraph is incoherent because the author has failed to explain how his support relates to the topic sentence. Does he mean that his roommate is annoying because he does not close the window in the morning? Or is he annoying because he opens the window every night, even in winter, thus causing the writer to be cold in the morning? Or what?

And who has dandruff, and who smokes? Is it the roommate or is it the author, who is upset because the roommate does not understand? After all, the author may be doing the best he can to get rid of the dandruff, and he is smoking heavily only because he is trying to distract himself after waking up every morning in a cold room.

By being incomplete, by not explaining the support fully, the paragraph demands too much of readers. Let's guess what the writer really meant and then revise the paragraph to add coherence.

Second Try

In the early morning, I am easily annoyed by my roommate. I have to shut the ice-covered windows *that John, my roommate, insists on opening every night, even during the winter.* A white tornado swirling around the room *shows me that his dandruff problem is still in full force.* A mass of smoke *from John's pack-a-day habit* hovers near the door. No wonder I find my roommate annoying.

We have now explained that John, the roommate, is guilty of the indiscretions. The coherence is improved greatly, but the paragraph still needs work.

REMINDERS OF THE OPINION IN THE TOPIC SENTENCE

In the preceding section, we learned not to assume that readers can read minds. In this section, however, we will make an assumption about readers: readers, like all of us, prefer being mentally lazy. They don't like remembering too much at once. While they are reading the support, they like occasional reminders of the opinion stated in the topic sentence so that they will remember why they are reading that support.

We can remind them of the opinion in the topic sentence with either of two techniques at the beginning of each item of support:

- We can repeat the exact words of the opinion.

- We can use other words that suggest the opinion.

In the sample paragraph about the roommate, we can use the word *annoy* in presenting each example, or we can use words such as *disgusted* or *choking on stale smoke,* which *suggest* annoyance. Notice the reminders in the revised paragraph.

Third Try

In the early morning, I am easily annoyed by my roommate. *I am annoyed* each time I have to shut the ice-covered windows that John, my roommate, insists on opening every night, even during the winter. A *disgusting* white tornado swirling around the room shows me that his dandruff problem is still in full force. *A choking mass of stale smoke* from John's pack-a-day habit hovers near the door. No wonder I find my roommate annoying.

By reminding the readers that each example presents something annoying, the paragraph becomes more coherent.

TRANSITIONS

Each example in the sample paragraph now has a clear explanation of the support and a reminder of the opinion in the topic sentence, but the paragraph is still rough. It moves like a train with square wheels, chunking along abruptly from idea to idea. To help the paragraph move more smoothly, we must add transitions.

Transitions are like road signs that tell readers where they are going. If you live in Louisville and wish to drive north to Indianapolis, you don't want to stop to consult a map to find out you are on the right road. You would rather have road signs.

Similarly, readers don't want to run into an example that slows them because they don't understand how it relates to the previous example or, worse yet, how it relates to the topic sentence. In a paragraph, the road sign could be *however* to tell readers that the next idea is going to contrast with the one just presented; or it could be *also* to tell readers that another idea like the preceding one is about to be presented; or it could be *therefore* to tell readers to prepare for a conclusion.

These and other transitions will keep your Indianapolis-bound driver from losing valuable time because he has to stop, or, if he takes a chance and presses on, from arriving nowhere, which is where he may end his trip in a paragraph without transitions.

Common Transitions

To add an idea: also, and, another, equally important, finally, furthermore, in addition, last, likewise, moreover, most important, next, second, third

To give an example: as a case in point, consider . . . , for example, for instance, as an illustration

To make a contrast: and yet, but, however, instead, nevertheless, nonetheless, on the contrary, on the other hand, still

To begin a conclusion: as a result, clearly, hence, in conclusion, no wonder, obviously, then, therefore, thus

---

A paragraph must have transitions, but where should these transitions be placed?

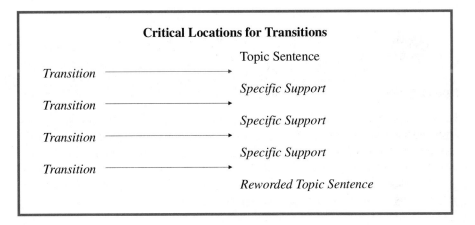

Critical Locations for Transitions

Topic Sentence

Transition ⟶

Specific Support

Transition ⟶

Specific Support

Transition ⟶

Specific Support

Transition ⟶

Reworded Topic Sentence

Sometimes you will find that no transition is necessary between the topic sentence and the first item of specific support because the second sentence of the paragraph is so obviously an example that a transitional expression seems too mechanical. For instance, you might be able to omit the first transition in this final revision of the sample paragraph about the roommate. The remaining transitions, however, are all desirable.

Final Version

In the early morning, I am easily annoyed by my roommate. *For example,* I am annoyed each time I have to shut the ice-covered windows that John, my roommate, insists on opening every night, even during the winter. I am *also* disgusted by a white tornado swirling around the room,

> which shows me that his dandruff problem is still in full force. *Most bothersome, though,* is the choking mass of stale smoke—from John's pack-a-day habit—that hovers near the door. *No wonder* I find my room-mate annoying.

Our sample paragraph is finally coherent. We have explained the support, reminded the reader frequently of the opinion in the topic sentence, and added transitions at the critical locations.

You're so familiar with the above paragraph by now, and it's so simple, you may believe the transitions aren't really necessary. Perhaps you're right. But what if you read a paragraph that began like this?

Poor Coherence

If you've ever bought a pomegranate, you probably know that it's one of the most difficult foods to eat. The juice is delicious and a beautiful ruby color. It drips everywhere, staining whatever it hits. The bitter, inedible pulp seems impossible to avoid. . . .

By now, you're probably lost. If the writer has trouble eating a pomegranate, then why start by telling us how delicious and beautiful it is? The writer knows why, but the readers don't because there aren't any transitions. Let's put them in:

Revised for Effective Coherence

If you've ever bought a pomegranate, you probably know that it's one of the most difficult foods to eat. *Although* the juice is delicious and a beautiful ruby color, it *unfortunately* drips everywhere, staining whatever it hits. *Also frustrating,* the bitter, inedible pulp seems impossible to avoid. . . .

The transitions (and the reminder *frustrating*) make the paragraph easy to understand the first time through.

Good writing shouldn't be an IQ test or a guessing game for the readers, so let them know what you're thinking as your ideas shift directions. For now, use the three techniques demonstrated in this chapter, even if they seem mechanical. As you gain experience as a writer, you will learn more subtle ways to link your ideas to each other and to the topic sentence. Your immediate goal now, though, is to communicate coherently with your readers.

> **Three Techniques for Coherence**
>
> - explanation of the support
> - reminders of the opinion in the topic sentence
> - transitions

EXERCISES

A. Outline this paragraph and indicate the *transitions* by filling in the blanks below. Merely summarize the topic sentence, the support, and the reworded topic sentence rather than writing them in full.

> A significant change I have noticed in myself since entering college is a fear of mathematics. The mere sight of a three-hundred-fifty-page math text, for instance, causes a cold shiver to run the length of my spine. As I cautiously open the front cover of the text, a myriad of complex formulas springs at me, quickly eliminating any trace of confidence I may have had. My dread of math is also strengthened each time I enter the small, dismal classroom. I can find no consolation in watching my classmates cringe behind open briefcases as they prepare to do battle with a common enemy capable of engulfing us all in a blanket of confusion. Finally, my greatest fears are realized as my instructor self-consciously adjusts his glasses and admits that he majored in English and never truly mastered, or even understood, calculus. Then I suddenly realize that the Cartesian plane has snared me in its nightmarish world for another semester.

Topic Sentence _____

    Transition _____

Specific Support _____

    Transition _____

Specific Support _____

    Transition _____

Specific Support _____

    Transition _____

Reworded Topic Sentence _____

The opinion the above paragraph demonstrates is *fear*. Circle all *reminders* of that opinion in the paragraph; that is, circle all words that either repeat the word or suggest the meaning of *fear*.

B. Outline this paragraph and show the *transitions* by filling in the blanks. Again, simply summarize the topic sentence, the support, and the reworded topic sentence rather than writing them in full.

> Since becoming a college student, I have learned many ways to study faster than I did in high school. As an example, I discovered that spending three-fourths of my study time sprawled across a desk in deep slumber has helped me find a sudden aptitude for instantly memorizing five chapters of chemistry the period before a test. Another way I have developed my study skills is reading magazines at the bookstore on free afternoons. When my classmates (and occasionally the professors) ask me to justify this practice, I calmly tell them that the rate at which I study is sure to increase if I study only in the evenings. But by far my most useful device for sharpening my study habits is my custom of writing my girlfriend during finals. What else could teach me to study an entire semester's material in only an hour and a half? So, since becoming a college student, I have developed many ways to study far faster than I ever had before.

Topic Sentence _____

    Transition _____

  Specific Support _____

    Transition _____

  Specific Support _____

    Transition _____

  Specific Support _____

    Transition _____

Reworded Topic Sentence _____

The opinion in the above paragraph is *study faster*. Circle all *reminder* words that either repeat the phrase or suggest the meaning of *study faster*.

C. Using another paragraph in this book assigned by your instructor, underline all the transitions and circle all the reminders..

D. Rewrite this paragraph, adding transitions and reminders of the opinion in the topic sentence. You also may need to add some support to fully explain the relationship of the support to the topic sentence.

> The city of Stockholm is among the loveliest in the world. Slum districts, prevalent in almost all large cities, are nearly nonexistent in Stockholm, having been replaced by government housing. The citizens are careful to dispose of their litter properly and to pick up litter other people may have dropped. Stockholm has a unique layout: it is built on twenty-three islands. Water winds throughout the city. The beauty of Stockholm makes it one of the most alluring cities in the world.

E. Follow the same instructions as for Exercise D.

Overnight camping can be disenchanting if you are a novice. Whether you hike in (carrying pounds and pounds of food and equipment on your back) or whether you drive (with all the monotony car trips are infamous for), you will probably be tired once you are ready to set up your camp. When you settle back to admire the stars at the end of the day, you will probably be besieged by bugs—mosquitoes and sand flies seem to prefer making their homes in scenic places. When you go to bed, you may find that your sleeping bag, especially if you have a cheap one, may be quite uncomfortable. Camping for newcomers can be quite different from a purely romantic adventure.

F. Write a paragraph that convinces readers that some*thing* (not some*one*) has a particular characteristic. On the final copy, underline all the transitions and circle all the reminders. Make sure you have met the other requirement for coherence by explaining your support fully. (The paragraph in Chapter 1 on the Boundary Waters Canoe Area could have been a response to this exercise.)

G. Write a paragraph that convinces readers of one significant way in which you have changed since entering college. Use examples from your own experience as support. On the final copy, underline all the transitions and circle all the reminders. Make sure you have met the other requirement for coherence by explaining your support fully. (Exercises A and B are on the same subject.)

H. Write a paragraph that convinces readers of one important characteristic you don't like your friends to have. Use examples from your experience as support. On the final copy, underline all the transitions and circle all the reminders. Make sure you have met the other requirement for coherence by explaining your support fully.

I. If you've held a job, try this exercise: Describe one important characteristic workers need at the place you work (or worked)—Patience? Stubbornness? Endurance? Intelligence? Something else?

Chapter 6

Tips on the Writing Process

So far, we've concentrated on what the final *product* of your writing should look like—a paragraph with a topic sentence, good support, unity, and coherence.

This chapter will give you a few tips on the *process* for getting there. To do that, we'll answer two questions:

- What is the writing process?
- What's the role of computers in that process?

THE WRITING PROCESS

The traditional way to think about the writing process is to divide it into three parts: *prewriting, writing,* and *rewriting.* Most teachers today think the process is more complicated than that, and we certainly agree with them.

Nevertheless, these three parts give us a convenient way to talk about the process in general.

Prewriting

Prewriting is the process of gathering your thoughts and preparing to write. You choose your topic, refine it, and consider ways of supporting it. You don't have to think your way all the way through the paper. In fact, most writers have trouble envisioning the entire paper—even only a one-paragraph essay—before the pencil hits the page. That's why writers do a little writing as part of the prewriting process.

Try some of these strategies to help with your prewriting:

- If you have no idea of a topic, and your instructor hasn't given you one, browse through some popular magazines. Just let your mind wander. You may write about something that isn't even in the magazines, but they'll have triggered ideas for you. Even better, browse through an encyclopedia.

- If you still don't have a good topic, talk to your friends. Tell them about your paper and start a general discussion. You might be surprised how some random conversation can get your mind going in the right direction.
- Once you have a general topic, try refining it into a good topic sentence (remember: a limited subject and a precise opinion). We suggest you actually write it down and then play around with it until it's just right.
- Now you need the support. One technique for getting good support—especially if the topic is about your personal experiences or uses invented material—is to brainstorm on paper. That is, spend a few minutes jotting down whatever comes to mind. Don't be judgmental at this point ("That doesn't make sense at all!"). Just let your thoughts flow. When you're through, look at what you have. Often you'll find something useful.
- Another way to get good support is to try a little free writing. That is, just start writing. Don't stop to think and don't stop writing. Make yourself write for perhaps five minutes, saying whatever comes to mind. If you're like us, a lot of absolute nonsense will appear on your page. But buried in that nonsense may well be a few nuggets that will become the actual support in your paper.

These techniques are all standard fare in the writing game—well known and often used. They take a little time—but only a little. And that small investment gets your brain in gear, ready to write.

Writing

So you have your ideas. Now is the time to get them on paper. If you already have some on paper from free writing or brainstorming, it's time to bring law and order to the page.

Here are some strategies for the writing stage:

- Have an outline. You don't need a formal one for your one-paragraph essay, but you should have at least an informal one you've jotted down.
- Next, remind yourself of the requirements for the one-paragraph essay so you'll meet the requirements of your assignment.
- Then . . . just start writing. Don't worry about errors and spelling—you can take care of them later. Just try to get the whole thing on paper, warts and all. Your goal here is to have a good flow of ideas. Try to write fairly quickly.
- Stop if your ideas aren't working at all, as any further writing will just waste your time. Instead, try some of the techniques of prewriting again. (Or take a break. Not too long, though!)

When you have a complete draft, breathe a sigh of relief. You have more work to do, but the hard part is finished.

Rewriting

In the writing stage, you put a premium on speed—getting everything down on paper. In the rewriting stage, the premium is on care. Few people slap down an "A" paper in one burst of creative effort. Most need to add some polish.

Here are some suggestions:

- First, check for the larger matters: Does your writing make sense? Does it follow the requirements for the one-paragraph essay? Is it unified? Coherent? Interesting?
- Then check for the smaller matters: Have you spelled the words correctly? Is your punctuation correct? Do your word choices seem good? These matters are small, but they can get big fast.
- Read your paper aloud. Don't read silently. Actually say the words. It's amazing how awkward phrases, missing ideas, and poor sentence structure stand out when you actually hear the words. Do you know that we read this entire book out loud several times when we prepared the first edition? And we're glad we did!
- Finally, set your writing aside. Do something else. Then come back to it. Your mind will be cleared of all the ideas you had when writing, and now you can see your writing through the eyes of someone else—or at least have a more objective view of what you wrote. Then, add the final polish that turns the funny looking rock into a real gem.

We began by saying the writing process is more complicated than prewriting, writing, and rewriting. That's true. The process often loops back and forth. For example, while you're in the writing stage, you might get stuck. That's a good time to head back for a few minutes in the prewriting stage.

Or you might do part of your paper and then set it aside. Before going on with more writing, you might begin (as we often do) by doing a little rewriting. That helps you ease into the actual writing by refamiliarizing yourself with what you've done.

THE ROLE OF COMPUTERS

By all means—if at all possible—use a computer!

If you already use one, you know what we mean. And if you don't use one, you can't really guess how beneficial it can be. You must actually try one—you'll see the benefit immediately.

The computer (and we include memory typewriters that act like computers) is effective at all stages of the writing process:

- *Prewriting.* Remember the writing we suggested you do as part of this process—free writing and brainstorming? That's all so easy with a computer. With paper and pencil (or an old typewriter), you soon end up with a page that's more like hieroglyphics than English—and just as hard to decipher. And the physical fatigue—"writer's cramp"—can make you unconsciously decide to take a break and do something less productive but more relaxing.

- *Writing.* Of course, the computer shines here. With an old-style typewriter, you have to worry about the ends of lines and making mistakes. With a computer, you don't care about these things, so you can concentrate fully on the task at hand: getting good ideas on paper. As a result, you usually get the words on paper much faster.

- *Rewriting.* The computer is, of course, famous for what it can do at this stage. Making changes is no longer dreaded, as it used to be in the days of ordinary typewriters. You can make changes with ease. And spelling checkers can help even good spellers who make typos while speeding through the writing stage of the process. Grammar checkers, which are especially useful in the business world, are becoming better and better for the classroom.

Try an Experiment

We ask our students to try at least one paper during the semester using a computer in our computer lab. At the end of the course, we then ask what happened. Almost without exception, students report that learning to write on a computer was one of the most important steps they've taken as a writer.
As an experiment, try writing one of your papers using a computer.

PRACTICAL WRITING

Let's look at each of the chapter's topics again—this time considering the writing you're likely to do after college.

The Writing Process

All too often you won't have time for an ideal writing process when you're at work. But there's also an advantage: you rarely need to think of a topic, either. At work, you don't write to learn how to write; you write because you need to tell somebody something.

The other techniques we covered—especially for the writing and rewriting stages—apply well. If you don't have time for them, at least you know you're varying from the ideal out of necessity.

And occasionally your writing project will be so important that you simply make the time to make the writing process the best you can.

The Role of Computers

The workplace depends on computers.

Several years ago, some bosses thought of the computer as a tool for secretaries, viewing it only as a fancy typewriter. And some bosses wouldn't let people who weren't secretaries use computers at all!

That attitude has changed almost entirely (except for a few benighted holdouts). Bosses now see the computer as replacing not only the secretary's typewriter but also the yellow legal pad executives used to prepare their drafts on.

So learning to use a computer for writing papers in this course won't be a wasted effort. It will be extraordinarily valuable for all your writing in school—and beyond.

EXERCISE

Write your next paper using a computer. Use it for all stages of the writing process: prewriting, writing, and rewriting.

Part Two

The One-Paragraph Essay (Stage II)

In this section you'll learn a slightly more sophisticated way to organize a one-paragraph essay. You'll find out when you reach Part Three that this new type of paragraph is actually a stepping-stone to larger themes and research papers. Once you learn how to write a Stage II paragraph, the full-length essay will be simple for you to learn.

Chapter 7

Overview of the One-Paragraph Essay (Stage II)

So how are Stage I and Stage II paragraphs different from each other? While a Stage I paragraph has only one opinion, the Stage II paragraph has more than one:

- the opinion in the topic sentence (which is the main opinion)
- the opinions in the subtopic sentences (these opinions help support the main opinion in the topic sentence)

Subtopic sentences are generalizations *within* the paragraph—and they help support the overall generalization, the topic sentence.

Let's look at an example. Here's a Stage II paragraph; we've underlined the subtopic sentences:

A Stage II Paragraph

Old-style computer manuals can be really frustrating to use. <u>For one thing, the indexes are usually frustrating because they are hard to decipher.</u> I remember when I was trying to find out how to print my paper: I tried to find the word <u>print</u> in the index. Believe it or not, the word wasn't even there. I finally asked the person next to me, who said the term for printing in that manual isn't <u>print</u>; instead, it's <u>concatenate</u>. No wonder I had trouble! <u>Aside from the indexes, the general quality of writing in the manuals themselves is frustrating.</u> The manual for my old spreadsheet program doesn't have any diagrams at all, asking me to visualize what a spreadsheet looks like. And my old word processing manual assumes I know as much as the software developers do. As you can tell, I think older computer manuals were user-<u>unfriendly.</u>

See how the subtopic sentences support the topic sentence? Now let's look at an outline of that paragraph:

Topic Sentence   Older computer manuals are frustrating.
  Subtopic Sentence   Indexes are hard to use.
    Specific Support   One index didn't use the word <u>print</u>.
  Subtopic Sentence   General quality of writing is poor.
    Specific Support   Spreadsheet program has no diagrams.
    Specific Support   Word processing program assumes too much.
Reworded Topic Sentence   Older computer manuals needed work.

Notice that each subtopic sentence has the kind of specific support we discussed in Chapter 2. We use examples here (a narrative example for the first subtopic sentence and two quick examples for the second one). But statistics and statements by authorities would do as well.

Notice also that if you remove the subtopic sentences above, you would have a Stage I paragraph. Sometimes the relationship between Stage I and Stage II paragraphs is not so simple. You could add subtopic sentences to the Boundary Waters Canoe Area paragraph in Chapter 1, but you would end up with a worse paragraph because the support is so meager—the paragraph would have more topic and subtopic sentences than support sentences.

Also, some Stage I paragraphs cannot become Stage II paragraphs because they were never divided into subtopic ideas. The sample paragraphs about fearing mathematics and learning to study faster in the exercises for Chapter 5, for example, do not have subtopic ideas, so you could not easily convert them into Stage II paragraphs.

Let's look now at a general model of the Stage II paragraph:

Model of the Stage II Paragraph

Topic Sentence
  Subtopic Sentence
    Specific Support
    Specific Support
  Subtopic Sentence
    Specific Support
    Specific Support
Reworded Topic Sentence

This outline is not rigid, of course. Your Stage II paragraph may have two, three, or four subtopic sentences, and each subtopic sentence may have one to four items of support, depending on the subject and your approach to it. The paragraph above, for instance, had just two subtopic sentences, and one of those topic sentences has just one item of support—a narrative example.

Our sample paragraph about computer manuals might have worked as a Stage I paragraph without subtopic sentences, but some paragraphs are so complex that they need subtopic sentences just to keep the readers (and maybe the writer) from getting lost. Look at this one:

No need to write a ¶ as long as this —
This could be divided into 3 ¶

Another Stage II Paragraph

Although apparently just an assortment of oddities from the National Museum of American History, a 1980 special exhibit called "The Nation's Attic" struck me as a tribute to American ingenuity. *One part of the exhibit demonstrated the ingenious ways Americans have found to shape everyday items.* For instance, a large collection of sewing accessories—hundreds of thimbles, needle cases, sewing cases, and pincushions—showed how simple things could be made more useful, more beautiful, or more entertaining. *More imaginative, though, were the things made apparently just because Americans wanted to accept the challenge of making them.* There was an intricate model of the U.S. Capitol constructed entirely of glass rods. Someone else had engraved the Lord's Prayer on a single grain of rice. And a group of chemical engineers even had managed to do the proverbial "undoable": they actually had created a silk purse from a sow's ear—just to prove it could be done. *The most interesting part of the exhibit to me, however, was some of the bizarre but ingenious failures among the models submitted for approval to the U.S. Patent Office.* I haven't been able to forget an early attempt at creating an electric razor. The inventor had mounted some razor blades on a rotating wheel so it looked something like the paddle wheel of a riverboat, and this wheel was attached to a small hand-held electric motor. There were no guards to control the depth at which the blades cut, so anyone foolish enough to use the razor no doubt would have lost much more than a few whiskers from his face. Still, although I would never have sampled this inventor's work, I had to respect his resourcefulness. This invention, like the other unusual items in "The Nation's Attic," showed the mark of American ingenuity.

Here is an outline of the paragraph:

Topic Sentence   "The Nation's Attic" was a tribute to American ingenuity.
  Subtopic Sentence   Some everyday items were ingenious.
    Specific Support   Sewing items.

Subtopic Sentence	Some items made just for the challenge were imaginative.
Specific Support	Capitol from glass rods.
Specific Support	Lord's Prayer on grain of rice.
Specific Support	Silk purse from sow's ear.
Subtopic Sentence	Some bizarre failures were ingenious.
Specific Support	Attempt to create electric razor.
Reworded Topic Sentence	The unusual items showed American ingenuity.

You might notice that the last sentence of the sample paragraph ties together the last item of support with all those that preceded it. That's not a necessary attribute of a reworded topic sentence, but it works nicely here.

Notice also that even though a paragraph follows a model, as does the paragraph above, it can still be very good writing.

EXERCISES

A. Outline this paragraph.

To play water polo well, you have to learn to cheat. The only way you can keep the ball is by making a few slightly illegal moves. Pushing off your opponent's stomach can give you the elbowroom necessary to make a good pass or score a goal. Likewise, kneeing your attacker in the ribs can keep him from stealing the ball while you are setting up a play. When the opposing team does get possession, the unapproved solution for retrieving the ball is again through cheating. Pulling back on your adversary's leg is an effective means of slowing him down to give you a fairer chance at guarding him. But the most effective method of getting the ball is simply to pull his suit down, which immediately stops all his competitive activity. Fortunately, water polo is played in the water, since it hides the cheating all players must do in order to be successful.

Topic Sentence   YOU MUST CHEAT TO PLAY WATER Polo WELL.

Subtopic Sentence   ILLEGAL MOVES ARE THE ONLY WAY TO KEEP THE BALL

Specific Support   PUSHING OFF AN OPPONENT'S STOMACH

Specific Support   KNEEING YOUR OPPONENT IN THE RIBS

Subtopic Sentence   CHEATING GETS THE BALL BACK

Specific Support   PULLING BACK ON OPPONENT'S LEG

Specific Support   PULLING DOWN HIS SUIT

Reworded Topic Sentence   THE CHEATING IT TAKES TO WIN IN WATER POLO GOES ON UNSEEN BECAUSE IT HAPPENS UNDER WATER.

B. Outline this paragraph:

　　　Giving a good speech takes a lot of work. For instance, it takes hard work just to prepare the content—to write it. Last year I had to give a speech to our entire graduating class in high school. I wanted to impress my friends and their families, of course, but the words I wrote always sounded phony—too "elevated" in tone. I wrote and wrote and rewrote until I finally decided not to be impressive but just to say the good things I felt about the school. I had spent more than hours; I had spent days getting the words right. Once I had the words, the hard part really started: practicing my delivery. I gave my speech to my empty room. I gave my speech to my mirror. I gave my speech to my twin sister. I even gave my speech to my parents! So don't let anybody tell you that giving a speech is easy.

Topic Sentence _IT TAKES A LOT of WORK TO GIVE A GOOD SPEECH_

Subtopic Sentence _PREPARING : WRITING IS HARD_

Specific Support _SAYING IT JUST RIGHT CAN TAKE DAYS_

Subtopic Sentence _DELIVERING ORATORY TAKES PRACTICE_

Specific Support _SPEAK TO AN EMPTY ROOM_

Specific Support _SPEAK TO A MIRROR_

Specific Support _SPEAK SPEECH TO SISTER_

Specific Support _SPEECH GIVEN TO PARENTS_

Reworded Topic Sentence _PREPALING : GIVING A GOOD SPEECH CAN TAKE A LOT OF TIME._

Chapter 8

Support: Subtopic Sentences

A subtopic sentence is very much like a topic sentence:

- A topic sentence and a subtopic sentence both state opinions that need specific support.
- And both are divisible into two parts: the subject (which must be limited) and the opinion (which must be precise).

Topic Sentences and Subtopic Sentences

A *topic* sentence is the main idea of your paragraph.

A *subtopic* sentence serves as a support idea. It helps show your readers that they should accept your main idea, the topic sentence.

Theoretically, if you can persuade your readers to accept each subtopic sentence, then they should accept your topic sentence as well.

The precise opinion in each subtopic sentence is usually identical to the precise opinion in the topic sentence. For example, we showed you a sample Stage II paragraph in the last chapter. These were the two subtopic sentences; notice that the opinions in them are identical:

- ■ For one thing, the indexes are usually *frustrating* because they are hard to decipher.

- ■ Aside from the indexes, the general quality of the writing is *frustrating* in the manuals themselves.

The rest of this chapter shows you three different kinds of subtopic sentences: subtopic sentences that answer the questions "Why?" "How?" or "When?"

There are other kinds of subtopic sentences than these, of course, but these three ways can get you started quickly.

SUBTOPIC SENTENCE: "WHY?"

One of the easiest ways to find a subtopic sentence is to state the topic sentence and then ask, "Why?"

Suppose this is your topic sentence: "Vegetable gardens take a lot of planning." If you ask yourself, "Why do vegetable gardens take a lot of planning?" you might come up with these two subtopic sentences:

■   Vegetable gardens take a lot of planning because the soil needs to be prepared.

■   Vegetable gardens take a lot of planning because the vegetables need to be planted at specific times.

Here is a possible outline, including the specific support you might want to use:

Topic Sentence —— { Vegetable gardens take a lot of planning.
Subtopic Sentence — { They take planning because the soil needs to be prepared.
Specific Support —— { Soil should be tilled in the fall, after the last harvest.
Specific Support —— { Soil should be tested in the spring, especially for acidity and nitrogen.
Subtopic Sentence — { They need to be planted at specific times.
Specific Support —— { Last year, I planted the lettuce too late, so that by the time it should have been ready for harvest, it had died. (Narrative example)
Reworded Topic —— { Therefore, you should plan your garden in advance.
Sentence

In this outline, the subtopic sentences give some reasons why the topic sentence is true; the specific support then gives the concrete support for the subtopic sentences.

By the way, subtopic sentences that answer the question "Why?" always can be joined to the topic sentence with the word *because:*

■   Vegetable gardens take a lot of planning *because* the soil needs to be prepared.

■   Vegetable gardens take a lot of planning *because* the vegetables need to be planted at specific times.

You don't have to use the word *because* to join the "Why?" subtopic sentence to the topic sentence, but you can. Whenever you write "Why?" subtopic sentences, you might want to test them by joining them to the topic sentence with the word *because.*

Notice that you can support your subtopic sentences with the same kind of specific support you learned in Chapter 2: examples (quick or narrative), statistics, and statements by authorities.

SUBTOPIC SENTENCE: "HOW?"

Another common type of subtopic sentence answers the question "How?" Look at this paragraph that has subtopic sentences answering the question "How?"

Topic Sentence —— { Heavy rush hour traffic brings out the worst in many drivers.

Subtopic Sentence —— { Traffic conditions make some drivers overly nervous.

Specific Support —— { Uncle Billy, usually a calm and careful driver, becomes so flustered in rush hour traffic that he can't carry on a conversation and forgets to check the rearview mirror when he changes lanes.

Specific Support —— { A 1987 study of traffic flow in the Los Angeles area showed that the average waiting time at freeway entrance ramps increased to 1.5 minutes during rush hour because of the number of drivers who were afraid to merge into the heavy stream of cars.

Subtopic Sentence —— { Heavy rush hour traffic reinforces the aggressiveness of some drivers.

Specific Support —— { Often drivers follow too closely during rush hour because they're afraid other drivers might slip in ahead of them.

Specific Support —— { Drivers continue into intersections on yellow lights even though they will get caught there and block cross traffic.

Specific Support —— { A psychologist who has studied driver reactions concluded that "stress conditions of rush hour traffic cause physical and emotional reactions like those of a soldier in combat."

Reworded Topic Sentence —— { Rush hour traffic conditions show many drivers at their worst.

Notice that these subtopic sentences clearly answer the question "How?" and not the question "Why?" "Why?" subtopic sentences probably would state something about the cause-effect relationship between rush hour traffic and the way drivers present themselves in it; "How?" subtopic sentences, on the other hand, show the results of the traffic on driver behavior.

We need to add a word of caution here. Sometimes subtopic sentences clearly answer "Why?" and sometimes they clearly answer "How?" At other times the questions appear to overlap. In other words, sometimes we can't be sure which of these two questions the subtopic sentences answer.

Don't worry. The fine distinctions you would have to make are more fitting for a class in philosophy or semantics than for one in composition. Treat these questions for what they are—a quick and effective way to find subtopic sentences.

SUBTOPIC SENTENCE: "WHEN?"

Another type of subtopic sentence answers the question "When?" For example, to show that your roommate is constantly sleepy, you could ask yourself "When?" The resulting paragraph might look like this one:

Topic Sentence —— { My roommate is constantly sleepy.
Subtopic Sentence —— { He is sleepy in the morning when he gets up.
Specific Support —— { He fumbles with the alarm clock.
Specific Support —— { He once put his trousers on backward.
Subtopic Sentence —— { He is sleepy when he is in class.
Specific Support —— { He once fell asleep in Math III and crunched his jaw on the desk.
Specific Support —— { He does not even remember the subject of the lecture he attended yesterday in chemistry.
Subtopic Sentence —— { He is sleepy in the evening.
Specific Support —— { His typical study position is a comatose sprawl with his head on his desk.
Specific Support —— { He is always in bed by 8:30 P.M.
Reworded Topic —— { My roommate is sleepy all the time.
Sentence

PARALLEL SUBTOPIC SENTENCES

In the examples in this chapter, all the subtopic sentences within a one-paragraph essay answer the same question: "Why?" "How?" or "When?" Your Stage II paragraphs should do the same.

In other words, if you are supporting the idea "Hitchhiking is dangerous" in a Stage II paragraph, do not answer the question "Why?" for one subtopic sentence ("Hitchhiking is dangerous because too many drivers are deranged") and the question "When?" for another subtopic sentence ("Hitchhiking is dangerous at night, when the streets are poorly lighted").

These ideas may both work to support your topic sentence, but they do not work well together. They are not parallel and seem like a mixture of apples and oranges when you are selling only apples.

Once you have outlined your Stage II paragraph, be sure your subtopic sentences answer the same question: "Why?" "How?" or "When?"

EXERCISES

A. For each of these topic sentences, invent subtopic sentences and specific support. Be sure all your subtopic sentences answer the same question: "Why?" "How?" or "When?"

1. Weather forecasting is definitely a science.

Subtopic Sentence (Why? or How? or When?)

> SATELLITE TECHNOLOGY HAS ALLOWED MAN TO
> PUT THE WEATHER UNDER A MICROSCOPE ALLOWING FOR

Specific Support (quick example) ITS VISIBLE MONITORING + RELATIVELY DEPENDABLE PREDICTION

> FOR EXAMPLE, HURRICANE TRAKING IS COMMONPLACE
> TODAY BECAUSE OF THE SATELLITES ABILITY TO
> MONITOR THEM

Specific Support (quick example)

> EMILY, THE DEVASTATING HURRICANE
> THAT RIPPED THROUGH FLORIDA IN 1991,
> TOOK VERY FEW LIVES BECAUSE OF THE
> SATELLITE'S ABILITY TO TRACK IT

Subtopic Sentence (Why? or How? or When?)

> DOPLER RADAL ALLOWS THE WEATHER SERVICE
> TO TRACK TORNADOC ACTIVITY AS WELL

Specific Support (statistics)

> 100% of ALL POTENTIAL LIFE LOSS IN HURICANE
> AREAS, & SOME 50% to 60% IN TORNADO
> AREAS CAN NOW BE AVERTED BECAUSE OF THESE
> MODERN WEATHER SCIENCE "EYES IN THE SKY."

Specific Support (statement by authority)

> "THE ABILITY TO TRACK WEATHER SYSTEMS TODAY
> BECAUSE OF SATELLITE DOPLER TECHNOLOGY HAS BROUGHT
> METEOROLOGY OUT OF THE GUESS WORK OF PROBABILITY
> INTO THE OBSERVABLE REALM OF INTELLICAL SCIENCE."
> (NATIONAL WEATHER SERVICE DIRECTOR, BOB SMITH)

2. Computers save people time.

Subtopic Sentence (Why? or How? or When?)

> THE COMPUTER'S EDITING FUNCTIONS OF DELETING &
> INSERTING TEXT CAN SPEED A WRITING PROJECT 3/4 FASTER

Specific Support (narrative example) THAN A TYPEWRITER'S TIME

Subtopic Sentence (Why? or How? or When?)

Specific Support (statistics)

Specific Support (statement by authority)

---

3. Twentieth-century medicine really works.

Subtopic Sentence (Why? or How? or When?)

Specific Support (statistics)

Specific Support (statistics)

Subtopic Sentence (Why? or How? or When?)

Specific Support (quick example)

_____

_____

_____

_____

Specific Support (quick example)

_____

_____

_____

B. If your instructor asks you to, outline the opposite of all the above topic sentences:

1. Weather forecasting is hardly a science.

2. Too often, computers waste people's time.

3. Twentieth-century medicine sometimes causes problems.

Use whichever type of subtopic sentence ("Why?" "How?" or "When?") and whichever type of specific support (examples, statistics, statements by authorities) you wish.

C. In Exercises A and B you outlined several Stage II paragraphs. Choose the one that interests you the most and use the support you invented to write the paragraph.

D. Write a Stage II paragraph convincing us that someone you know has a positive (pleasant, good) or a negative (unpleasant, bad) characteristic. Since you're writing about someone you know, don't use invented support for this exercise.

E. Write a Stage II paragraph explaining how something you have observed impressed you. The sample paragraph in Chapter 7 about "The Nation's Attic" could have been a response to this exercise. Since you're writing about something you've observed, don't use invented support for this exercise.

F. Write a Stage II paragraph about one of these topics (using, if you wish, invented support):

birds	Native Americans
brothers or sisters	nursing homes ✓
a building you know well	railroads
extracurricular events	restaurants
landscaping	vacation spots
losing teams	winning teams

G. If you've held a job, try this exercise. Write a Stage II paragraph characterizing your workplace—Hectic? Rewarding? Frustrating? Something else?

CHECKLIST FOR THE ONE-PARAGRAPH ESSAY

Topic Sentence

_____ Does your paragraph begin with a topic sentence?

_____ Does your topic sentence have a limited subject?

_____ Does your topic sentence have a precise opinion?

Support

_____ Does your support begin with the second sentence of the paragraph?

_____ Is your support detailed enough?

_____ Do all your items of support clearly belong with the topic sentence (unity?)

_____ Do you explain your spport fully so the relation to the topic is clear (coherence)?

_____ Does each item of support include a reminder of the opinion in the topic sentence (coherence)?

_____ Do you have transitions at the critical locations (coherence)?

Conclusion

_____ Does the last sentence of the paragraph reword the topic sentence?

Other

_____ Is your paragraph convincing?

_____ Is your paragraph interesting?

_____ Have you checked the spelling of the words you're unsure of?

_____ Is your paper neatly done so it's easy to read?

Part Three

The Five-Paragraph Essay

A five-paragraph essay is a handy device for learning to write longer papers. The first and last paragraphs are the introduction and conclusion, two new types of paragraphs most longer papers need. The three central paragraphs provide enough material to justify a full-length introduction and conclusion but still keep the paper short enough to be manageable—for both you and your instructor.

You'll also begin writing about more serious topics in this part. So far you've depended on your own experiences for much of your support; you'll still present your experiences here, but you'll supplement them with occasional support from books and magazines. Of course, we don't expect you to learn the fundamentals of the multiparagraph essay and the fundamentals of documentation at the same time, so we present in this section a simplified system of documentation you can use until you study the research paper in Part Five.

Chapter 9

Overview of the Five-Paragraph Essay

Are your paragraphs turning into monsters? Are they getting longer and longer, seeming more like small themes instead of one-paragraph essays?

If so, you're ready to take the next step: learning to write the *five*-paragraph essay. Actually, the five-paragraph essay is a lot like a Stage II paragraph. This diagram shows you how:

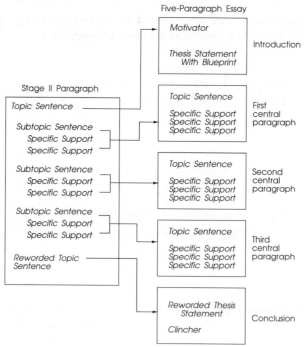

PARTS OF A FIVE-PARAGRAPH ESSAY

A five-paragraph essay has these parts:

- an introduction (1 paragraph)
- central paragraphs (3 paragraphs)
- a conclusion (1 paragraph)

Let's look at each of these briefly. (We'll discuss them in greater detail in the next few chapters.)

[handwritten: En essays or research paper Consists of the same elements of a paragraph. This will make it simple]

Introduction

[handwritten: Aristotle claimed that every story (research paper) can be reduced to a SINGLE SENTENCE.]

[handwritten: Aristotle said it best: A GOOD STORY HAS A BEGINNING, A MIDDLE- ; AN END.]

An introduction is, of course, the first paragraph of the essay. In a way, the topic sentence of your one-paragraph essay served as an introduction, but now that you're about to write longer papers, you'll want something more substantial at the beginning.

[handwritten: with purpose unity]

Introductions have three parts: a *motivator,* a *thesis statement,* and a *blueprint.*

Motivator

A motivator is the beginning of the introductory paragraph. Its purpose is simply to get the reader interested in reading more—in other words, in *motivating* the reader.

Thesis Statement *[handwritten: — BEGINNING A statement you want to make.]*

A topic sentence carries the main idea of a one-paragraph essay, right? Well, a thesis statement carries the main idea of the five-paragraph essay.

Blueprint

A blueprint is simply a quick summary of the main points you are about to present in the essay. Since a five-paragraph essay has three central paragraphs, your blueprint will have three points, one for each of the central paragraphs.

Central Paragraphs

There are three central paragraphs in a five-paragraph essay, and each central paragraph supports the essay's main point (or thesis statement).

A central paragraph is like a one-paragraph essay, with a topic sentence at the beginning and specific support following. Normally, though, central paragraphs don't have reworded topic sentences.

Conclusion

Remember the reworded topic sentence at the end of a one-paragraph essay? That sentence gave your one-paragraph essay a sense of finality. The conclusion—the last paragraph of a five-paragraph essay—also gives a sense of finality. A conclusion has two parts: a *reworded thesis statement* and a *clincher.*

[handwritten: SENTENCE REWORDING OF your intro.]

Reworded Thesis Statement

A reworded thesis statement simply does what it says: rewords the thesis statement. It's intended to be a reminder to your readers, saying, in effect, "You've just been reading my three central paragraphs. Once again, let me tell you what those three paragraphs were supporting." Then you tell them.

Clincher

A clincher is simply a finisher, a final sentence or two that leaves no doubt in the reader's mind that the essay has reached its end.

A SAMPLE FIVE-PARAGRAPH ESSAY

Now let's look at a "real" five-paragraph essay. As you read it, notice the points we've been discussing: the motivator, the blueprint, and so forth.

Motivator — Do you realize that newly born children are not even aware that parts of their bodies belong to them? I learned this fascinating fact in my psychology course from a book that says a baby "lies on his back, kicking his heels and watching the little fists flying past his face. But only very slowly does he come to know that they are attached to him and he can control them" (Mary Ann Spencer Pulaski, *Understanding Piaget,* p. 21). Children have a lot of

Thesis Statement — learning to do before they can see the world—and themselves—through grown-up eyes. As children pass through this remarkable process of growing up, they often do some humorous things, especially in learning to speak,

Blueprint — in discovering that all objects do not have human characteristics, and in trying to imitate others around them.

Topic Sentence — Not surprisingly, one area in which children are often humorous is in learning to speak. I remember one time I was talking to a friend on the phone while my little sister, Betsy, seemed to be playing inattentively on the floor nearby. After I hung up, Betsy asked me, "Why is the teacher going to give Janet an old tomato?" At first I

Specific Support — couldn't figure out what Betsy was talking about. When I asked her what she meant, she said, "You said if Janet doesn't hand in her homework, the teacher is going to give her an old tomato." Finally I caught on. The word I had used was *ultimatum!*

Topic Sentence — Children also can be funny in the way they "humanize" the objects around them. According to my psychology book, "Up to four or five years old, the child believes

Specific Support — anything may be endowed with purpose and conscious activity. A ball may refuse to be thrown straight, or a 'naughty' chair may be responsible for bumping him"

Specific
Support ——————
(Pulaski, *Understanding Piaget,* p. 45). I, myself, still can remember one vivid and scary afternoon when I was sure the sun was following me around, just waiting for the right

Specific
Support ——————
moment to get me. I also can remember a time, not scary, when Betsy stood at the top of the stairs and yelled to her shoes at the bottom, "Shoes! Get up here!"

Topic
Sentence ——————
Another way in which children are sometimes funny is in their attempts to imitate what they see around them. All

Specific
Support ——————
children look pretty silly when they dress up like their mothers and fathers and play "house." My psychology book tells of a more interesting example, though. The famous psychologist Jean Piaget wrote of the time his sixteen-month-old daughter quietly watched a visiting little boy throw a tantrum in trying to get out of his

Specific
Support ——————
playpen. Piaget's daughter thought it would be fun to try the same thing: "The next day, she herself screamed in her playpen and tried to move it, stamping her foot lightly several times in succession. The imitation of the whole scene was most striking" (quoted in Pulaski, *Understanding Piaget,* p. 81).

Reworded
Thesis ——————
Little children are funny creatures to watch, aren't they? But as we laugh, we have to admire, too, because the humorous mistakes are but temporary side trips that children take on the amazingly complicated journey to

Clincher ——————
maturity—a long way from the beginning, where they lay in wonder, silently watching the strange, fingered spacecraft passing, back and forth, before their infant eyes.

Now let's look at an outline of that essay:

Introduction

> *Motivator*   Children have many things to learn and adjust to as they grow up—including the awareness of the parts of their bodies.
>
> *Thesis*   Children often do humorous things.
>
> *Blueprint*   They're often humorous in learning to speak, in discovering that all objects do not have humorous characteristics, and in attempting to imitate others.

First Central Paragraph

> *Topic Sentence*   Children are often humorous in learning to speak.
>
> *Specific Support*   Betsy mistook *ultimatum* for *old tomato.*

Second Central Paragraph

Topic Sentence   Children "humanize" the objects around them.
Specific Support   Book says children blame balls and chairs as though the things were conscious.
Specific Support   I thought the sun was out to get me.
Specific Support   Betsy ordered her shoes to climb the stairs.

Third Central Paragraph

Topic Sentence   Children attempt to imitate what they see.
Specific Support   They dress like their parents.
Specific Support   Piaget's daughter imitated a tantrum a visiting child threw.

Conclusion

Reworded Thesis   Children are funny creatures to watch.
Clincher Reminder of the motivator that children have a lot of learning and adjusting to do.

PRELIMINARY DOCUMENTATION

Until now, you've been writing most of your papers based on your personal experience. Those papers can be interesting and important.

At some time in your life, though, you need to learn to write about other topics—about the ideas and the words of other people. When you use the ideas and words of others, you need to let the reader know where. In other words, you need to learn about documentation.

You need to document any time you use the ideas or words of other people. However, we don't want to ask you to learn the fundamentals of the five-paragraph essay and the fundamentals of documentation all at once. On the other hand, we want you to be able to use the ideas and words of others now.

As a result, we've devised what we call a "preliminary system of documentation"—a temporary and easy way for you to acknowledge your sources. Later in the book we devote two chapters to a more formal way of documenting your writing.

Here's our preliminary system:

- Put quotation marks around all words you take directly from a source.
- At the end of every sentence in which you use someone else's words or ideas, identify the source in parentheses. To identify the source, simply use the

author's name (if there is one), the title of the book or article, and the page number: (Dick Francis, <u>Forfeit</u>, p. 143) or (<u>The Columbia-Viking Desk Encyclopedia</u>, pp. 45–58) or (George Miller, "The Magical Number 7, Plus or Minus 2," p. 81).

Proper documentation serves two purposes: it tells your readers that you are using words or ideas of others; and it tells your readers where they can find your source. Our preliminary system serves only the first purpose well, because your parenthetical information simply isn't complete. As a result, your instructor may ask you to keep your sources handy.

The sample essay in this chapter has good examples of preliminary documentation. If you have any questions at all, please ask your instructor.

PRACTICAL WRITING

You don't find many five-paragraph essays in business and technical writing, but you see variations that come quite close.

Busy readers like the main point up front—for the document as a whole and for the sections of a document. In other words, something like a thesis statement at the beginning of a document is helpful. And something like topic sentences at the beginnings of sections can be helpful, too.

And as long as a document has sections, why not name those sections up front, right after the main point? Naming the sections is (you guessed it) a blueprint. Business writers sometimes call it a "road map."

Let's look at an example of business writing that resembles our five-paragraph essay.

Here's the situation: a manager writes a memo to her boss, asking permission to buy an expensive kind of printer and software that does fancy word processing.

This is the memo she actually wrote (and the vice president approved the purchase, too!):

```
              Using the Principles
          of the Five-Paragraph Essay

From:     Janet Chambers
To:       Ed Malone
Subject:  A Proposal for a PostScript Printer and
          Desktop Publishing

We need to improve the quality of the documents and
proposals we're producing in our division. To add the
polish and professional look we need, I recommend we
buy a PostScript laser printer plus additional
purchases that will let our secretaries do desktop
```

publishing. This memo will cover why we need the laser printer, why we need the additional purchases, and what our implementation plan will be.

First, I recommend we buy a PostScript laser printer. The cost would be $3,400. The printer will give us two main benefits: It will add a graphics capability to both graphics work and desktop publishing. In fact, desktop publishing almost requires a PostScript printer for efficient and timely work. The PostScript printer is also fairly fast, so it will give us the crucial speed we need for rapid turnaround of final documents and proposals. It will make possible those last minute additions and changes that often improve the final presentation.

Next, we'll need additional purchases to do desktop publishing on the laser printer. Here's specifically what we'll need:

2 copies of software	$550/copy	$1,100
2 mouse set ups	100/mouse	200
2 graphics boards	200 each	400
2 training slots	500/person	1,000
	Total	$2,700

The desktop publishing will give our documents a professional appearance plus it can easily combine text and graphics. That way the appearance of our documents will truly express the professional quality of our work.

Once we get a PostScript laser printer and the additional purchases, here's what our implementation plan will be: We'll add the PostScript printer to our network so it's widely available to the staff. We'll install the other hardware and software on the workstations belonging to the two secretaries. One secretary is ready to do desktop publishing as soon as we get her a mouse and a graphics board. She already has software, training, and experience publishing a proposal. The other secretary needs to take the training first. That training is offered 3 weeks from now. When she's trained, we should have an excellent start for desktop publishing.

```
I'll be glad to talk this over with you whenever you
like.
```

The principles of the five-paragraph are all there, aren't they? Did you notice the main point and blueprint in the first paragraph? The topic sentences at the beginning of each major paragraph? The detailed support?

Now try to imagine that memo another way—<u>without</u> all those good techniques of organization. And imagine you're the vice president getting it (and you're having a busy day!). You'd be much less likely to read it quickly, wouldn't you? And when you did read it, you'd probably have to struggle a bit, too.

So the five-paragraph essay is a learning tool—and the principles it teaches can help you all your life.

EXERCISE

Outline this five-paragraph essay:

When a person thinks of that old-time, small-town doctor, he usually envisions a mannerly, dignified gentleman. However, this image did not fit my Uncle Rodney, a doctor in the small town of Bandon, Wyoming. Instead, Dr. Rodney was an obnoxious person because he had an annoying habit of speaking in crude, incoherent sentences; he had sloppy eating habits; and he was a messy smoker.

Probably Dr. Rodney's most irritating trait was his crude way of speaking. For example, I recall a particularly embarrassing moment during a family reunion at my mother-in-law's house when Dr. Rodney was asked to say a blessing before dinner. He managed a "Hump, bump, grump," or so it sounded, and almost immediately added "Goddammit" as he knocked over a bowl of grated corn he was grabbing. As a result, my mother-in-law—a very religious person—was mortified. On another occasion, Dr. Rodney's nurse said, "It's a good thing I can interpret what Dr. Rodney says and smooth over the rough feelings, or we would be out of patients."

Additionally, Dr. Rodney bothered many people with his messy eating habits. He shoveled food into his mouth at such an alarming rate that often he could not catch his breath. My brother-in-law once remarked, "When I see Uncle Rodney eat, I think of jackals devouring their kill." Furthermore, Dr. Rodney always finished his meal long before anyone else; then he would make a nauseating slurping sound by sucking air and saliva through the gaps between his top front teeth while he waited for everybody else to finish. Because of his atrocious eating habits, none of Dr. Rodney's neighbors invited him to dinner.

Dr. Rodney also was disliked because he was an inconsiderate smoker. Everywhere he went, he left a trail of ashes, a terrible stench, and wet, chewed-up cigar butts. After his death, the office cleaning lady confided that the townspeople used to bet on how many days would pass before anyone saw Dr. Rodney without a spot of tobacco juice on his shirt. Naturally, all the local children learned not to be downwind from him because no one could easily tolerate his odor of stale tobacco.

Clearly, Dr. Rodney was an obnoxious person whose talking, eating, and smoking habits alienated him from even his own family. He was indeed lucky that the town had only one doctor, or he might not have been employed.

Introduction

```
Motivator
Thesis
Blueprint
```

First Central Paragraph

```
Topic Sentence
   Specific Support
   Specific Support
```

Second Central Paragraph

```
Topic Sentence
   Specific Support
   Specific Support
   Specific Support
   Specific Support
```

Third Central Paragraph

```
Topic Sentence
   Specific Support
   Specific Support
   Specific Support
```

Conclusion

```
Reworded Thesis
Clincher
```

Chapter 10

Techniques of Layout

At the beginning of this part of the book, we asked if your paragraphs had turned into long monsters. Well, without special care, the paragraphs in a five-paragraph essay can do the same thing.

In this chapter, we'll offer three suggestions to help your writing *look better* (layout is the word for the *look* of the page):

- headings
- paragraphs that show breaks in thought
- indented lists (like this one)

The popularity of the computer has made good layout common even for school papers, because the computer lets us experiment until we get the layout just right. So now, the computer (something new) can work with the five-paragraph essay (something old) to produce something even better.

Let's look more closely at these three techniques of layout.

HEADINGS

The word just above this sentence ("Headings") is a heading—the name for the "title" of a section of writing. In fact, we like to think of a heading as a *label* for a section's content.

One advantage of a heading is that it adds some white space to your text, signaling your reader that you're moving to a new topic. That way, your layout visually reinforces your words.

Another advantage is that a heading gives the main idea of the section. In the model of the five-paragraph essay we just showed you, paragraphing showed new ideas. But sometimes paragraphs have minor changes in thought within them. If you've used headings to announce the topic of a section, you then can have paragraphs *within* that section. That way, the reader can see all the minor shifts in organization, such as moving to a new item of specific support.

And the reader shouldn't get confused: the headings clearly show the various major sections of the paper.

You may wonder how to make headings. We suggest simply using initial capital letters and starting on the left margin. Here's a sample paper using headings:

A Sample Paper With Headings

XXXXX XXXXXXXXX XXXXXX XXX XXXXXXXXX XXXX XXXXXX XXXXXXX XXXXXX XXXXXXXXXXXXXX XXXXXX XXXXXXXXXXX XX XXXXXXXXXXX XXXXX XXXXXXXXXX XXXXXX XXXXXX XXX XXXXXXXXX XXXX XXXXXX XXXXXXX XXXXXX XXXXXXXXXXXXXX XXXXXX

This Is a Heading

XXX XXXXXXXXXX XXXX XXXXXX XXXXXXX XXXXXXX XXXXXXXXXXXXXX XXXXXX XXXXXXXXXXX XX XXXXXXXXXXX XXX XXXXXXXXXX XXXX XXXXXX XXXXXXX XXXXXXX XXXXXXXXXXXXXX XXXXXX XXXXXXXXXXX XX XXXXXXXXXXX XXX XXXXXXXXXX XXXX XXXXXX XXXXXXX XXXXXXX XXXXXXX XXXX XXXXXX XXXXXXX XXXXXXX

XXX XXXXXXXXXX XXXX XXXXXX XXXXXXX XXXXXXX XXXXXXXXXXXXXX XXXXXX XXXXXXXXXXX XX XXXXXXXXXXX XXX XXXXXXXXXX XXXX XXXXXX XXXXXXX XXXXXXX XXXXXXXXXXXXXX XXXXXX XXXXXXXXXXX XX XXXXXXXXXXX

This Is Another Heading

XXX XXXXXXXXXX XXXX XXXXXX XXXXXXX XXXXXXX XXXXXXXXXXXXXX XXXXXX XXXXXX XXX XXXXXXXXXX XXXX XXXXXX XXXXXXX XXXXXXX XXXXXXXXXXXXXX XXXXXX XXXXXXXXXXX XX XXXXXXXXXXX XXXXX XXXXXXXXXX XXXXXXXXXXXXXXXXX XX XXXXXXXXXX XXX XXXXXXXXXX XXXX XXXXXXXXXXX

XXX XXXXXXXXXX XXXX XXXXXX XXXXXXX XXXXXXX XXXXXXXXXXXXXX XXXXXX XXXXXXXXXXX XX XXXXXXXXXXX XX XXXXXXXXXXX XXXXX XXXXXXXXXX XXXXXXXXXXXXXXXXX XX XXX XXXXXXXXXX XXXX XXXXXX XXXXXXX XXXXXXX XXXXXXXXXXXXXX XXXXXX XXXXXXXXXXX XX XXXXXXXXXXX

You can have either a single paragraph or several under a heading.

> **Tips on Headings**
>
> - If you use a computer or newer typewriter, make all your headings **bold.** Don't use bold elsewhere in the paper (simply underline) or else you'll distract your reader's eyes from your headings.
> - Put one more space above a heading than below it. That way your heading is visually part of the text it labels.
> - Use at least two headings—never only one. Headings show subordinate ideas, so—just as with outlines—you need two or more.

SHORTER PARAGRAPHS

Once you use headings, you can then use shorter paragraphs that show breaks in thought. For example, consider this paragraph from our sample five-paragraph essay in the last chapter:

Sample Paragraph Without Organizational Breaks

Children also can be funny in the way they "humanize" the objects around them. According to my psychology book, "Up to four or five years old, the child believes anything may be endowed with purpose and conscious activity. A ball may refuse to be thrown straight, or a 'naughty' chair may be responsible for bumping him" (Pulaski, *Understanding Piaget,* p. 45). I, myself, still can remember one vivid and scary afternoon when I was sure the sun was following me around, just waiting for the right moment to get me. I also can remember a time, not scary, when Betsy stood at the top of the stairs and yelled to her shoes at the bottom, "Shoes! Get up here!"

But if that paragraph had a heading (and the paragraph after had another heading), then we could show the small organizational breaks this way:

Sample Paragraph With Organizational Breaks

Discovering Objects Aren't Human

Children also can be funny in the way they "humanize" the objects around them. According to my psychology book, "Up to four or five years old, the child believes anything may be endowed with purpose and conscious activity. A ball may refuse to be thrown straight, or a 'naughty' chair may be responsible for bumping him" (Pulaski, *Understanding Piaget*, p. 45).

> I, myself, still can remember one vivid and scary afternoon when I was sure the sun was following me around, just waiting for the right moment to get me. I also can remember a time, not scary, when Betsy stood at the top of the stairs and yelled to her shoes at the bottom, "Shoes! Get up here!"

Now the writer can easily signal the shift from one item of support to the next.

So when you use headings in your writing, your paragraphs don't always have to begin with topic sentences: the headings show the boundaries of your ideas. Then your paragraphs can show the lesser organizational breaks, giving additional help to your readers.

INDENTED LISTS

Lists help show—that is, visually emphasize—a pattern of organization *within* a paragraph.

To make them, use a bullet symbol (a hyphen will do fine, as will a lower-case letter *o*). Then use the same sort of spacing you see on the sample papers in the next section.

A SAMPLE FIVE-PARAGRAPH ESSAY USING GOOD LAYOUT

Now let's see what good layout can do for a paper we saw in the last chapter.

> **A Paper With Good Layout**
>
> Do you realize that newly born children are not even aware that parts of their bodies belong to them? I learned this fascinating fact in my psychology course from a book that says a baby "lies on his back, kicking his heels and watching the little fists flying past his face. But only very slowly does he come to know that they are attached to him and he can control them" (Mary Ann Spencer Pulaski, Understanding Piaget, p. 21).
>
> Children have a lot of learning to do before they can see the world--and themselves--through grown-up eyes. As children pass through this remarkable process of growing up, they often do some humorous things, especially
>
>   - in learning to speak

        - in discovering that all objects do not have
          human characteristics
        - and in trying to imitate others around them

Learning To Speak

    Not surprisingly, one area in which children
are often humorous is in learning to speak. I
remember one time I was talking to a friend on
the phone while my little sister, Betsy, seemed
to be playing inattentively on the floor nearby.
After I hung up, Betsy asked me, "Why is the
teacher going to give Janet an old tomato?"

    At first I couldn't figure out what Betsy
was talking about. When I asked her what she
meant, she said, "You said if Janet doesn't hand
in her homework, the teacher is going to give her
an old tomato." Finally I caught on. The word I
had used was ultimatum!

Discovering Objects Aren't Human

    Children also can be funny in the way they
"humanize" the objects around them. According to
my psychology book, "Up to four or five years
old, the child believes anything may be endowed
with purpose and conscious activity. A ball may
refuse to be thrown straight, or a 'naughty'
chair may be responsible for bumping him"
(Pulaski, Understanding Piaget

    I, myself, still can remember one vivid and
scary afternoon when I was sure the sun was
following me around, just waiting for the right
moment to get me. I also can remember a time, not
scary, when Betsy stood at the top of the stairs
and yelled to her shoes at the bottom, "Shoes!
Get up here!"

Imitating Others Around Them

Another way in which children are sometimes funny is in their attempts to immitate what they see around them. All children look pretty silly when they dress up like their mothers and fathers and play "house."

My psychology book tells of a more interesting example, though. The famous psychologist Jean Piaget wrote of the time his sixteen-month-old daughter quietly watched a visiting little boy throw a tantrum in trying to get out of his playpen. Piaget's daughter thought it would be fun to try the same thing: "The next day, she herself screamed in her playpen and tried to move it, stamping her foot lightly several times in succession. The imitation of the whole scene was most striking" (quoted in Pulaski, Understanding Piaget, p. 81).

Conclusion

Little children are funny creatures to watch, aren't they? But as we laugh, we have to admire, too, because the humorous mistakes are but temporary side trips that children take on the amazingly complicated journey to maturity— a long way from the beginning, where they lay in wonder, silently watching the strange, fingered spacecraft passing, back and forth, before their infant eyes.

It looks good, doesn't it? And for those of you who use computers, you can play around with the layout of your paper until you get it just right.

SINGLE SPACING AND DOUBLE SPACING

There used to be one way to space papers in school—double spaced. That has the advantage of giving your instructor room to make detailed comments.

There's another camp now, however. Some instructors prefer single spacing because it can show more of the paper at once. Particularly if the paper has headings in it, it's possible for the instructor to understand the organization better—more words and ideas are on each page. That way, the instructor is less likely to miss the forest because trees get in the way.

PRACTICAL WRITING

Everything in this chapter is highly relevant to writing both in college and beyond:

- In college, these techniques can help your instructors follow your longer papers and examinations.
- Beyond college, these techniques are prevalent in all types of business, technical, and other professional writing.

In a sense, then, this entire chapter could fall under the heading "Practical Writing."

EXERCISE

Apply the three techniques of layout to this paper we showed you in the last chapter (you may need to do just a little rewording in places to get indented lists):

```
From:      Janet Chambers
To:        Ed Malone
Subject:   A Proposal for a PostScript Printer and
           Desktop Publishing

We need to improve the quality of the documents and
proposals we're producing in our division. To add the
polish and professional look we need, I recommend we
buy a PostScript laser printer plus additional
purchases that will let our secretaries do desktop
publishing. This memo will cover why we need the laser
printer, why we need the additional purchases, and
what our implementation plan will be.

First, I recommend we buy a PostScript laser printer.
The cost would be $3,400. The printer will give us two
main benefits: It will add a graphics capability to
both graphics work and desktop publishing. In fact,
desktop publishing almost requires a PostScript printer
```

for efficient and timely work. The PostScript printer is also fairly fast, so it will give us the crucial speed we need for rapid turnaround of final documents and proposals. It will make possible those last minute additions and changes that often improve the final presentation.

Next, we'll need additional purchases to do desktop publishing on the laser printer. Here's specifically what we'll need:

2 copies of software	$550/copy	$1,100
2 mouse set ups	100/mouse	200
2 graphics boards	200 each	400
2 training slots	500/person	1,000
	Total	$2,700

The desktop publishing will give our documents a professional appearance plus it can easily combine text and graphics. That way the appearance of our documents will truly express the professional quality of our work.

Once we get a PostScript laser printer and the additional purchases, here's what our implementation plan will be: We'll add the PostScript printer to our network so it's widely available to the staff. We'll install the other hardware and software on the workstations belonging to the two secretaries. One secretary is ready to do desktop publishing as soon as we get her a mouse and a graphics board. She already has software, training, and experience publishing a proposal. The other secretary needs to take the training first. That training is offered 3 weeks from now. When she's trained, we should have an excellent start for desktop publishing.

I'll be glad to talk this over with you whenever you like.

Chapter 11

Thesis Statement With Blueprint

The thesis statement with blueprint is an essential part of your five-paragraph essay. As the name suggests, it has two components:

- the main idea *(thesis statement)*
- the outline of your support *(blueprint)*

Let's look at each of these two components in more detail.

THESIS STATEMENT

The thesis statement is the main idea of your five-paragraph essay, the single idea your entire essay will support. Sound familiar?

The *topic sentence* was the main idea of a one-paragraph essay. Now, the *thesis statement* is the main idea of anything larger than a one-paragraph essay—in this case, the main idea of the five-paragraph essay.

Like the topic sentence, the thesis statement can have the form of *"limited subject* is *precise opinion."* Here's the introduction to our sample five-paragraph essay—we've underlined the thesis:

Introduction With Thesis Statement

Do you realize that newly born children are not even aware that parts of their bodies belong to them? I learned this fascinating fact in my psychology course from a book that says a baby "lies on his back, kicking his heels and watching the little fists flying past his face. But only very slowly does he come

---

> to know that they are attached to him and he can control them" (Mary Ann Spencer Pulaski, *Understanding Piaget,* p. 21). Children have a lot of learning to do before they can see the world—and themselves—through grown-up eyes. <u>As children pass through this remarkable process of growing up, they often do some humorous things</u>, especially in learning to speak, in discovering that all objects do not have human characteristics, and in trying to imitate others around them.

The limited subject is *children as they grow up;* the precise opinion is *humorous.*

BLUEPRINT

What is a blueprint for an essay? As we mentioned in the last chapter, a blueprint is a summary of the main points you are about to present in the body of your paper. In other words, *the blueprint is a summary of the topic sentences for your central paragraphs.*

The Meaning of the Term *Blueprint*

As the name *blueprint* suggests, the blueprint is like an architect's pattern for the structure she intends to build . . . only in this case, you are the architect, and the structure you intend to build is your essay.

Suppose you have this organization in mind for your five-paragraph essay:

Thesis Statement	Overly competitive sports can damage a child psychologically.
Topic Sentence	They can damage a child's view of himself.
Topic Sentence	They can damage a child's view of his peers.
Topic Sentence	The can damage a child's view of adults.

Now, to form a blueprint, simply combine the basic ideas from the three topic sentences:

■ Because they can damage a child's view of himself, of his peers, and of adults,

Now let's combine the blueprint with the thesis statement to get the result this chapter is about—the thesis statement with blueprint:

■ Because they can damage a child's view of himself, of his peers, and of adults, overly competitive sports can damage a child psychologically.

Finally, let's look at the introduction to the sample theme from the last chapter—we've underlined the blueprint:

Introduction With Thesis and Blueprint

Do you realize that newly born children are not even aware that parts of their bodies belong to them? I learned this fascinating fact in my psychology course from a book that says a baby "lies on his back, kicking his heels and watching the little fists flying past his face. But only very slowly does he come to know that they are attached to him and he can control them" (Mary Ann Spencer Pulaski, *Understanding Piaget,* p. 21). Children have a lot of learning to do before they can see the world—and themselves—through grown-up eyes. As children pass through this re-markable process of growing up, they often do some humorous things, especially in learning to speak, in discovering that all objects do not have human characteristics, and in trying to imitate others around them.

BLUEPRINTS ANSWERING "WHY?" "HOW?" AND "WHEN?"

The five-paragraph essay is really just an expanded Stage II paragraph, so you could use the same kind of support for both of them. Let's examine sample blueprints answering each of the questions "Why?" "How?" and "When?"

"Why?" Blueprint

If we ask "Why?" about a thesis statement, the answer will usually begin with *because.* In fact, our sample about competitive sports being psychologically damaging to children is a "Why?" blueprint, isn't it?

Let's look at another example: *Why do vegetable gardens take a lot of planning?*

Blueprint Answering "Why?"

Because the soil needs to be prepared, *because* the vegetables need to be planted at the right times, and *because* the fertilizing must take place on schedule, [then the thesis follows].

"How?" Blueprint

A "How?" blueprint usually can begin with *by, with,* or *through.* Also, since "How?" blueprints are sometimes similar to "Why?" blueprints, they both can begin with *because.*

For example: *How does Wanda distract you?*

Blueprints Answering "How?"

By singing, eating, and talking as I try to study,

or

With her singing, her eating, and her talking,

or

Through her singing, her eating, and her talking,

or

Because of her singing, her eating, and her talking,

"When?" Blueprint

Finally, you usually can begin a "When?" blueprint with, yes, the word *when*. *When is your roommate constantly sleepy?*

Blueprint Answering "When?"

When he gets up in the morning, sits in class, or studies in the evening,

---

DIFFERENT FORMS OF THE THESIS WITH BLUEPRINT

So far, we've shown you blueprints as part of the same sentence as the thesis, with the blueprint coming at the beginning of that thesis:

Thesis With Blueprint in the Same Sentence

Because they can damage a child's view of himself, his peers, and adults, overly competitive sports can damage a child psychologically.

Actually, though, you can present the thesis with blueprint many different ways:

Different Forms of the Thesis With Blueprint

Overly competitive sports can damage a child psychologically because they can damage a child's view of himself, his peers, and adults.

or

> Overly competitive sports can damage a child psychologically: they can damage a child's view of himself, his peers, and adults.
>
> or
>
> Overly competitive sports can damage a child psychologically. They can damage a child's view of himself. They can damage a child's view of his peers. They even can damage his view of adults.

Please notice, though, that for each example, each item in the blueprint has the same structure. In the last example, each was an entire sentence.

This is a poor blueprint because the blueprint items do not have the same structure:

Poor Blueprint

Overly competitive sports can damage a child psychologically. They can damage a child's view of himself and of his peers. They even can damage his view of adults.

A reader probably would be confused. Is the writer going to talk about two ideas or three? There seem to be three ideas (view of self, peers, adults), but there are just two blueprint sentences following the thesis statement.

You can avoid confusing your reader by using the same structure—all sentences, all clauses, or all phrases—for each of your blueprint items. If you want more information, see the chapter on parallelism in Part Seven.

PRACTICAL WRITING

We've already discussed the value of the main point in writing for the business world. The blueprint is a valuable technique, too—especially when the content gets complicated.

Here's a sample from a very specialized magazine on computers, *UNIX Review:*

A Blueprint on Problems With Computer Security

I've organized the problems into five categories:

- What can I do to mess up one of those system configuration files?
- You mean there's something special about **setuid** programs?
- What's so important about physical security anyway?
- Are these manuals really useful for installing a system?

- That can't be a security breach! I've got a provably secure UNIX system!

[The article then has sections on each of the blueprint items.]

In the last chapter, we talked about indented lists such as the one *UNIX Review* used for its blueprint. Businesses often use indented lists for blueprints; that way, the blueprint gets extra visibility, extra emphasis. In most writing, a blueprint is an especially important list deserving emphasis.

The next example shows an implied blueprint; that is, instead of actually naming the items coming up, it just says how many there are and then plunges into writing about them. That's a good technique, too. Here's the example—also from *UNIX Review* (we've underlined the implied blueprint):

An Implied Blueprint

Computer (and UNIX) security matters can be broken down into <u>four general areas of concern</u>:

<u>Preventing unauthorized access</u>. This is perhaps the most important aspect of security: people who are not authorized to use the system. . . . [This section continues for several more sentences.]

<u>Preventing Compromise</u>. This is another important security concern: users, authorized or unauthorized, must. . . . [This section continues for several more sentences.]

[And so forth, for four total sections. Notice there is no explicit blueprint—just the statement that the writer will discuss four areas.]

So when in doubt, use blueprints. They take little space and can do a lot of good. In fact, you can find them at the beginning of many of our chapters.

EXERCISES

A. Combine the thesis statement and ideas for topic sentences to produce a thesis with blueprint.

   1. **Thesis**   Amusement parks have a variety of attractions.
      Idea for Topic Sentence   rides
      Idea for Topic Sentence   shows

Idea for Topic Sentence   food

Thesis With Blueprint _____

_____

_____

2. **Thesis**   Magazine advertisers use several ways to get your attention.
   Idea for Topic Sentence   large print
   Idea for Topic Sentence   eye-catching color
   Idea for Topic Sentence   beautiful people

   Thesis With Blueprint _____

_____

_____

3. **Thesis**   Computers have many uses.
   Idea for Topic Sentence   writing
   Idea for Topic Sentence   numbers
   Idea for Topic Sentence   games

   Thesis With Blueprint _____

_____

_____

4. **Thesis**   American "hard-boiled" mysteries have many things in common.
   Idea for Topic Sentence   tough private eyes
   Idea for Topic Sentence   uncooperative police
   Idea for Topic Sentence   lying clients

   Thesis With Blueprint _____

_____

_____

_____

5. **Thesis**   Beach vacations are ideal for relaxing.
   Idea for Topic Sentence   watching waves
   Idea for Topic Sentence   lying in the sun
   Idea for Topic Sentence   reading long books

   Thesis With Blueprint _____

_____

_____

B. Choose any one of the items from Exercise A and write a thesis statement with blueprint three different ways. See the last section of the chapter, "Different Forms of the Thesis With Blueprint," for some ideas. Use an indented list for one blueprint.

C. Each item below gives a thesis statement. Invent three ideas for topic sentences. Then combine those ideas with the thesis statement to produce a thesis statement with blueprint.

1. **Thesis**   Older people are more active these days.

   Topic Sentence _____

   Topic Sentence _____

   Topic Sentence _____

   Thesis With Blueprint _____

   _____

   _____

2. **Thesis**   Finding a part-time job is frustrating.

   Topic Sentence _____

   Topic Sentence _____

   Topic Sentence _____

   Thesis With Blueprint _____

   _____

   _____

3. **Thesis**   Winter is the best season here for having fun.

   Topic Sentence _____

   Topic Sentence _____

   Topic Sentence _____

   Thesis With Blueprint _____

   _____

   _____

   _____

Chapter 12

Central Paragraphs

Because your purpose in a theme is always to persuade the reader to accept your thesis, you need space to make your point. Generally, the more fully you develop your support, the more persuasive you'll be. Central paragraphs, which form the body of your theme, give you the needed space.

Each central paragraph, which is like a Stage I or Stage II paragraph, develops an opinion that in turn helps develop the thesis statement. Specific evidence in a central paragraph supports the paragraph's topic sentence, and the topic sentences, taken together, support the thesis. Therefore, if each central paragraph supports its own topic sentence, and if the topic sentences are properly related to each other and to the thesis, then the central paragraphs should persuade the readers to accept that thesis statement.

Three of the paragraphs of a five-paragraph essay are central paragraphs. Similarly, all but two paragraphs of any multiparagraph essay are central, or body, paragraphs. The two exceptions, introduction and conclusion, are discussed in Chapters 13 and 14; until you study these chapters, the thesis statement with blueprint will suffice for both the introduction and conclusion. For the moment, then, consider the form of the five-paragraph essay to be the following:

Thesis Statement With Blueprint

First Central Paragraph

Second Central Paragraph

Third Central Paragraph

Thesis Statement With Blueprint

Central Paragraphs

A central, or body, paragraph is very similar to a one-paragraph essay; that is, each one presents a topic sentence followed by specific support. You already know, for the most part, how to write this type of paragraph.

This chapter deals with two differences between central paragraphs and the one-paragraph essay: *omission of the reworded topic sentence* and *additions to the topic sentence.*

OMISSION OF THE REWORDED TOPIC SENTENCE

Every State I and Stage II paragraph essay, a unit complete in itself, has three basic parts: topic sentence, specific support, and reworded topic sentence. The reworded topic sentence provides a mark of finality to the argument.

A central paragraph, however, does not require this same mark of finality. Remember that a central paragraph does not present the entire argument of the theme. Instead, the development of the thesis is complete only after all central paragraphs are presented. Therefore, the mark of completion is one of the special functions of the concluding paragraph. Each central paragraph, then, ends *without* a reworded topic sentence; when the last item of specific support of a central paragraph is finished, so is that paragraph.

ADDITIONS TO THE TOPIC SENTENCE

Like a topic sentence for a one-paragraph essay, the topic sentence for a central paragraph presents the *main idea of the paragraph* in the basic form of *"limited subject* is *precise opinion."* However, the central-paragraph topic sentence has two additions—a *transition* from the preceding paragraph and a *reminder of the thesis.*

The first addition, the *transition,* provides theme coherence. Just as sentences within any paragraph must move smoothly from one to another, paragraphs within a theme must also flow together. The pieces of the total argument will not seem to combine unless the paragraphs that contain the pieces of the argument also combine.

The second addition to the topic sentence, the *reminder of the thesis,* helps fit the central paragraph's main idea to the theme's main idea. The total argument will come together more easily if each central paragraph's idea (its topic sentence) connects to the theme's idea (the thesis statement). This addition, then, helps provide both coherence and unity.

Therefore, the topic sentence for a central paragraph should have these three parts:

- a transition
- a reminder of the thesis statement
- the main idea of the paragraph

EXAMPLES OF CENTRAL PARAGRAPHS

Let's look at some examples of central paragraphs. Here's the *first* central paragraph from the sample theme in Chapter 9. Can you find the three parts of the topic sentence?

First Central Paragraph

Not surprisingly, one area in which children are often humorous is in learning to speak. I remember one time I was talking to a friend on the phone while my little sister, Betsy, seemed to be playing inattentively on the floor nearby. After I hung up, Betsy asked me, "Why is the teacher going to give Janet an old tomato?" At first I couldn't figure out what Betsy was talking about. When I asked her what she meant, she said, "You said if Janet doesn't hand in her homework, the teacher is going to give her an old tomato." Finally, I caught on. The word I had used was *ultimatum*!

Here are the three parts:

Transition "one area"
Reminder "children are often humorous"
Main idea "learning to speak"

Notice also the specific support for the topic sentence: a narrative example telling the brief story of Betsy's funny question. A central paragraph should have the same detailed support as a one-paragraph essay.

Now let's look at the *second* central paragraph from the sample theme:

Second Central Paragraph

Children also can be funny in the way they "humanize" the objects around them. According to my psychology book, "Up to four or five years old, the child believes anything may be endowed with purpose and conscious activity. A ball may refuse to be thrown straight, or a 'naughty' chair may be responsible for bumping him" (Pulaski, *Understanding Piaget,* p. 45). I, myself, still can remember one vivid and scary afternoon when I was sure the sun was following me around, just waiting for the right moment

> to get me. I also can remember a time, not scary, when Betsy stood up at the top of the stars and yelled to her shoes at the bottom, "Shoes! Get up here!"

Here are the three parts of the topic sentence:

Transition   "also"
Reminder   "children . . . can be funny"
Main idea   "the way they 'humanize' objects"

This paragraph has a variety of support: a statement by an authority and two quick examples.

Finally, let's look at the *third* central paragraph:

Third Central Paragraph

Another way in which children are sometimes funny is in their attempts to imitate what they see around them. All children look pretty silly when they dress up like their mothers and fathers and play "house." My psychology book tells of a more interesting example, though. The famous psychologist Jean Piaget wrote of the time his sixteen-month-old daughter quietly watched a visiting little boy throw a tantrum in trying to get out of his playpen. Piaget's daughter thought it would be fun to try the same thing: "The next day, she herself screamed in her playpen and tried to move it, stamping her foot lightly several times in succession. The imitation of the whole scene was most striking" (quoted in Pulaski, *Understanding Piaget,* p. 81).

Here are the three parts of the topic sentence:

Transition   "Another way"
Reminder   "children are sometimes funny"
Main idea   "their attempts to imitate what they see around them"

This paragraph has an interesting form of support: a narrative example that's stated by an authority—Piaget.

Because you must have space to develop your argument, you break it into parts—the arguments of the central paragraphs. Yet, like a jigsaw puzzle, a theme will never seem complete unless you connect the pieces. The additions to the topic sentence of each central paragraph help you to fit the central-paragraph main ideas to each other and to the thesis statement, creating a whole, the body of your theme.

EXERCISES

A. Let's say you're writing a five-paragraph essay with this thesis support:

Thesis   Installing carpets requires expertise.

For each topic sentence below, identify the transition, the reminder of the thesis, and the main idea.

First Topic Sentence   For one thing, measuring the rooms where the carpet will go requires expertise.

Transition _____

Reminder _____

Main Idea _____

Second Topic Sentence   Also, cutting the carpet into exact dimensions requires skill.

Transition _____

Reminder _____

Main Idea _____

Third Topic Sentence   Finally, laying the carpet in odd-sized spaces requires special techniques.

Transition _____

Reminder _____

Main Idea _____

B. Do the same thing for this thesis statement:

Thesis   The linebacker position on a football team requires a versatile athlete.

First Topic Sentence   As a play begins, the linebacker must be intelligent enough to diagnose the offensive team's plan.

Transition _____

Reminder _____

Main Idea _____

Second Topic Sentence   As the play develops, the linebacker must be agile enough to move in any direction.

Transition _____

Reminder _____

Main Idea _____

Third Topic Sentence   And to end the play successfully for his team, he must be strong enough to stop the ball carrier.

Transition _____

Reminder _____

Main Idea _____

C. Do the same thing for this thesis statement:

Thesis   Meteorologists—more commonly known as weather forecasters—have important technical advantages today.

First Topic Sentence   For one thing, historical records kept on computers tell seasonal patterns.

Transition _____

Reminder _____

Main Idea _____

Second Topic Sentence   Also, satellite photography tracks wind and cloud movements.

Transition _____

Reminder _____

Main Idea _____

Third Topic Sentence   Furthermore, modern communications give immediate access to weather data from all over the world.

Transition _____

Reminder _____

Main Idea _____

D. Here's a thesis statement and three main ideas for central paragraphs. Use these main ideas to write complete topic sentences—including transitions and reminders of the thesis.

Thesis   Restoring old houses is rewarding.
Main Idea   Discovering the original interior is exciting.
Main Idea   Working with one's hands is relaxing.
Main Idea   Viewing the completed project is satisfying.

First Topic Sentence _____

Transition _____

Reminder _____

Second Topic Sentence _____

Transition _____

Reminder _____

Third Topic Sentence _____

Transition _____

Reminder _____

E. Do the same with this thesis and three main ideas:

Thesis   Numbers in advertisements can seduce the consumer.
Main Idea   Digits in the product's name lure the consumer.
Main Idea   Statistics from surveys tempt the buyer.
Main Idea   Other numbers sprinkled throughout the advertisements awe the consumer.

First Topic Sentence _____

Transition _____

Reminder _____

Second Topic Sentence _____

Transition _____

Reminder _____

Third Topic Sentence _____

Transition _____

Reminder _____

F. For Exercises A–E, you've written topic sentences for a number of central paragraphs. Choose the one that interests you the most, and—inventing the support—write one central paragraph.

G. Recall for a minute the sample theme in Chapter 9 on the humorous things children do. In a way, the writer of that theme was an "expert" on children's funny behavior: she had been a child herself, and she had observed her sister (and undoubtedly many other children) growing up. She did not depend in that theme on any expertise in psychology, only on the behavior of children she had observed. The expertise she did use—from the book on Piaget—was highly interesting, of course, but it was not an essential part of the thesis statement, nor was it the only support.

You, too, are probably an "expert" in something. Perhaps you play golf well or understand how to tune an automobile engine or know every record the Beatles recorded. Choose something you know well and say something *significant* about it. Once you have something significant to say about your topic, turn that statement into a thesis statement with blueprint. Then, letting the thesis statement with blueprint serve as both the introduction and the conclusion, write the three central paragraphs of the five-paragraph essay (you'll write the full-length introduction and conclusion later as exercises for Chapters 13 and 14).

Be sure to use the same kind of detailed support for each central paragraph that you would use for a one-paragraph essay, and be sure that each of your topic sentences contains a transition from the previous paragraph, a reminder of the thesis statement, and the main idea of the paragraph.

If you use outside sources, use them only to find support, not to find a thesis. Otherwise, you'll merely be paraphrasing someone else. Also, be sure to place quotation marks around all words you borrow directly. At the end of every sentence containing borrowed words or ideas, acknowledge your source in parentheses (look again at Chapter 9 if you've forgotten the rules for the preliminary documentation system).

H. Using your first job (or any job you've held) as a topic, devise a thesis statement. Perhaps your thesis could be about an important lesson you learned at work. Or what you learned not to do. Or how the job changed your attitude toward school or your friends or your parents.

Regardless, let the thesis with blueprint serve as both the introduction and the conclusion. Then write the three central paragraphs of the five-paragraph essay (you'll write the full-length introduction and conclusion later as exercises for Chapters 13 and 14).

Also, be sure to follow the advice for support and documentation in Exercise G.

Chapter 13

Introduction

Your introduction serves two important purposes:

- It gets your reader's attention.
- It tells your reader what your main idea is (and how you will develop it).

The part of your introduction that gets your reader's attention is called a *motivator.*

The part that tells your reader what your main point is (and how you will develop it) is called the *thesis statement with blueprint.*

Since we've just discussed thesis statements with blueprints, we'll concentrate on motivators in this chapter.

Here's the introduction from our sample theme in Chapter 9. Can you find the motivator—the part that gets the reader's attention?

Introduction to a Five-Paragraph Essay

Do you realize that newly born children are not even aware that parts of their bodies belong to them? I learned this fascinating fact in my psychology course from a book that says a baby "lies on his back, kicking his heels and watching the little fists flying past his face. But only very slowly does he come to know that they are attached to him and he can control them" (Mary Ann Spencer Pulaski, *Understanding Piaget,* p. 21). Children have a lot of learning to do before they can see the world—and themselves— through grown-up eyes. As children pass through this remarkable process of growing up, they often do some humorous things, especially in learning to

---

> speak, in discovering that all objects do not have human characteristics, and in trying to imitate others around them.

The motivator is all but the last sentence, isn't it? The writer hopes to interest you by telling you something intriguing—that infants don't know that parts of their bodies belong to them.

As you practice writing and look carefully at the writing of others, you'll find many good ways to motivate your reader. Here are three good ways—which we'll discuss in this chapter:

- the opposite opinion
- a brief story
- an interesting statement

THE OPPOSITE OPINION

A really easy way to begin your paper is to state the opinion your paper opposes and then make a transition to your thesis statement with blueprint. In other words, your introduction has this flow to it:

- what the opposition says
- transition
- what you say

Transitions With the Opposite Opinion

The transition is particularly important in this kind of introduction because you must move clearly from the position you oppose to the position you support.

Here's a sample introduction to an essay showing that smoking is not a good habit:

Motivator ——— { Some people think that smoking makes them appear sophisticated and mysterious, perhaps even seductive. They become Humphrey Bogart in *Casablanca* or Lauren Bacall in

Transition ——— { *To Have and Have Not.* Those people, however, are wrong.

Thesis With Blueprint ——— { As far as I am concerned, smoking is really a disgusting habit—messy, irritating to others, and even harmful to nonsmokers.

Notice the strong transition ("Those people, however, are wrong.") And notice that the thesis statement and blueprint are obvious. Readers know clearly they have read the main idea of the paper and how it will be developed.

Here is another introduction using the opposite opinion as the motivator:

Motivator ——— As I was walking down the hall yesterday, I overheard a professor complaining about computers: "Those things are going to ruin the writing of our students. A computer is just a fancied-up TV and arcade game disguised as an 'educational

Transition ——— tool.'" But my experience with computers is entirely different.

Thesis With Blueprint ——— As word processors, for example, they can be immensely helpful with each stage of the writing process: prewriting, writing, and rewriting.

A BRIEF STORY

We all enjoy stories, so one of the most interesting ways to begin a paper is to tell your readers a brief story somehow related to your thesis statement. That way you've engaged their attention right from the start. By the time they've finished the story, sheer momentum carries them into the rest of your paper.

Here's a sample introduction that begins with a brief story:

Motivator ——— I walked into the living room, picked up a magazine, and settled back into my recliner. When I opened the cover, I was confronted by a sensuous blonde slinking toward me, her eyes staring straight into mine. "I like a Marlboro Man," she seemed to whisper provocatively. Believe me, I was ready to start

Transition ——— smoking. I never did, though, because—Marlboro men

Thesis With Blueprint ——— notwithstanding—I've always thought of smoking as a disgusting habit: messy, irritating to others, and even harmful to nonsmokers.

Notice that the introduction has a transition ("I never did, though . . .") between the motivator and thesis with blueprint.

Some introductions need a transition—like the one above, and all those that begin with opposite opinions—while others move smoothly from the motivator to the thesis with blueprint without any explicit transition words:

Motivator ——— I remember the first time I used a computer—or "word processor"—to do some writing. I was at a neighbor's house, so I just began a "letter" (one I wasn't planning to mail) to my friend. Instead of pausing frequently to think of things to say, I just wrote. The words seemed to come easily since I knew I could make changes later with no problem. Since then, I've

Thesis With Blueprint ——— used computers for most of my writing, and I've come to believe that they can be immensely helpful to us at each stage in the writing process: prewriting, writing, and rewriting.

AN INTERESTING STATEMENT

Another easy way to get your reader's attention is to begin with a statement that's interesting, either because the idea is intriguing or because, perhaps, the tone is angry. The introduction to the five-paragraph essay in Chapter 9 begins with an interesting statement, one that's intriguing: "Do you realize that newly born children are not even aware that parts of their bodies belong to them?"

The next example is a motivator that's interesting because the tone is angry (after all, if we're walking along and hear somebody yelling, we would probably stop because we're curious):

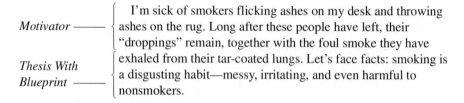

Motivator ——— { I'm sick of smokers flicking ashes on my desk and throwing ashes on the rug. Long after these people have left, their "droppings" remain, together with the foul smoke they have

Thesis With Blueprint ——— exhaled from their tar-coated lungs. Let's face facts: smoking is a disgusting habit—messy, irritating, and even harmful to nonsmokers.

The last example is only two sentences long, showing that an introduction can be effective even if it's fairly short:

Motivator ——— { Computers can *really* make a difference in how quickly and how easily you can get words on paper. In fact,

Thesis With Blueprint ——— computers—used as word processors—can be immensely helpful with each stage of the process: prewriting, writing, and rewriting.

The motivator for this introduction is interesting because the writer seems enthusiastic. If you convey your enthusiasm for your topic, your beginning will often be interesting, too.

When you are writing the introduction to your paper—whether you choose the opposite opinion, a brief story, or an interesting statement—be sure you fulfill the two important purposes of all introductions: interest your readers, and tell them the main idea of your paper (and how you will develop it).

EXERCISES

A. In Exercise A for Chapter 11 ("Thesis Statement With Blueprint"), you wrote five thesis statements with blueprints. Choose one and write three introductions for it: one with the opposite opinion, one with a brief story, and one with an interesting statement.

B. For Exercises G and H in Chapter 12 ("Central Paragraphs"), you wrote a thesis statement with blueprint followed by three central paragraphs. Now, using any of the three types of motivators we just discussed, write a full-length introduction for one of those exercises (G or H). You may need to change the wording of the original thesis statement with blueprint for it to fit smoothly with your motivator, but be sure not to change the essential meaning.

Chapter 14

Conclusion

The conclusion, like the introduction, serves two purposes:

- It reminds the reader of the main point of your essay.
- It gives the reader a sense of finality.

The part that reminds the reader of the main point is the *reworded thesis statement.*

The part that gives finality is the *clincher.*

Let's look at the conclusion to the sample five-paragraph essay you saw in Chapter 9. Can you find the reworded thesis and the clincher?

Conclusion of a Five-Paragraph Essay

Little children are funny creatures to watch, aren't they? But as we laugh, we have to admire, too, because the humorous mistakes are but temporary side trips that children take on the amazingly complicated journey to maturity—a long way from the beginning, where they lay in wonder, silently watching the strange, fingered spacecraft passing, back and forth, before their infant eyes.

The reworded thesis is the first sentence; the clincher is the last one.

You already know how to write a reworded thesis statement: it resembles the reworded topic sentence that you worked with on the one-paragraph essay. Therefore, this chapter concentrates on the clincher. We'll discuss two types:

- the reference to the motivator
- the interesting statement

THE REFERENCE TO THE MOTIVATOR

The simplest—and most common—clincher reminds the readers of the motivator you used in your introduction. This clincher has the advantage of bringing the paper full circle, an unmistakable signal that the paper is over.

The last chapter showed you three sample introductions with the thesis that smoking is disgusting. Let's look at those introductions again. Each begins with a reworded thesis. Then each finishes by referring to the motivator:

Introduction to Essay 1 (Opposite Opinion)

Some people think that smoking makes them appear sophisticated and mysterious, perhaps even seductive. They become Humphrey Bogart in *Casablanca* or Lauren Bacall in *To Have and Have Not.* Those people, however, are wrong. As far as I am concerned, smoking is really a disgusting habit—messy, irritating to others, and even harmful to nonsmokers.

Conclusion to Essay 1

Reworded Thesis ——— *Clincher* ———

I am glad I never began such a disgusting habit, and I wish others had not started, either. I hope my sophisticated friends soon find out that Humphrey Bogart and Lauren Bacall were mysterious and appealing in spite of their habit, not because of it.

*   *   *

Introduction to Essay 2 (Brief Story)

I walked into the living room, picked up a magazine, and settled back into my recliner. When I opened the cover, I was confronted by a sensuous blonde slinking toward me, her eyes staring straight into mine. "I like a Marlboro Man," she seemed to whisper provocatively. Believe me, I was ready to start smoking. I never did, though, because—Marlboro men notwithstanding—I've always thought of smoking as a disgusting habit: messy, irritating to others, and even harmful to nonsmokers.

Conclusion to Essay 2

Reworded Thesis ——— *Clincher* ———

I am glad I never began such a disgusting habit, and I wish others had not started, either. I no longer have the magazine with the sexy blonde. Even though I miss her, I've never missed cigarettes.

*   *   *

Introduction to Essay 3 (Interesting Statement)

I'm sick of smokers flicking ashes on my desk and throwing ashes on the rug. Long after these people have left, their "droppings" remain, together with the foul smoke they have exhaled from their tar-coated lungs. Let's face facts: smoking is a disgusting habit—messy, irritating, and even harmful to nonsmokers.

Conclusion to Essay 3

Reworded Thesis ———
Clincher ———

I'm glad I never began such a disgusting habit. If other people had not started smoking, then neither their houses nor mine would be littered with smokers' "droppings," and we would all be healthier.

AN INTERESTING STATEMENT

The last chapter showed you how to *begin* papers with interesting statements; an interesting statement is a good way to *end* a paper, too. Your statement might be interesting because of the information or because of the tone. Here's a conclusion that has an interesting statement because of the information:

Reworded Thesis ———
Clincher ———

I am glad I never began such a disgusting habit, and I wish others had not started, either. I hope my sophisticated friends soon find out that Humphrey Bogart, mysterious and appealing though he might have been, unfortunately died of cancer of the throat—possibly caused by smoking!

And here's a conclusion with an interesting—even angry—tone:

Reworded Thesis ———
Clincher ———

I am glad I never began such a disgusting habit, and I wish others had not started, either. Then the only smoking would take place at the fire-eater's show at the carnival—a spectacle that would give smoking the kind of dignity it deserves.

So to finish your five-paragraph essay, simply reword the thesis statement and end with unmistakable finality: the clincher.

A Note of Caution

When you write your conclusion, be careful not to state any new, unsupported generalizations that your reader might question.

EXERCISES

A. Chapter 12 presents three introductions to a paper about word processors. Using the *reference to the motivator* as a clincher, write a conclusion to each one.

B. Again, for the sample introductions in Chapter 12 on computers, choose one introduction and write a conclusion that has an interesting statement as your clincher.

C. For Exercise B in Chapter 12 you wrote an introduction to the three paragraphs you had written for Exercises G or H in Chapter 11. Now finish your five-paragraph essay by writing the conclusion. Use either type of clincher. As you prepare the paper, pay special attention to the three techniques of layout you read about in Chapter 10: headings, paragraphs that show breaks in thought, and indented lists. In reality, then, your "five-paragraph essay" may have more than five paragraphs!

CHECKLIST FOR THE FIVE-PARAGRAPH ESSAY

Introduction

_____ Does your introduction begin with a motivator?

_____ Does your introduction have a thesis statement with blueprint?

_____ Does your thesis statement have a limited subject?

_____ Does your thesis statement have a precise opinion?

_____ Are the items in your blueprint in the same order as your central paragraphs?

_____ Do the items in your blueprint all answer the same question "Why?" "How?" or "When?"

Central Paragraphs

_____ Does each central paragraph begin with a topic sentence?

_____ Does each topic sentence have a transition from the previous paragraph?

_____ Does each topic sentence have a reminder of the thesis?

_____ Does each topic sentence state the main idea of the paragraph?

_____ Is your support specific enough to be convincing?

_____ Do all your items of support clearly support the topic sentence (unity)?

_____ Do you explain your support fully so the relation to the topic sentence is clear (coherence)?

_____ Does each item of support include a reminder of the opinion in the topic sentence (coherence)?

_____ Do you have transitions at the critical locations (coherence)?

Conclusion

_____ Does your conclusion have a reworded thesis statement?

_____ Does your conclusion end with a clincher?

Layout

_____ Have you considered headings?

_____ If you use headings, do your paragraphs show breaks in thought?

_____ Have you considered using indented lists?

Other

_____ Is your essay convincing?

_____ Is your essay interesting?

_____ Have you checked the spelling of the words you're unsure of?

_____ Is your paper neatly done so it's easy to read?

Beyond
The Model Essay

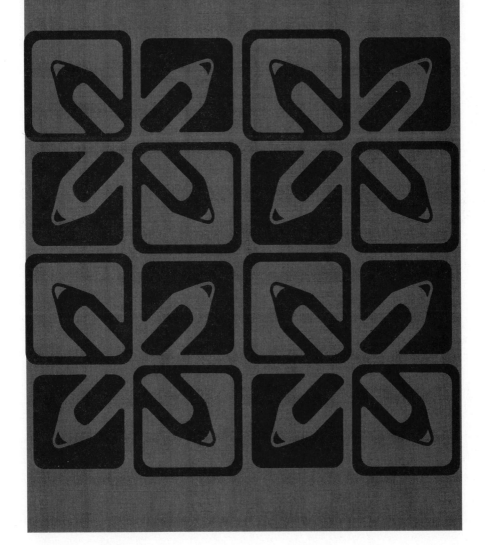

Part Four

More Patterns
of Development

In Part Three you began your transition to the research paper by learning how to write longer papers and how to use a simple method of documentation. You'll continue that transition here, learning two new skills:

- First, you'll find out about four different ways to develop a paper: process, classification, comparison and contrast, and cause and effect.

- Second, you'll learn some easy ways to vary from the five-paragraph essay. Our sample essays in this part clearly grow out of the five-paragraph essay, but they all have differences from it.

The sample essays in this part share another thing: they all use the techniques of layout (short paragraphs, headings, lists) we showed you in Chapter 10. You'll see that those techniques are especially important to help readers make their way through new patterns of development.

Because these essays usually have headings or lists, they often run more than five paragraphs. But they still have clearly identifiable *sections,* and these sections are very similar to the paragraphs in the five-paragraph essay. And each central section begins with a topic sentence, just as central paragraphs did in a five-paragraph essay.

Chapter 15

Process

There are really only two kinds of processes. In simple language:

- how people do something (like change a tire or use a computer)
- how something works (like an automobile engine or a computer)

The first of these we know as *instructions*. We follow them almost every day in our lives, and almost every day we give some sort of instructions to others.

The second of these (how something works) we call a *description of a mechanism in operation*. "Mechanism" can mean a machine (an automobile), something natural (photosynthesis or how a volcano erupts), something abstract (how an appeals court handles cases), or even something historical (how Hitler's army invaded Poland).

Learning to describe a process is important because it's a very common writing task.

INSTRUCTIONS

Let's look first at instructions—telling people how to do something.

Common Instructions

Regulations are instructions. So are computer manuals. And so are the notes we get from teachers and supervisors telling us how to prepare a paper or how to deal with customers.

Here's a sample paper discussing how to give instructions. As you read it, notice both *what* it says and *how* it says it.

How To Write Instructions

One of the most important things to keep in mind while writing instructions is simply this: "Don't waste your reader's time." Everything in a set of instructions should follow that advice.

So let's begin by looking at a brief paragraph of terrible instructions. It's from a computer manual on a word processing program:

Attributes may be assigned to the elements of a document either directly or indirectly; these two ways of assigning attributes are referred to as "direct formatting" and "styles." Direct formatting has a direct effect on document layout. Assigning a style tells [the word processor] to look on a style sheet to acquire direct formatting.

Would you like to try following those instructions? I'm sure most people didn't try, because the later versions of the manual changed those instructions dramatically--to make them "reader friendly."

You should try to make your instructions "reader friendly," too. Here are four steps that will help you reach that goal:

1. <u>Organize the instructions into a step-by-step procedure</u>. If you truly understand the instructions you are about to give, this should be easy to do. And steps are much easier for the reader to follow than continuous narrative. This paper is using steps right now.

2. <u>Start each step with a verb (as in this sentence)</u>. Instructions tell people what to do, what action to take. Verbs are action words. So starting each step with the specific action gets

right to what the reader needs to know. Virtually
all good computer manuals (and there are many
good ones) start each step with a verb.

3. Use a layout that clearly shows the steps.
   Headings, bulleted paragraphs, and numbered
   paragraphs are all easy techniques to let the
   reader see the steps in the process you're
   describing.

4. Test your instructions on somebody else. Try to
   choose somebody who is typical of the people you
   really plan to instruct. It's amazing how easy it
   is to leave out steps when you're writing. Early
   computer manuals gained their deservedly terrible
   reputation because they didn't test the
   instructions adequately. Now the top-notch
   computer companies test their manuals extensively
   before publishing them.

If you follow these easy steps, you'll have a
good chance of writing instructions that work.

That sample has an extremely clear organization—the same kind we showed you in the chapter on the five-paragraph essay. That is, there's a clear beginning, a clear ending, and a clear structure in the middle.

The list with underlining really helps, too, doesn't it?

Now let's look at another set of instructions, this one telling you how to prepare to paint a room. Especially notice the benefit of the headings.

Getting Ready To Paint a Room

Nearly everyone has to paint a room at some time
or other--at home, in a dorm, in a first apartment.
You can make the painting simple if you follow these
steps to get ready.

Protect Furnishings in the Room

Clearly, the best time to paint a room is when
it's empty. If you're in that fortunate situation,
skip to the next step.

But if your room isn't empty, your first step is
to protect what's there:

1. Move all the furniture away from the walls and
   into the center of the room, stacking wherever
   possible to use as little floor space as you can.

2. If the carpet is not fastened down, roll it from
   each end to the middle of the room. If it is
   fastened down, cover it with a drop cloth.

3. Use drop cloths. Cover all furniture and the
   floor. The best drop cloths have fabric on the
   top and plastic on the bottom. Drop cloths that
   are all plastic don't absorb spilled paint, so
   they stay messy. On the other hand, drop cloths
   that are all fabric can leak through to what's
   underneath.

Remove Electrical Covers

The next step is to remove cover plates for wall
switches and outlets. The covers are usually held in
place with one or two screws, so remove the screws and
place them in a plastic bag.

Use Masking Tape

Tape over anything you want to stay free of
paint--windows, woodwork, door hinges, door knobs,
etc. You'll want to use a sharp knife to cut the tape
precisely rather than just tearing it. Also, check the
stickiness of the tape--some is so sticky that it can
remove the paint underneath it, the paint you want to
save! "Artist's tape" is only lightly sticky, so you
might want to try that.

Profit From Your Preparations

These few steps can be time consuming, but anyone
who has tried skipping them can tell you a cautionary

```
tale with the moral of "haste makes waste." And the
time you spend preparing is saved many times over
during the next two stages of the painting process:
putting the paint on the wall and (especially)
cleaning up!
```

Again, notice the importance of layout to signal the organization. And notice the obvious organization that echoes the clear structure you learned for the five-paragraph essay.

DESCRIPTION OF A MECHANISM IN OPERATION

The second kind of process paper tells how something works. Technical writers call this a "description of a mechanism in operation." And a mechanism can be almost anything that has parts to it and does something: from a jet engine to a rubber-band motor, from a reflecting telescope to an overhead projector.

To write a description of a mechanism in operation, you follow basically the same guidelines as for writing instructions: organize the process into steps, use an appealing layout on the page, and just stop when you're through.

There are a couple of differences, however, between mechanism descriptions and instructions. First, you really cannot lead with verbs as you could with instructions: you have to say "Step One: The jet engine . . ." rather than "Step One: [You] *organize* the. . . ."

Also, the background section now becomes virtually mandatory. For the sample paper on "How to Write Instructions," we gave—as background—an excerpt of some bad instructions from a word-processing program. That kind of background is nice, even important, but not always necessary.

For a description of a mechanism in operation, though, you use the background section to describe the parts of the mechanism. Then, the way those parts function together—the way the mechanism operates—will be the step-by-step part of your paper.

Let's consider a paper telling how a reflecting telescope operates. The introduction would, no doubt, describe the purpose of a reflecting telescope. The background section would then briefly describe the important parts of the telescope: the primary mirror, the secondary mirror, and the magnifying lens. The rest of the paper would describe how those parts operate. Here's a skeletal model of such a paper:

> Introduction
>
> The purpose of the reflecting telescope

```
┌─────────────────────────────────────────────────────────────┐
│                         Background                          │
│                                                             │
│   The parts: primary mirror, secondary mirror, magnifying lens │
│                                                             │
└─────────────────────────────────────────────────────────────┘

┌─────────────────────────────────────────────────────────────┐
│                         First Step                          │
│                                                             │
│          The light hitting the primary mirror              │
│                                                             │
└─────────────────────────────────────────────────────────────┘

┌─────────────────────────────────────────────────────────────┐
│                        Second Step                          │
│                                                             │
│          The light hitting the secondary mirror            │
│                                                             │
└─────────────────────────────────────────────────────────────┘

┌─────────────────────────────────────────────────────────────┐
│                         Third Step                          │
│                                                             │
│            The light magnified by the lens                 │
│                                                             │
└─────────────────────────────────────────────────────────────┘

┌─────────────────────────────────────────────────────────────┐
│                         Conclusion                          │
│                                                             │
│          A summary of the telescope's operation            │
│                                                             │
└─────────────────────────────────────────────────────────────┘
```

There's one more important difference between writing instructions and writing descriptions of mechanisms in operation: visual aids. You can see that a drawing of the telescope and how it operates—that is, the path the light takes—would be immensely helpful for the paper we just outlined.

Although it's really beyond the intent of this book to go into detail on how to construct good visual aids, the main keys are these: *keep visual aids simple* and *label everything.* Here's a sample visual for the paper we just outlined:

Here is a sample paper about ceiling fans. Note how the visuals fit into the text as an integral part of the paper. Putting them close to the writing that refers to them is a convenience for the readers.

How a Ceiling Fan Works

The ceiling fan — familiar from films like <u>Casablanca</u> — is not quite the simple device it appears to be. A well-designed ceiling fan does more than just add some ambience and a breeze. It also can save on utility costs (summer <u>and</u> winter) and make life indoors more comfortable.

In this description, we'll assume the reader doesn't need to know how to install the fan or how to connect the fan to the electrical circuits.

<u>The Parts</u>

To understand how a ceiling fan works, we must first look at the parts that constitute it (see Figure 1).

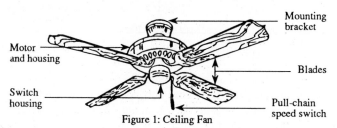

Figure 1: Ceiling Fan

<u>Mounting bracket.</u> Beginning at the top, nearest the ceiling, the first part is the mounting bracket and covering canopy. The mounting bracket connects the fan to the ceiling electrical outlet; the canopy covers the bracket and wires and makes the fan look better.

<u>Motor, housing, and blades.</u> The second part — and key to the fan's operation — is the motor, its housing, and the fan blades:

- The electric motor normally weighs about 14 pounds and uses 75 watts of power at its highest speed. Since a fan often is mounted in an inaccessible place, the motor usually will have permanently lubricated bearings that require no maintenance.

- Covering the motor assembly is the motor housing. The design of the housing varies from highly ornate embossed brass to painted sheet metal. Since its function is largely decorative, selection is a matter of taste for the purchaser. Regardless of design, however, the fan housing also serves to dampen noise and to keep dirt out of the motor.

- Mounted on the lower, outer edge of the rotating motor are the fan blades, made of wood or plastic (see Figure 2). Usually four blades, with a diameter of 30 to 52 inches, provide enough force to move the air, although fans installed in small areas sometimes have six blades.

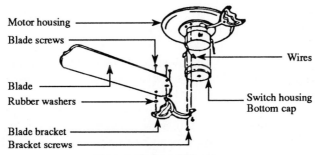

Motor housing
Blade screws
Blade
Rubber washers
Blade bracket
Bracket screws
Wires
Switch housing
Bottom cap

Figure 2: Blades and Mounting

The crucial factor in blade mounting is the pitch of the blade, the angle it is turned from absolutely flat horizontal. The most common pitch for a good fan is 12 degrees, although some larger ones have a pitch of 14 degrees. Any pitch less than 8 degrees will not move enough air to make the fan worthwhile. Such a low pitch is the mark of a cheap fan that will merely look good and have little positive effect on cooling.

Switches. The third important part of the fan is made up of the directional and speed switches, and their housing (see Figure 3):

- Although it's merely a simple slide switch, the directional switch makes the fan an energy-saving device, for it changes the flow of air during warm or cold weather.

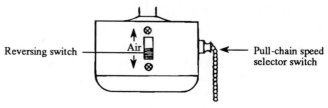

Figure 3: Fan Switches

- The pull–chain switch controls the speed of the fan's operation. Most fans have three speeds, from about 95 revolutions per minute to about 350 rpm. Pulling the chain moves the switch through the three speeds one after the other — low, medium, high.

Operation of the Ceiling Fan

  Fans are useful in the summer, of course — in fact, most people think of them as useful <u>only</u> in the summer. But fans have a benefit in the winter, too.

  <u>Summer Operation.</u> During warm weather, set the fan's switch to direct air downward to create a cooling breeze. This cooling results from the phenomenon known as wind–chill: as air moves across the skin, we sense a chill factor of 6–8 degrees.

  <u>Winter Operation.</u> In cold weather, adjust the fan so the air moves upward. Because heat rises, the temperature in the area near the ceiling may be as much as 15 degrees higher than at floor level. By pulling air upward, the ceiling fan gently pushes the warm air from the ceiling and back to the floor where the people are. In circulating the heated air trapped at the ceiling, the fan reduces the temperature differential to about 2 degrees. Thus, the furnace or other heater will have to come on less often, thereby reducing heating costs.

  When the world watched <u>Casablanca</u> in the 1940s, the ceiling fans added to the exotic atmosphere. Today, we know the fans add comfort and save money, too.

VARYING FROM THE MODEL THEME

The five-paragraph essay you learned earlier in this book is highly organized, as are the samples in this chapter. The main differences from the five-paragraph essay are these:

- The samples don't limit themselves to three central parts as the five-paragraph essay does.
- The samples use headings and lists to show the parts clearly.
- The samples occasionally use visuals to replace or reinforce words.

In other words, the samples in this chapter keep the underlying fundamentals of a five-paragraph essay (introduction, clear organization, thesis statement, conclusion) *but let the form vary to fit the content.*

The content is also different from most of the earlier essays we've shown you. The samples in this chapter are mainly *informative* instead of *persuasive.* That is, they simply try to explain something to you, not convince you. Therefore, most central sections don't begin with the three-part topic sentence you've learned. Yet you always know clearly in the samples what the topic of a section is—the heading or first sentence lets you know.

EXERCISES

A. Let's say you're going to give instructions on how to change a tire. Without writing the paper, simply list the various steps, in order, that you think someone should follow. If you don't know anything about changing tires, then list the steps for making a left turn in a car at a four-way stop (i.e., an intersection with stop signs at all four entrances to the intersection).

B. Now let's say you're going to describe how a simple mechanism—a mercury thermometer—operates. You'll probably have to look in an encyclopedia for this one, if you don't know offhand. List the parts (which would be the material for the background section) and outline how it operates. Just list and outline—you don't actually have to write the paper.

C. Now, write the paper for Exercise A.

D. And now write the paper for Exercise B.

E. Everyone knows something other people don't know but might be interested in. Perhaps you're good at golf, computers, or gardening. Choose something you know how to do and write a clear, concise set of instructions that tells your readers how to do it. You might try out these instructions on a friend before you hand in your paper. It's amazing how easily people (including all of us, of course) can go wrong unless the instructions are absolutely unambiguous.

F. Part of the special knowledge we all possess includes mechanisms others may know little about: the golf ball washer, the computer disk drive, the lawn sprinkler.

Choose something you know about and write a clear description of how it operates. Again, you might read your description to a friend just to be sure you've been clear: often, we know exactly what we mean while others (our readers or our listeners) are just confused. By the way, you might include a simple visual aid or two, just to be even clearer.

Chapter 16

Classification

Often we find ourselves with a long list of items we'd like to talk about but with no simple way to discuss them. We do know we could handle the items if we put them into three or four groups. This process of grouping a long list into categories is *classification.*

Consider this example. At the end of classes on Friday you look for a way to tackle all the studying you need to do over the weekend. Some of the work is so simple that you can do it right away before you go to a movie. You want to save some of the assignments for Sunday so the lessons will be fresh in your mind on Monday morning. And there are a couple of small research projects that would be good for a library session on Saturday.

To cope with the amount of studying you have to do, you classify the assignments under these headings:

Things to Study Friday
Things to Study Saturday
Things to Study Sunday

Now you've reduced a long list to three groups, but the important idea is that the groups all answer the same question: When is a good time to do this work? In other words, you've classified according to *one* characteristic related to all the items in the list.

If you classify on the basis of a different characteristic related to the items, you'll get a different listing. For example, as usual you don't study as hard over the weekend as you planned to on Friday afternoon; late Sunday night you find yourself with most of the work to do. Perhaps you make a new list, like this:

Put Off Until Next Weekend
Put Off Until Final Exams

Put Off Forever

Now the groupings are based on how long you can avoid doing the work, so this listing will not be identical with the one you made on Friday afternoon.

Classifying

Dozens of times each week we organize items by classification. We classify when we sort laundry into piles for machine wash, hand wash, or dry clean; or when we put the machine wash into piles for hot water, cold water, or medium temperature. We think of automobiles in groupings by size (sub-compact, compact, intermediate, and so on), by cost (under $12,000, $12,000 to $20,000, and so on), or by expected use (individual, family, or commercial). Because classification is such a common way of thinking, it is also a popular type of theme development. The groupings automatically provide us with the theme's *organization* and help us see what we want to say about the groups, our *thesis*.

ORGANIZATION

Since it breaks a topic into packages, classification results in a simple pattern that matches the model for the multiparagraph essay. Each category forms a central section:

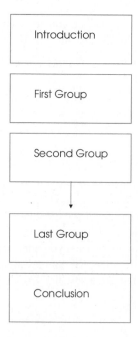

Introduction

First Group

Second Group

Last Group

Conclusion

You'll see a theme using a pattern similar to this one later in the chapter.

Yet, easy as the pattern of development is, you need to avoid its three potential pitfalls. You can tumble into any one of them if you're not careful when you classify.

The first problem is limiting the subject you intend to classify. A subject that is too broad could contain hundreds of items. You could put these hundreds into two or three groups, but the groups probably wouldn't be useful since each would still include a long list of items. On the other hand, you could classify hundreds of items into a large number of groups (say, fifteen), but then you'd have to write a theme with fifteen central paragraphs. In either case, you might as well not classify. Instead, limit the subject until it includes a workable number of items. For example, you choose "Ethnic Groups" as your subject. The world has too many ethnic groups for you to work with. You limit to "Major Ethnic Groups in the United States," but the number of items still seems endless. Limiting the subject to "Major Ethnic Groups in San Francisco" should solve the problem.

The second and most common problem is related to unity. Remember that to classify is to group on the basis of *one* characteristic related to each item. If more than one kind of grouping shows up in your theme, you've failed to maintain unity; and readers who are troubled by the groupings themselves probably will not be convinced by your argument. Consider this list of categories for types of car:

American	Italian
Japanese	Luxury
German	

"Luxury" is not a country of origin. The grouping is unacceptable.

Finally, you need to realize that many classifications that work well for grouping items actually have minor flaws. For instance, we often put motorized passenger vehicles that run on land into three convenient groups: cars, trucks, and buses. Yet this classification does not cover the special vehicle that looks like a large station wagon (a car) but is built on a truck chassis (a truck) and can carry nine adults (a small bus).

There's no simple rule for dealing with this problem; however, there is a reasonable procedure to follow when you find an exception to your classes.

First, judge the importance of the exception. If the exception destroys the point you are trying to make (the thesis of your argument), then rethink your groupings.

And if a single exception brings to mind dozens more, then again you must regroup.

Finally, if the exception remains a minor flaw, you may want to acknowledge the complication somewhere in your paper.

Or you may be able to exclude the exception by the way you word your subject. For example, if you write about "Religions on My Campus," you'll have to deal with all of them, including that of the single student who has made an idol of the oak tree on the campus mall; but if you write about "Major Religions on My Campus," you eliminate the minor exceptions to your categories.

THESIS

Classification leads logically to one of two types of thesis. The classification may itself be the thesis. Or the classification may be only the means of organizing the argument that persuades the readers to accept the thesis. The first is easier to write, but the second generally makes a better theme.

If your classification reveals striking groupings, the classification itself may be the thesis. Such a thesis takes the general form of "There are *(number of groups)* for *(topic)*." For example, "There are three types of teacher," or "There are two types of politician." Not very interesting, really. Still, sometimes the groupings themselves reveal your stand on the topic. Then the "there are" thesis may work. Consider this example:

■   Today there are two types of politician: the dishonest and the half-honest.

Implicit in these classes is the thesis that no politician today is completely honest.

Often, however, the "there are" thesis is not satisfying by itself. The readers yawn and mutter, "So what?" What they are really asking is why the writer bothered to classify items. Consider this thesis:

■   There are four types of door locks available for home use.

If your readers happen to be interested in locks, the thesis may work. Probably more interesting would be a theme that uses the types of door locks to make a more important point, such as this:

■   Although there are four types of door locks available for home use, an expert burglar can fool any of them.

Now the thesis is that the locks are not foolproof; the writer will develop the theme with a central section for each type of lock, but he'll be showing in each case that the locks will not stop a determined burglar.

When you develop a subject by classification, you'll have to judge the value of your classification. Will the readers care that you've identified groups? Or do the groups merely help reveal something more important?

Here's a sample theme in which the classification serves as an organizational stepping-stone to get to the thesis idea.

The Waistland of TV Advertisements

Like thousands of Americans, my compulsive drive to eat keeps me continually on a diet. When I told a friend that I eat if I'm happy, sad, or just sort of blah, he said I need to occupy my mind. He suggested that when I'm hungry I should watch television. This solution seemed particularly appropriate, for I enjoy television when I'm happy, when I'm sad, and when my mind is too dull to feel much of anything. My friend was right about the television shows; even the worst of them draws my attention away from food.

But my friend forgot about the advertisements. Whether commercials for food in restaurants or for food to take home, these television advertisements represent cruel and all-too-usual punishment for the dieter.

Ads for Restaurants

Numerous restaurant ads provide seemingly continuous reminders of a world of eating enjoyment, all of it forbidden on my 1,200-calorie diet. There are so many restaurant ads that I can turn from channel to channel during commercial time and usually be assaulted with only one laundry detergent ad, one pet food ad, but four ads for restaurants.

After a week on my diet, I'm jealous of the kitten in the cat chow commercial; imagine what the barrage of restaurant ads does to me. There are commercials for steak (with salad, potato, and toast), pizza (thick or thin crust, with dozens of toppings to choose from), fish or clams, chicken (with fixin's), hamburgers (with or without cheese, decorated with catsup and mustard, sprinkled with chopped onions and lettuce, topped with a pickle, stuffed in a lightly toasted bun), roast beef or ham sandwiches (for a change from the hamburger habit), and tacos or burritos (as well as related Mexican foods that I've never heard of but begin to crave anyway when I see them on TV).

Need I go on? Probably by now even your stomach has started to rumble, and you've had more for supper than my spoonful of cottage cheese on half a small peach (made more appetizing by a scrap of wilting lettuce for decoration).

Ads for Take-home Food

Less numerous than restaurant ads but more enticing are the commercials for the foods I can buy to take home.

When I've been starved for carbohydrates for a few days, the convenience of the take-home foods appeals to the remnants of my ability to reason. You see, if my willpower wavers and I go to a restaurant-- even a quick-order place--someone who knows I'm dieting may catch me, but it's easy to dart into a grocery store, ice-cream parlor, or doughnut shop and dash home without being seen.

Besides, the TV ads for foods to take home are so inviting. For example, you may remember seeing the advertisement for one of the doughnut shops in town. As the TV camera pans slowly across a counter laden with bakery goodies, I begin to drool. The commercial's sound track broadcasts a man calling to his wife to run to the TV to see the panorama of food laid out before his--and my--impressionable eyes.

He says that the sight of the doughnuts will "drive him crazy," and his voice sounds as though he's already slightly deranged because of what he sees. He proclaims the scene "heavenly," but I know it's a dieter's hell.

I've always assumed he demands that his wife give him her car keys so he can rush to the doughnut shop; I say "assumed" because I've never stayed at my TV set long enough to hear the end of the commercial. I'm on my way out the door to beat that crazy fool to the best of the doughnuts.

Just Deserts

You're reading the rantings of a dieter too often distracted by hunger and too long provoked by TV commercials for food.

Yes, I confess--stop the torture--the ads are obviously effective. I salivate right on cue for all the food advertisers. But in my few remaining rational moments I can still judge those advertisements for restaurants and take-home foods. To the dieter they're cruel. They play on the dieter's weakness, his compulsion to eat.

But I'll have my revenge, in my own limited way. My friend has invited me to his apartment tomorrow to watch TV, as he puts it, "to relieve the depression" of my latest diet. I'll sit calmly in his favorite chair; I'll stare innocently at his television. But

> when the first commercial for food comes on, I'm going
> to cut the plug off his set.
>   While he's paralyzed by shock, I'll go into his
> kitchen to make myself a sandwich.

Behind the writer's humorous mask is a pattern of development dependent upon classification. Because he recognizes that there are too many different food ads to deal with individually, the writer has classified them into two groups—foods to eat in restaurants and foods to eat at home.

Are you bothered by the fact that some of the foods he classifies as restaurant foods could be taken home? Probably not, because the inconsistency will not damage his thesis. And besides, for him the classification may well be valid; some types of foods he consistently eats at restaurants (though he could take them home) and some types he buys for his pantry.

What we should recognize is this: Classifications are arbitrary, but they do allow us a reasonable means to organize material. All in all, the classification in this theme is reasonable. It allows the writer to package his support material so that he can get to his thesis.

VARYING FROM THE MODEL THEME

Did you notice the minor differences in the sample theme for this chapter? For one, the thesis is not a simple statement of *"limited subject* is *precise opinion,"* but we could still tell that the writer would need to show that the food ads are numerous and that they are "cruel."

You may have noticed that the first central section is the Stage I type, whereas the second central section, which uses subtopic ideas, is a Stage II type.

Finally, in the conclusion no single sentence fully restates the thesis; nevertheless, the first five sentences of the conclusion as a whole do remind us of the thesis.

As you can see, the general pattern of the multiparagraph essay remains, even though there are deviations from the model.

EXERCISES

A. Circle the class in each list below that breaks the unity of the classification.

1. **Topic** Books
   Classes fiction
   poetry
   paperbacks
   history

2. **Topic** Students

Classes   sophomores
gymnasts
juniors
freshmen

3. **Topic**   Furniture
Classes   rugs
chairs
tables
desks

4. **Topic**   Buildings
Classes   sheds
barns
garages
apartments

B. Each subject below is too broad to classify easily. First limit the subject and then name at least three classes.

Example: **Topic**   Music

Limited topic   Classical music _____

Classes   Early Renaissance _____

Late Renaissance   Solo

Eighteenth Century   OR   Small Group

Romantic   Symphonic

Early Modern

1. **Topic**   Furniture

Limited topic _____

Classes _____

_____

_____

_____

_____

_____

_____

2. **Topic**   Computers

Limited topic _____

Classes _____

_____

_____

_____

_____

Topic   Shoes

Limited topic _____

Classes _____

_____

_____

_____

_____

4. **Topic**   Games

Limited topic _____

Classes _____

_____

_____

_____

_____

C. Choose one of the limited topics from Exercise B and write an essay that you organize by classification. Remember that you can make your writing more interesting if you use classification to develop a thesis other than the classification itself.

D. Use classification to develop an essay about one of the following topics. You'll need to limit the topic before you attempt to classify it, just as you did in Exercise B.

    Advertising
    Books
    Clothes
    Trees
    Stores

If you use outside sources for support, be sure to document them with the preliminary system you learned in Chapter 10.

Chapter 17

Comparison and Contrast

Comparison and contrast aren't new to you; they are extremely common ways of thinking. Whenever you examine how things are similar, you compare them. And when you look at their differences, you contrast them.

Sometimes you use comparison and contrast to talk about something new: by telling your readers how a thing is similar to or different from something they know, you can help them understand the new thing. For instance, to explain a rotary automobile engine, you'd probably compare and contrast it to the conventional automobile engine.

However, besides explaining something new, comparison and contrast also appear frequently in decision making: because A and B share some characteristics but differ in others, one is better. You compare and contrast brands when you shop for groceries, stereos, automobiles, and so forth. When you chose the college you're attending, you probably compared and contrasted available schools, and you're likely to use comparison and contrast again when you choose your major. The list of examples could be endless.

The comparison-and-contrast theme, then, is really quite practical.

THESIS

Comparison and contrast lead logically to a thesis because you usually won't bother to compare and contrast unless you have some purpose in mind. You could, of course, stop once you note that A is like B or C is different from D. But your readers probably will want to know what the similarity or difference amounts to. You could write this for a thesis:

■ The rotary automobile engine is different from the conventional automobile engine.

However, once you've noted the difference, the readers will see that you've merely stated the obvious. Much more useful would be one of the following:

■ Although the mechanical structure of the rotary automobile engine is obviously different from that of the conventional automobile engine, the rotary engine offers little worthwhile improvement.

or

■ Although they both depend on internal combustion, the rotary automobile engine is a significant improvement over the conventional automobile engine.

Thus, comparison or contrast for its own sake is generally pointless, but both are extremely useful to develop support for a thesis.

APPROACHES TO COMPARISON AND CONTRAST

As you may have noticed in the preceding sample thesis statements, there are two general approaches to the comparison-and-contrast paper. First, you can note the difference between items but *concentrate on their similarity* (comparison).

■ Although the mechanical structure of the rotary automobile engine is obviously different from that of the conventional automobile engine, the rotary engine offers little worthwhile improvement.

Here the writer acknowledges that the engine types are different. Does the difference mean that the newer one—the rotary engine—is better? The writer says it isn't; the engines are really comparable. We can expect the theme to concentrate on the similarities of the engines.

For the second approach you can note the similarity between items but *concentrate on their differences* (contrast).

■ Although they both depend on internal combustion, the rotary automobile engine is a significant improvement over the conventional automobile engine.

Now the writer acknowledges one similarity—that the two engines have the same type of combustion—but she is concerned with showing that the rotary engine is better than the conventional engine.

Notice that with either similarity or difference you acknowledge the opposite. Why? You need to establish a reason for bringing the two items together. Noting that the items seem different gives you a reason for comparing them, and noting that the items appear to be similar establishes a reason for contrasting them. In both cases, the opposite can provide the motivator section of your theme's introduction.

At the same time, you must decide where in the theme you're going to discuss the similarities and differences. The thesis establishes your primary purpose, which you'll concentrate on; you'll obviously discuss that side in the central sections.

Yet, how will you deal with the opposite? You have two choices. If the opposite is well known, let the introduction handle it. But if the opposite is not generally understood, you may need to develop it in the body of the theme. In that case cover it *first* in your central sections. Doing it this way leaves the primary idea in the position of emphasis, the end of the theme.

CENTRAL PARAGRAPH ORGANIZATION

When you've decided whether to concentrate on comparison or contrast, you still must decide *how* to do it. Suppose you want to contrast two brands of automobile to decide which to buy; you'll consider such subtopics as price, mileage per gallon, and maintenance record. You must decide whether to devote the central paragraphs to whole items (the cars) or to their various elements (price, mileage per gallon, and maintenance record).

The diagram shows the two most likely organizational types (we've used two items with three elements per item, but other combinations are certainly possible):

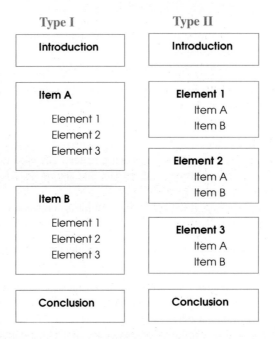

Order of Your Subtopics

Whether you choose the Type I or Type II organization for the central sections of your theme, make sure that you always cover the same subtopics in the same order. As with parallelism within a sentence (see Chapter 37), this symmetry will clearly show the relationships that are important for your ideas.

Which pattern is preferable? Well, notice that the Type I organization gives a sense of each item as a whole; however, the readers may have difficulty relating the elements. For example, suppose you compare a Nissan and a Toyota on the basis of seven elements. By the time the readers get to element five of the second car, the Toyota, they've forgotten what they read about element five of the Nissan. As a result, Type I organization is better for short papers dealing with only a few items and elements.

On the other hand, Type II organization destroys the sense of the whole item as it builds the relationships of the elements. Still, Type II development can handle more items and more elements, so it's more useful than Type I for a longer comparison or contrast paper.

So which type is better? There's no absolute answer, but you'll see more papers using Type II organization, probably because people are more concerned with element-by-element similarities and differences.

Type I

To demonstrate the difference, we've included a Type I essay comparing kinds of school classes. Note how the writer, one of our students, deals first with one kind of class and its elements (teacher, students, results), then another. The essay is short enough that we as readers don't get lost in all the differences.

```
        Learning or Not: Active and Passive Classes

    Everyone who has gone to school knows that some
classes are better, more interesting, livelier than
others. We have all sat through classes where we
learned little, except the facts and to be quiet. We
also have been part of classes where we actively
learned by being challenged by teachers and the
subject to learn for ourselves.
    Although classes often seem outwardly alike in
having a teacher, in having some students, and in
producing some results, the differences between
passive and active classes are enormous.


Passive Classes

    The passive kind of class usually has a teacher
who lectures, puts outlines and terms on the
chalkboard, and dispenses information to the students.
Like my sophomore biology teacher, Mrs. Noguida, who
```

rarely looked up from the orange notebook in which she
had carefully typed all her lectures, teachers in a
passive classroom simply dictate information and
answers. They tell the students how to think and what
to think. They pour facts into the students like water
into a sieve. The students are forced, usually by the
teacher's authority, to sit, listen, take notes, and
regurgitate only what the teacher has said.

The only kinds of questions are about form: "What
is the work in subpoint 3,a,(1)?" or "How do you spell
photosynthesis?" The results in such a class are
measured by multiple-choice or true-false questions,
or questions that require memorized answers: "What is
Newton's First Law?" "What are the three causes of the
American Civil War?"

The results in such classes are also measured by
the quickness with which students forget the facts
they had poured into them.

Active Classes

The other kind of class, the active kind, usually
has a teacher who stimulates the students to learn for
themselves by asking questions, by posing problems,
and most of all by being a student, too.

Such a teacher might plan the outline of a
course, but doesn't force the class in only one
direction. Instead, like Ms. Cerrillo, my junior
history teacher, a teacher in an active class uses the
discussion to lead to learning. Instead of lecturing
on the causes of the Civil War, Ms. Cerrillo gave us a
list of books and articles and said, "Find out what
caused the Civil War." We had to search for ourselves,
find some answers, then discuss what we found in
class. From the discussions, we all learned more than
just the facts; we learned the facts but we also
learned how complex the causes were.

Students in active classes like that become more
involved in their learning; they ask questions about
why and how. The results in the active class are
usually measured by essay answers, individual
projects, and a change in attitude on the students'
part. Learning becomes fun; although students may
forget the facts just as quickly, their attitudes

toward learning and their excitement in developing answers for themselves don't end with the last class.

We all remember having to learn that "4 x 9 = 36" and having to memorize dates like 1914-1918, 1776, and 1492. And those kinds of classes are important for laying some groundwork, but not much true learning takes place there. There is a difference between knowing a fact and understanding it. Despite their outward similarities, the passive kind of class is clearly inferior to the active one for helping students understand the world around them.

Type II

Here's a sample theme that compares two characters in literature. We've selected this theme because English instructors sometimes ask you to write about literature; as you'll see, a theme comparing two fictional characters is fairly easy to organize. You'll also see how well the Type II organization works for comparing a large number of subtopic elements, even though there are only two items.

Holmes and Dupin

Although Sir Arthur Conan Doyle created Sherlock Holmes in 1886, Holmes remains one of the most popular of detective characters. Moreover, Holmes' personality influenced the characterizations of other fictional detectives, both in Doyle's time and later. For example, Agatha Christie's Hercule Poirot is similar to Holmes.

Yet many readers of the Holmes stories don't realize that Holmes isn't entirely original. Holmes is very much like Chevalier C. Auguste Dupin, a character Edgar Allan Poe introduced in 1841. Of course, Holmes and Dupin have their differences; Holmes himself calls Dupin "a very inferior fellow" (Doyle, A Study in Scarlet and The Sign of Four, p. 25).

Nevertheless, pushing aside Holmes' criticism of Dupin, we can find numerous similarities between the two characters. Both in professional situation and in personality, Holmes is a copy of Dupin.

Conditions of Their Work

The conditions under which Dupin and Holmes work are alike. Both Dupin and Holmes are "consulting detectives," to use Holmes' name for the profession (Doyle, p. 23). This may not seem important, but we should notice that most other detective characters take cases on their own. On the other hand, Dupin works on cases for Monsieur G--, Prefect of the Parisian police, and Holmes (at least when he first appears) works on cases that have stumped Scotland Yard detectives.

In addition, both characters dislike the policemen they work for, and for the same reason. In "The Purloined Letter," Dupin says that the police are "persevering, ingenious, cunning, and thoroughly versed in the knowledge which their duties seem chiefly to demand" but that they fail because they cannot adapt their methods "to the case and to the man" (Poe, Great Tales and Poems of Edgar Allan Poe, pp. 208-09). Similarly, Holmes says the Scotland Yard detectives are "both quick and energetic, but conventional--shockingly so" (Doyle, p. 28).

Still, Dupin and Holmes somehow control their scorn while they solve cases for the police. The "consulting detectives" have the satisfaction of solving puzzles, but let the police steal the glory.

Their Personalities

Holmes' personality also matches Dupin's. Both characters are loners; they accept the company of the narrators of their stories, but of no one else. Poe writes in "The Murders in the Rue Morgue" that Dupin is "enamored of the night for her own sake"; in fact, Dupin and the narrator close the shutters of their house during the day and usually go out only at night (Poe, pp. 106-07). This love of darkness emphasizes Dupin's physical withdrawal from society. In Holmes' case, the withdrawal and gloominess lead to cocaine addiction; when Holmes isn't on a case, he withdraws from ordinary life as well as from society.

Of course, the detectives become active in society to solve cases, but each withdraws again when

his case is over. At the opening of the second Dupin
story, the narrator says that after his first case
Dupin "relapsed into his old habits of moody revery"
(Poe, p. 144). And Holmes at the end of The Sign of
Four calls for his cocaine so he, too, can withdraw.

Even when Dupin and Holmes actually enter society
to solve puzzles, they remain mentally separate from
other men. On a case, both Dupin and Holmes show
energy unknown to most people. This energy involves
them in society, but it doesn't mean that they
actually join society. Instead, each stays separate by
remaining unemotional; unlike ordinary men, they
appear to be minds without feelings. In "The Murders
in the Rue Morgue" the narrator describes the working
Dupin as "frigid and abstract," with eyes "vacant in
expression" (Poe, p. 107).

Doyle is more obvious about Holmes. In The Sign
of Four Holmes says that "detection is, or ought to
be, an exact science and should be treated in the same
cold and unemotional manner" (Doyle, p. 137). Like
Dupin, then, Holmes prefers to have a mind free of
emotions.

Holmes as Copy

Thus, the number of similarities between the two
characters shows that the 1886 Holmes is a copy of the
1841 Dupin. They take their cases for the same reason
and handle them with the same dislike for their police
associates. Neither character can stand the world of
normal men, choosing instead to withdraw into a secret
shell. And even when they work with ordinary men, they
remain aloof, emotionless.

These similarities are too numerous to be
accidental. Clearly Doyle owes a large debt to Poe.

VARYING FROM THE MODEL THEME

There are two sample essays in this chapter, the one on active and passive classes and
the one you just read on Holmes and Dupin.

Both follow the general form of the five-paragraph essay rather closely. These,
of course, are the main differences:

- They use *sections* instead of *paragraphs* (like most of the other sample essays you've seen in this part). Both samples have two central sections.
- They use headings to help readers see the organization.

The similarities with the five-paragraph essay are these:

- They have a thesis statement and blueprint in the introduction.
- They begin each section with a topic sentence.
- They use detailed support throughout the sections.
- They conclude with a reminder of the thesis statement.

So although there's a little variation from the five-paragraph essay, there's a lot of similarity, too.

EXERCISES

A. For each of the two topics below, first limit the topic and then write *two* thesis statements, one for each approach to a comparison-and-contrast paper.

Example: Topic   Emotions

Limited topic   Emotional responses _____

Acknowledge the difference and concentrate on the similarity

Although the intensity of emotional response to pleasure and to pain are obviously

different, the chemical and physical effects are very much alike.

Acknowledge the similarity and concentrate on the difference

Although all emotions are every much alike in their physical and chemical effects,

the responses to pain and pleasure differ in intensity.

1. **Topic**   Automobiles

   Limited topic   _____

   Acknowledge the difference and concentrate on the similarity   _____

   _____

   _____

   _____

   _____

   _____

   Acknowledge the similarity and concentrate on the difference   _____

   _____

_____

_____

_____

_____

2. **Topic**   Students

Limited topic _____

Acknowledge the difference and concentrate on the similarity _____

_____

_____

_____

_____

_____

Acknowledge the similarity and concentrate on the difference _____

_____

_____

_____

_____

B. Choose one of the thesis statements you developed for Exercise A and outline the central sections for a theme to support the thesis. Make your outline conform to either the Type I or the Type II organization: for each central section you will need to show a topic item with subtopic elements (Type I) or a topic element with subtopic items (Type II).

C. Here are some possible topics for comparison-and-contrast papers:

Commercial products	Music
Computers	Radio
Food	Relatives or friends
Literature	Schools

First, limit the topic; then, write a thesis that concentrates on comparison or contrast. Organize your support with the Type I or Type II pattern, and then write the theme. If you wish to vary from the model theme, do so. And if you use outside sources for support, be sure to document them (you can use the preliminary system, as the second sample theme in the chapter does).

Chapter 18

Cause and Effect

Remember the "Why?" subtopic sentences you studied in Chapter 8? Maybe you didn't realize it at the time, but you were studying one kind of cause-and-effect paper. We'll examine cause-effect papers more closely in this chapter.

A *cause* is a reason something happens; an *effect,* then, is whatever happens. As a simple example, we might say, "Because the television set is unplugged, it doesn't work." The *cause* is that the set is unplugged; the *effect* is that the set doesn't work.

Kinds of Cause-Effect Papers

You can write three kinds of cause-effect papers: you can state that the effect is true and examine the *cause* in detail; you can state that the cause is true and examine the *effect* in detail; or you can attempt to show that the *entire cause-effect statement* is true.

EXAMINING THE CAUSES

Sometimes the controversial part of a cause-effect statement is the cause, so your paper naturally will examine that part in detail. Let's say you've decided to write about this thesis: "The aggravated assault rate here at Gila Monster Maximum Security Prison has decreased dramatically because of the warden's innovations."

The effect—that the aggravated assault rate has dropped—shouldn't be controversial, so take care of that part quickly with a statistic or two in your introduction: "In the last year, the aggravated assault rate at Gila Monster Maximum Security

Prison has plummeted from nineteen per month to only four per month." After dispensing with the effect, spend the rest of your paper telling us about the warden's policies and why they work.

How? Write a section about each of the warden's important policies. Your outline might look something like this:

Thesis ——————	{ Because of the warden's innovations, the aggravated assault rate at Gila Monster Maximum Security Prison has decreased dramatically.
Topic Sentence ——	{ The warden's new leathercraft shop allows inmates a constructive way to spend their time.
Topic Sentence ——	{ The warden has started an intramural sports program that permits the prisoners a physical outlet for their pent-up emotions.
Topic Sentence ——	{ The new coed jail cells allow the inmates the chance to discuss relevant social issues with members of the opposite sex.

Did you notice that the thesis begins with *Because*? That word clearly established that the essay will examine cause and effect. Another way of saying it is this: if you want to write a cause-and-effect paper, you must have the word *because* somewhere in the thesis statement.

Of course, you don't need to have exactly three central sections. Two especially well-developed sections or four or five shorter ones could work also.

EXAMINING THE EFFECTS

Sometimes the cause is fairly straightforward, but the effect needs elaboration. What if your thesis is that "Because Napoleon's wars killed many young men who otherwise could have worked a lifetime, Europe's standard of living dropped markedly"? Not many people would doubt that the wars killed many young men who could have done a lot of work, but people still might doubt that the standard of living actually did drop. You need to state the cause as a fact and then elaborate upon the effect.

You then could begin the theme by mentioning in the introduction (perhaps using the "striking statement" motivator) how many young men were slaughtered. Then you could develop the theme by discussing the effect ("Europe's standard of living dropped markedly") in three or four European countries. Here's a possible outline:

Thesis ——————	{ Because Napoleon's wars killed many young men who otherwise could have worked a lifetime, Europe's standard of living dropped markedly.
Topic Sentence ——	{ After Napoleon's wars, Russia had a lower standard of living.
Topic Sentence ——	{ Austria also had a lower standard of living.
Topic Sentence ——	{ Even Napoleon's home, France, had a lower standard of living.

Sometimes you have to deal with ideas that require a little more complexity. The cause may be a general assertion, but the effects are real and often complicated. In this sample paper by one of our students, though it deals with technical matters and borrowed ideas, you will find a thesis and three topic sentences.

```
           The Search for Extraterrestrial Life

      When the first hominid stood upright, we
   speculate that it must have looked up to the heavens
   in wonder, for we find ourselves doing so today. As we
   look at the nighttime sky with all its stars and
   spaces, we can't help wondering about life out there.
      Perhaps the curiosity, the need to know, which
   motivated our ancestors to explore this planet, to go
   into the most forbidding jungles, or to sail the most
   hazardous seas, also motivates us. We think that what
   happened here on Earth might have happened elsewhere
   in the cosmos, and we follow our interest to press
   farther into the universe searching for life.
      Because of our enduring quest to know the
   unknown, our search for extraterrestrial life, a
   search that already has taken people to the moon, will
   grow in the years ahead. Whether in the form of
   interplanetary probes, radio and radar signals in
   outer space, or interstellar travel, the human race
   will continue to look up to the heavens looking for
   life beyond this Earth.


   Interplanetary Probes

      "The search for extraterrestrial life," according
   to Isaac Asimov, "took its first flying leap in 1969
   when man walked on the moon" (Extraterrestrial
   Civilization, p. 183). This great step proved that we
   were not destined to spend the rest of our existence
   earthbound.
      Subsequent successful moon landings demonstrated
   our race's ability to traverse space to the moon and
   return safely. More distant planets also were out
   there to be explored. Viking I and II, for example,
   were sent to Mars in 1975 to test the planet for the
   possibility for life. Landing in 1976, they found
   Martian soil not unlike Earth's "but richer in iron
```

and less rich in aluminum" (Asimov, p. 59). The bad news was the absence of carbon, which is essential for life as we know it.

Consequently, the search for life beyond Earth turned to other planets and other means--long-distance radio and interstellar travel.

Radio and Radar Signals

Attempts at interstellar communications have been going on for many years, but they take a long time. Because radio waves travel at the speed of light, it would take over a hundred years for a question to be asked and answered from a near star only fifty light-years away. And when we send out radio signals we have no way of knowing if anyone is even listening. But despite the long delays, astronomers have been sending radio signals for almost twenty years using "single or arrayed radio techniques, sensitive radio detectors, advanced computers for processing received information, and the imagination and skill of dedicated scientists" (Carl Sagan, "The Quest for Extraterrestrial Life," Smithsonian, May 1978, p. 39). They listen for meaningful sounds from outer space because scientists theorize that any civilization akin to ours would learn to use radio signals most readily. The largest listening dish in the world--in the Russian Caucasus--is devoted to this search for intelligent life beyond our planet (Sagan, p. 43).

Interstellar Travel

An even more dramatic attempt to find life in space will come with interstellar travel. Both the United States and the USSR have put crews in space for months at a time.

However, the barriers to interstellar exploration are enormous, both technically and humanly. For example, according to NASA, an interstellar spacecraft would need a totally efficient fuel, one that hasn't been developed yet. It may even have to wait for the discovery of antimatter. Almost certainly such a fuel would require metal alloys to withstand heat beyond anything we now know (NASA, Interstellar Communications, 1963, pp. 144-50).

Both these problems likely will be overcome; human intelligence and the quest for knowing probably will meet those challenges as we have in the past.

The real barrier to interstellar travel, however, is that same human being. We do not know if humans can endure the extreme durations of space travel. Not only would travelers be confined to cramped quarters with limited exercise and have little variety to see, but also the crew might well suffer mentally from the confinement.

Furthermore, if Einstein's theory of relativity is correct, the phenomenon of "time delation" will mean that the Earth from which travelers leave will be far different from the one to which they return. "Time delation" means that the rate at which time seems to progress slows with increased speed; this phenomenon would mean that a traveler hurtling through space would live what seemed to him or her a normal lifetime, while 5,000 years elapsed on Earth (Asimov, pp. 231-32).

Thus, a traveler searching for life on other stars would return to an Earth that had no family, or friends, perhaps not even the nation that sent out the explorer.

Continuing the Search

Despite the barriers (and the limited success), the search for extraterrestrial life will continue. The chances seem too great that somewhere in the estimated 280 billion planetary systems in our galaxy (Asimov, p. 109) intelligent creatures also have developed.

With the technological advances we already have made united with the never-ending quest to explore the unknown, our search for extraterrestrial life in the great expanse of space will go on. It must, just as much as it was inevitable that the first hominid looked up to the heavens so long ago.

EXAMINING THE ENTIRE CAUSE-EFFECT STATEMENT

Sometimes cause-effect papers examine the entire statement instead of only half of it. Perhaps both cause and effect are controversial, or perhaps neither is controversial but the fact that they have a cause-effect relationship is.

Let's look first at a cause-effect statement in which both parts are controversial and need elaboration. What if we say that "Because Colorado land developers have no long-term stake in the development they sell, customers often end up with property they cannot inhabit"? We'll have to persuade the readers of two ideas: that the developers do not have any long-term interests in development and that the new landowners can't live on their property. Both parts need support.

One simple way to organize the support is to write a section on the cause and a section on the effect. We could show in the first central section that Colorado developers do not have any long-term interests in the land; in the next section, then, we could show that the new owners often can not use their property.

However, we probably could write a better paper by examining both parts of the cause-effect statement in the same section. How? We could use examples. We'll make each central section a narrative example of the entire cause-effect statement.

One section might be about Pyrite Acres, a development bulldozed out of the desert at the base of the Sangre de Cristo mountains. The developer, after selling the last site, disappeared into Arizona with all the money. He had not found time to tell the new owners that the underground water supply was so low it could last for only another year or two. Then—if our thesis is really valid—we should be able to present a section on each of two or three similar situations with other developers. Extended examples can be effective any time both the cause and effect need support.

Extended examples can help in another case—one in which both the cause and the effect are fairly straightforward, but their relationship is not.

Consider this statement: "Because many mountain climbers are elated after a difficult climb, they are in danger from carelessness after the difficulty is past." We can accept easily that climbers are elated after a difficult ascent; we also can accept that climbers who are careless afterward are in danger. We probably would like to see support for the idea that the elation from a difficult climb produces that carelessness.

The following sample theme uses extended examples to provide such support.

```
              The Matterhorn Effect


     Only a little over a century ago, some people in
Europe thought that the Matterhorn--that awesome,
beautiful pinnacle--was the highest mountain in the
world. Many climbers from many nations had raced to
climb it, but none had succeeded. Then in 1865, an
Englishman, Edward Whymper, and six others reached the
summit, but only Whymper and two others lived to tell
about it. The rest, careless from elation and fatigue,
```

died when one climber slipped on a relatively easy part of the descent and carried three others over a 4,000-foot cliff.

That carelessness, a mental letdown that climbers tend to experience after succeeding at something hard, is called the "Matterhorn effect." I've seen it myself.

The Matterhorn Effect--And Me

I remember how pleased I was when I first climbed Borderline, a hard route up a 150-foot spire in the Garden of the Gods, Colorado. Only six others had ever climbed it. My forearms were so cramped from exertion that I could barely pull the rope up as my climbing partner, Leonard Coyne, seconded the route.

After reaching the top, Leonard mentioned that he knew the descent route was fairly hard, though the previous climbers had disdained using a rope for it. Filled with overconfidence, I simply tossed the rope to the ground below. We had just done the tough ascent, so surely we did not need a rope either. Then I started down the nearly vertical face.

Suddenly Leonard yelled, "Your handhold is loose! Grab my leg!" There I was--unroped, 150 feet above the ground, and apprehensively holding a couple of loose flakes of rock--when my foothold broke. I still don't know what kept me on the rock, but apparently as my foothold gave way, my foot slipped into a barely visible toehold.

I didn't fall, but if I hadn't been overconfident from the hard ascent, I would never have ventured into that dangerous position without a rope.

The Matterhorn Effect--And Leonard

I've seen the Matterhorn effect almost claim Leonard, too. Last summer, he, Gary Campbell, and I had just finished climbing the northwest face of Half Dome, a magnificent 2,000-foot vertical cliff in Yosemite, California. We'd been climbing, eating, and sleeping on the face for three days, and finally we were on top--well, almost.

> Actually we were about 30 feet from the top, but
> that part was really easy. We untied, coiled the
> ropes, and stowed our climbing hardware. Leonard slung
> on one of the packs--a rather unwieldy thing with a
> sleeping bag tied precariously to the outside--and
> started up the last 30 feet. As he began to haul
> himself onto a five-foot shelf, the pack shifted on
> his back, almost jerking him off the rock.
>
> Two thousand feet above the ground, he
> balanced--like a turtle about to flip on its back--for
> what seemed like a minute before he rolled slowly
> forward onto the shelf. Three days of numbing fatigue
> and the elation of doing such a hard climb had caused
> us all to have a mental letdown; we had put away the
> ropes too soon. That letdown almost cost Leonard his
> life.
>
> The point is clear to me: the Matterhorn effect
> is real for anybody who has just done something hard,
> but especially for climbers. I've seen it in myself
> too many times and too many times in others. But--so
> far, at least--I've been fortunate not to learn about
> it in the way Edward Whymper and his companions did.

Each extended example in this sample theme presents the entire cause-effect relationship. The cause (the author's elation and fatigue on Borderline and Leonard's on Half Dome) seems to lead quite naturally to the effect (the near-accidents).

PITFALLS OF THE CAUSE-EFFECT THEME

In Chapter 16 you learned not to choose a subject that is too general for your classification paper. That advice is also true for cause-effect papers. In a theme, you could never hope to convince disbelievers of this thesis: "Because the United States wanted to ensure the freedom of South Vietnam, it went to war against North Vietnam." You'd need a book, or a substantial chapter in one, to support that statement.

You also must be careful that your cause-effect statement presents the important cause and not just a secondary one. We'd be foolish to blame a field-goal kicker for losing an important game just because he missed a thirty-two-yard attempt during the last five seconds. The team may have lost in part because of that missed attempt, but what about the quarterback who threw an interception during the first quarter, the defensive lineman who missed a key tackle, or the coach who canceled practice last Wednesday? Be sure, in other words, that your cause is really the main cause.

VARYING FROM THE MODEL THEME

As you saw in the preceding chapters, one of our purposes in Part Four is to help you learn how to vary from the model theme. How does our sample about the Matterhorn effect differ from the model five-paragraph essay you learned in Part Three? Before we discuss the differences, look back at that sample and underline the thesis, blueprint, and topic sentences. Then read on.

You probably underlined this sentence as the thesis: "That carelessness, a mental letdown that climbers tend to experience after succeeding at something hard, is called the 'Matterhorn effect.'" It doesn't exactly state the main idea of the paper (that the Matterhorn effect is real), but certainly it implies it. Readers expect the rest of the paper to convince them that the Matterhorn effect exists.

Did you find a blueprint? The last sentence of the introduction—"I've seen it myself"—is not really a blueprint of the topic ideas for each paragraph, but it certainly *implies* the development. We know we are about to read some examples.

The topic sentence for the first central section also is implied, not by any one sentence but by the entire section. A stated topic sentence isn't nearly as important as unified support and coherence. As long as you *could* write a topic sentence for a section—the section, in other words, is unified—and as long as the readers have no doubt what they are reading and why, a topic sentence is not necessary.

EXERCISES

A. Use these topics to answer the items below:

Air bags in automobiles
Bank robbers
Educating children at home
City parks
Public swimming pools
Shopping malls
Sex education

1. Write a cause-effect thesis with a cause that is controversial but an effect that isn't. Then write three proposed topic sentences to show how you could develop your thesis.

Thesis _____

_____

Topic Sentence _____

_____

Topic Sentence _____

_____

Topic Sentence _____

_____

2. Write a cause-effect thesis with an effect that is controversial but a cause that isn't. Again, write the topic sentences you would use.

Thesis _____

_____

Topic Sentence _____

_____

Topic Sentence _____

_____

Topic Sentence _____

_____

3. Write a cause-effect thesis that has both a controversial cause and a controversial effect. Write the proposed topic sentences.

Thesis _____

_____

Topic Sentence _____

_____

Topic Sentence _____

_____

Topic Sentence _____

_____

B. Find your own support and write a cause-effect theme using this thesis: "Because they try to dupe me, I object to car advertisements." Choose some other kind of advertisement if you like, but attach the advertisements to your paper when you hand it in. If you wish to vary from the model theme, do so.

C. Choose something that had a significant effect on you and write a cause-effect paper. If you use outside sources for support, be sure to document them. You can use the preliminary system you learned in Chapter 9.

D. Choose one of the topics in Exercise A (not necessarily one you outlined) and write the theme. If you use outside sources for support, be sure to document them. You can use the preliminary system you learned in Chapter 9.

Part Five

The Research Paper

You've probably been having nightmares about the research paper ever since we first mentioned it. Actually, you already know most of the skills involved. You know the fundamentals of organization and support, and you may have looked at the punctuation and expression chapters. You've even used some outside sources and a simple method of documentation. The only new skills you need to learn are efficient ways to find your support in the library, organize it, use it in the paper, and document it. You'll find these new skills demand more time and patience than you needed for your earlier papers, but they are not difficult to learn.

Chapter 19

Overview of the Research Paper

Sooner or later the longer paper comes to us all, usually because it's assigned, or perhaps because we find ourselves interested in a subject. But regardless of the reason, we're all faced with the same problem: How do we say anything intelligent for five or ten pages or more?

Either we write about a subject we know intimately, or we go to some other source—an interview with an eyewitness, perhaps, or a book in the library. When we must use sources outside our own minds or experience, we rely on research.

Unlike some of the earlier exercises and paragraphs in this book, the research paper has *no invented evidence.* You must find the specific support for your research paper by consulting real sources, not imaginary ones.

By now you may be worried because of stories you've heard about research papers. A research paper can be long, and it can be a lot of work. It can be particularly troublesome if you put it off until the last minute. The process of research and writing requires a number of careful steps. You'll find it hard to compress all of them into a long night's work—or even a day or two.

What a Research Paper Is and Isn't

It's not

- a rehash of encyclopedia articles
- a string of quotations, one after another, like sausages
- a mass of invented support
- a mystical kind of writing that's more difficult than the kinds you've been doing

---

It is

- an organized statement about a subject, using support from sources outside your own experience
- a paper that credits sources with thorough documentation
- a normal requirement in many college courses and professional jobs
- the next step in your development as a writer

THE SHAPE OF THE RESEARCH PAPER

Like the writing you did for Part Four, the research paper is an expanded form of the five-paragraph essay. Of course it's longer, but the basic structure is still the same. The chart on the next page shows the relationship between a five-paragraph essay and a longer research paper.

Not every paragraph must have exactly three items of specific support, nor must every main idea have exactly three paragraphs of support. Some may have more and some less. Whatever the number, the support paragraphs help persuade your readers to accept one of the major topic sentences in the same way specific support helps persuade them to accept the topic sentences in a five-paragraph essay. And the major topic sentences in the research paper help convince your readers of the thesis. By now you've learned that a model is simply a guide, a handy way to begin thinking about your paper. Treat this model the same way.

THE RESEARCH PAPER'S PURPOSE

Why write a long paper? A research paper could be:

- to explore a particular problem (the major cause of the British defeat at Singapore in World War II, for example)
- to inform readers about a development (the effects of an increase in the minimum wage)
- to trace the history of a situation (how America became involved in the Panama Canal)
- to present the solution to a problem (how we can deal with the effects of pollution on buildings and monuments)

Research papers are a means of presenting a large amount of information about a particular topic, information gathered from outside the writer's own knowledge and experience. And the purposes of these papers can be as varied as are the reasons for presenting large amounts of information.

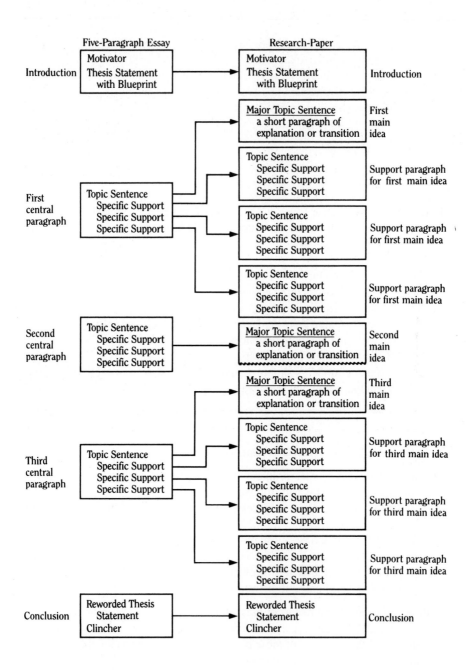

Practical Applications for Research Papers

A research paper is not just a classroom exercise. It has many practical uses. Businesses use research reports as marketing studies and reports to stockholders. The military services call them staff studies and intelligence reports. Inspectors and auditors call them reports of findings. Doctors call them case studies. Professors sometimes call them monographs. Whatever the names, reports that present large amounts of information from research or investigations of some sort are likely to remain part of your life beyond the classroom.

A SAMPLE RESEARCH PAPER

To see what is possible in a research paper of about 1,500 words, look at the sample paper that follows. Comments on pages facing the paper highlight points you'll learn more about in subsequent chapters.

For the most part the page layout in the sample paper follows the guidance in the third edition of the *MLA Handbook for Writers of Research Papers.* In a few places, however, we've departed from the MLA page format guidance because it restricts layout techniques. Nevertheless, we've noted those places in the comments facing the pages so you'll know the MLA rules if your instructor wants your paper to adhere strictly to the MLA guidance. Of course, we've also explained why we departed from the MLA format to help you judge the effect of the alterations.

Some instructors want their students to submit outlines with their final papers. Chapter 22, which discusses outlining, shows a formal sentence outline for this sample research paper.

The MLA page format, which your instructor may want you to use, calls for your last name and the page number one-half inch from the top of each page and flush with the right margin. You'll see this style illustrated on page 2 and subsequent pages of the sample paper. MLA guidance calls for this information on page 1 as well, but we've deleted it. Traditionally, the first page of a document bears no page marking.

MLA research paper guidance also calls for identifying information in the upper left corner of the first page, as you see it here. Include your name, your instructor's name, the course number, and the date. Your instructor may ask you to include this information on a title page instead.

MLA guidance also directs you to double space from the last line of the identification block, type the title of the paper, and double space to begin the first line of text in the body of your paper. The result is a solid-looking mass of type that doesn't provide visual separation for the paper's title. We've added extra space before and after the title, setting it off for readers to see. Using white space in this way is a simple design technique that enhances the appearance of a paper.

A

Jennifer James
Professor Wilson
English 111
15 April 1990

Hostages of Testing

The school system my sisters attend uses
standardized tests for final examinations. Last
year, two weeks before my younger sister took
her seventh-grade history final, her teacher
drilled the students on lists of names, dates,
and places that would be on the test. The
teacher even told them that if they saw certain
questions, to provide certain answers. I've
learned since that this is called "teaching to
the test," although "cramming to the test" would
seem more appropriate. The problem is a typical
result when schools use standardized tests for
large numbers of students and the stakes are
high for students and teachers.

But when my tenth-grade sister took her
minimum competency test to qualify for eventual
high school graduation, I realized how serious
testing could be. Across the United States,
thousands of students are subject to minimum

The thesis statement for this paper is in two sentences: "Despite their appeal to the public, minimum competency tests are of questionable value for the students. They hold at risk the quality of education of all students—not just those who fail one or more times—making them hostages to the testing system." The second sentence could stand on its own as the thesis, of course, but readers get the full meaning of the thesis statement from the two sentences in combination.

This paper puts the blueprint in a separate paragraph with bullets to mark the blueprint items. The blueprint also would work if it were part of the previous paragraph and had no bullets. However, the layout here leaves no doubt about what is to follow. This type of overt organizational device is particularly important in business and technical writing—and it can add to other types of writing as well.

Marked here is a first-level (or major) heading. In Chapter 10, you saw what a single level of headings could do to help readers grasp the information in a short paper. A longer paper may need more levels—this one has two.

The heading at the beginning of the first block of "body" text provides a benefit for the introduction as well. Commonly, the first paragraph of a short research paper is one paragraph—beginning with a motivator and ending with the thesis statement with blueprint. The sample paper has the necessary parts, but they are divided into three paragraphs for easier reading—instead of one long paragraph. The heading at the *end* of the introduction keeps readers from confusing introductory and body paragraphs.

MLA page format does not address headings. However, MLA guidance does call for consistent double spacing throughout the research paper. Presumably, then, it would allow no extra space before or after headings within the body of the paper. As you can see, we advise using extra space before and after headings.

That spacing is an important design technique. The white space signals to readers that you're moving to a new topic and sets off the heading, focusing on the title it provides for the following material. In this way, layout reinforces your words.

Documenting borrowed material is one of the new skills you'll learn in studying the research paper. Notice that the information from the Madaus article has an introduction ("George Madaus provides. . . .") so that readers can tell where the borrowed material begins. The parenthetical reference at the end of the borrowing—"(614)"—marks where the borrowing ends and tells specifically which part of the Madaus article the writer drew upon.

Notice also that the parenthetical reference—the page number in parentheses—comes before the period that ends the sentence.

You'll learn more about presenting and documenting borrowed material in Chapters 23 through 25.

James 2

competency tests, yet those tests lead to a
number of problems, among them "teaching to the
test." Despite their appeal to the public,
minimum competency tests are of questionable
value for the students. They hold at risk the
quality of education of all students--not just
those who fail one or more times--making them
hostages to the testing system.

Why the minimum competency tests interfere
with learning will become clear from a
discussion of:

- why the tests were adopted
- what minimum competency tests are
- problems the tests generate for the
  classroom
- how the testing holds students at risk

WHY MINIMUM COMPETENCY TESTS WERE ADOPTED

Minimum competency tests make the most
sense if we understand the setting in which they
were created. George Madaus provides an overview
of the events that led to competency testing. In
the 1960s and early 1970s, the public became
convinced that the quality of education in the

See the parenthetical reference at the end of the first sentence? Where did the summary begin? Your obligation to your readers is to be sure they always know where borrowed material begins and ends. No problem here. Clearly, the borrowed material begins at the start of the paragraph. However, if you think readers may question where your borrowed material begins, introduce the borrowing by mentioning the source's author or title.

The second sentence of the paragraph ("What the public wanted. . . .") is the writer's own. Readers can tell that because the first sentence ends with a parenthetical reference and the third sentence begins with an introduction to another borrowing.

The parenthetical reference at the end of the first sentence—"(Salganik 608)"—has both the name of the author of the source and the page number for the borrowing. This is a "standard" parenthetical reference. All the other parenthetical references in the sample paper have only page numbers. Why? When an introduction to a borrowing identifies the source in the Works Cited listing, the parenthetical reference needs only the page designation. You'll learn more about parenthetical references and this streamlining technique in Chapter 24.

G

Quotations that require four or fewer lines of typing in your paper will be incorporated into the flow of your paper, but set off with quotation marks to designate the exact words from your source. Longer quotations, like this one, are indented as a block. Notice that the indented quotation does *not* begin and end with quotation marks; the block indentation functions in the place of quotation marks to set off the exact words of the source from your own words.

Notice also that the parenthetical reference—"(608)"—comes *after* the ending punctuation for the quotation. For long, indented quotations, space twice after the ending punctuation of the quotation, provide the parenthetical reference, and put *no* punctuation after the closing parenthesis of the reference. Note: this is the style *only* for quotations set off with block indentation.

James 3

United States was inadequate. Employers claimed
high school diplomas were meaningless. News of
declines in Scholastic Aptitude Test scores
convinced many that schools weren't doing their
jobs. And, of course, education costs continued
to rise (614). The public wanted proof that
youth were being prepared for life and that tax
dollars weren't being wasted.

Attempts in the 1960s to develop detailed
activity plans and report progress to parents
proved too complex for most parents (Salganik
608). What the public wanted was simplicity--
scores they could understand and proof that
money spent on education brought improvement. As
Laura Salganik notes:

> in the new climate of uncertainty
> about the adequacy of the schools (and
> thus about the competence of
> educators), testing introduced a
> welcome simplicity to the task of
> restoring both educational quality and
> public confidence in the schools. Few
> people were willing to argue with the
> use of tests as a means of insuring
> quality control. (608)

F

G

James 4

To policy makers, standardized testing appeared
to offer accurate, unbiased assessment tools. As
Andrew Strenio explains, standardized tests
appear to be "objective," because they are
scored by machine rather than by a person, and
to many that equates to "scientific" (63-65,
192-94). To policy makers and school
administrators, the standardized tests appeared
to offer a convenient, cost-effective way of
improving education and especially of pleasing
the public. And if you're trying to demonstrate
that students graduate from high school with at
least minimal skills, what better way to show it
than to administer a minimum competency test?

WHAT MINIMUM COMPETENCY TESTS ARE

Minimum competency tests are standardized
examinations, almost always multiple-choice,
developed to ensure that students have developed
minimal proficiencies. In most states the tests
are on reading, writing, and math, with a few
adding other skills. Usually the tests are
connected to some serious consequence, such as
promotion to a higher grade; the most common

This short quotation is incorporated into the flow of the student writer's work. Notice that the quoted material, which is set off with quotation marks, does not begin with a capital letter. That is, the first portion of the quotation is itself not a full sentence, although it is set into the student's writing so that there is a complete sentence structure. You can, and should, trim the material you quote to fit it into your own writing as support for your points. The quotations should fit into the grammar and sense of your own writing. Of course, it's *not* acceptable to edit the original material in such a way that you misrepresent what its author said or wrote— for example, by leaving out *not* or *never*. Chapter 23 explains techniques for dealing with quotations: omitting words, adding words, adding emphasis, verifying quotation accuracy, and altering final punctuation.

Notice also that the parenthetical reference here—"(8)"—follows the quotation marks but precedes the ending punctuation for the sentence. This technique apples to quotations incorporated into the flow of your paragraphs, but not to long, indented quotations.

"Time Lost to Coaching" and the two headings that follow are second-level (or minor) headings. The heading style this simple research paper employs is one good way to make headings in a typed paper. As Chapter 22 illustrates, if your computer or word processor permits changes in type sizes, faces, and styles, you can make fancier headings. But even if you have only a standard typewriter, you can create the types of headings here. The important point is that a major heading should stand out more on a page than a minor heading does.

If you compare the heading levels in this paper with its formal sentence outline (in Chapter 22), you'll see that the writer has employed first-level headings for each major block (Roman numeral outline level) of the body plus the conclusion. She has provided second-level headings only for the sub-blocks (capital letter outline level) within one major block. Why? This major block on problems the testing generates has three clearly defined subordinate sections; the second-level headings help readers grasp that material. The other major blocks, especially the one on what minimum competency tests are, do not have this same type of separation within the blocks—so minor headings would not be functional. Don't feel you have to provide a subheading for every division of your final outline. But do use headings to focus attention on the contents of your paper where such focus is appropriate.

connection is to high school graduation. Karen
Klein reports that by 1984, 40 states had some
type of minimum competency testing program,
about half of them a requirement for graduation
(565).

PROBLEMS THE TESTS GENERATE FOR THE CLASSROOM

The American Association of School
Administrators noted the most serious drawback
of the minimum competency movement: "its almost
total reliance on testing. Testing alone cannot
guarantee that students will become more
competent" (8). What the testing does, however,
is create serious problems for the educational
process in the classroom. Critics of minimum
competency testing point out these problems:
time lost in coaching students, narrowing of the
material taught, and deflection in the
curriculum overall.

Time Lost to Coaching

When a test has serious consequences for
either students or teachers, significant

classroom time goes into preparing the
students--time taken away from other studies.
This is "teaching to the test." For example,
George Madaus reports that the department of
education in New Jersey admitted providing local
districts with the previous year's test and that
some teachers coached students for weeks or even
months (616). For students who fail a minimum
competency test, the loss of normal class time
can be greater. Michael Henry reports that 33 to
50 percent of Maryland's students fail the
citizenship competency test at least once. As a
result, a student who hasn't passed by the end
of the junior year can have been taken out of 15
weeks of normal classroom work in world
geography, world history, and U.S. history (11).

Narrowing of the Curriculum

Teachers also report that the tests lead to
narrowing, or trivialization, of the curriculum.
Michael Henry charges that the Maryland
competency test has reduced the concept of
citizenship to "an exercise in trivia": "The
test requires a commitment to memory of hundreds

of details--information probably forgotten
before the last test booklet has been packed and
shipped back to the state board of education"
(11). The problem results because test makers
have difficulty designing multiple-choice
questions that go beyond identification of
correct rules or facts or of simple
computations. Thus, composition becomes rules of
grammar and punctuation, not actual writing. As
Gerald Bracey notes, "It is difficult to present
science as an ongoing process of discovery, as a
detective story, when test items converge on the
recall of a single right answer" (686).

Deflection in the Curriculum

    The third major effect of minimum
competency testing is deflection in the
curriculum. Deflection results when emphasis is
placed on preparing students for test material
rather than on other curriculum areas of equal
or greater merit. Most competency tests focus on
reading, writing, and math; that leaves the arts
and social sciences, for instance, without
emphasis. It even ignores courses such as shop

J

Just as headings allowed the writer to divide the introduction into three paragraphs without risk of confusing readers about the paper's organization, headings allow the writer to break a long paragraph into two at this point. Clearly both paragraphs have to do with "Deflection in the Classroom."

and home economics that are designed to prepare
students for later life.

J

     Charles Suhor cites a survey of the effects
of testing in Florida in 1977. Results showed
that because of the focus on basic skills, there
had been reduced emphasis on literature,
language, and composition (639). Gerald Bracey
provides a particularly apt example: The
Virginia math competency test assessed
recognition of parallel lines, but not of
perpendicular lines. One version of the test,
however, included a question on perpendicular
lines, and student performance on that question
dropped significantly (685). The conclusion is
simple: if the test covers an item, it receives
classroom attention, yet other areas--even
closely related ones--may be ignored.

      HOW MINIMUM COMPETENCY TESTING HOLDS STUDENTS
                       AT RISK

     The problems we have just covered are
likely to result to some degree from any
standardized testing. Without doubt, however,
they become more acute when the stakes are high,

Tables and figures often will not fit exactly where you'd like them to go in your final paper. For that reason, it's best to prepare them so they can "float" freely within the paper—that is, so you do not have to place them in only one particular place. Refer to a table (or figure) by number—as with "(see table 1)." Then place the table (or figure) where you'd like it to go if it will fit there. If it won't fit, you can place it intact at the top of the next page (or on a separate page for a very large table or figure).

Prepare a table as the sample paper shows it. Give the table a number and a title; show the source, if necessary, at the end of the table, set off by a short line dividing it from the table contents. You may want to put tables and figures within boxes to separate the graphics from your text; many computer word processing programs provide such a capability. Illustrated here is a technique of setting the table off with single lines above and below—a layout technique you can achieve with only a standard typewriter.

The MLA format for a table differs somewhat from what you see here. If you need to follow MLA guidance exactly, make these changes: Type the table designator and title on separate lines as shown, but place them flush left at the left margin of your paper. Double space *throughout* the table. Use full ruled lines (margin to margin) in the place of the partial lines you see in this sample table. Do not set the table off from your text with lines or a box, and do not provide extra space above or below the table.

James 9

K

as they are with minimum competency testing.
How, then, can these tests be defended?
Advocates and the public seem to be convinced by
increases in scores. James Popham provides
figures of improvement associated with
competency testing (see table 1). Gerald Bracey
argues against a simple interpretation of such
data. He points out that when students are
threatened with failure and teachers with loss
of jobs, "it is something less than miraculous
to find that test scores rise" (686).

L

				Percent
Table 1				
Test Score Improvements for Localities Using Competency Tests				
Locale	Subjects	Grade	Period	Improvement
Alabama	Reading, Writing, Math	11	1983-85	4-8
Connecticut	Reading, Writing, Math	9	1980-84	6-16
Detroit	Reading, Writing, Math	12	1981-86	19
Maryland	Reading, Writing, Math	9	1980-86	13-25
	Citizenship	9	1983-86	23
New Jersey	Reading, Math	9	1977-85	16-19
	Reading, Math	10	1982-85	8-11

Source: James W. Popham, "The Merits of
Measurement-Driven Instruction," <u>Phi Delta
Kappan</u> 68(1987) : 682.

A vocal advocate of minimum competency testing, James Popham accepts that the tests affect teaching and wants to push things further. He advocates using tests with serious consequences to drive curriculum, to determine what teachers will teach. This, he feels, will overcome mediocre teaching in the classroom (680-81). But let's consider what he's asking for. So teachers will teach certain things in certain ways, their students should be held at risk; then outsiders can be assured the teachers are doing what is required of them. This is a hostage situation.

Finally, we should consider research about the effect of minimum competency testing on earnings after high school graduation, especially since the tests were adopted partially because of employer complaints about student quality. Karen Klein cites two studies of the relationship of math and reading scores of students not attending college to their earnings after leaving high school. Those studies showed scores and earnings were totally unrelated. However, she points out that other research shows people between 16 and 21 are

$\boxed{\text{M}}$

The introduction to the paper does not need a heading to announce where it starts (although it benefits from the heading for the beginning of the paper's body, which also marks where the introduction ends). The conclusion, however, needs a heading to separate it from the body of the paper.

Would "Conclusion" work as the heading? Yes, but not well. "Conclusion" would mark the move from the paper's body to its conclusion. But good headings should be more than mere place marks. They're also titles that lead readers into the substance of the material that follows.

twice as likely to be unemployed if they have no diploma. And as Klein notes, for most students who are going to college, the minimum competency tests are just a "formality" (566). So who actually benefits from the tests?

M

MINIMUM COMPETENCY TESTS DO NOT PROMOTE LEARNING

The minimum competency tests, it seems, provide simple statistics that appear to "prove" the usefulness of the tests. Yet, when we go behind those statistics to see what the impact is on the classroom and on the preparation of students for life, the results are very different. The tests indeed appear to force students to learn bits of information, and--not surprisingly--overall improvement on retaining bits of information improves as a result. But do those bits equate to learning? Many educators say no. At the same time, the cost to all students is severe. Time that could be spent on developing thinking and reasoning is spent on memorization. Vital subjects are reduced to bare minimums that can be tested easily, so that the minimum level for competency becomes the maximum

James 12

level for teaching. Courses and activities that
do not lead to test preparation begin to be
ignored. In this way, the quality of education
of American students is held hostage by the
minimum competency testing process.

The Works Cited page begins on a separate page from the text of the research paper. Chapter 25 explains in detail the style for Works Cited entries.

If you need to follow MLA page layout guidance exactly, begin the section title—"Works Cited"—one inch from the top of the paper and double space to get to the line for the first entry. That is, do not provide additional space between the section title and the beginning of the entries. We've shown extra space for the same reason we set off the paper's title, the headings, and the table—to let white space signal breaks and highlight the material set off.

N

James 13

Works Cited

American Association of School Administrators. The Competency Movement: Problems and Solutions. By Shirley Boes Neill. AASA Critical Issues Report. Sacramento: Education News Service, 1978.

Bracey, Gerald W. "Measurement-Driven Instruction: Catchy Phrase, Dangerous Practice." Phi Delta Kappan 68 (1987): 683-86.

Henry, Michael. "A True Test or a Trivia Game?" Newsweek 22 Jun. 1987: 10-11.

Klein, Karen. "Minimum Competency Testing: Shaping and Reflecting Curricula." Phi Delta Kappan 65 (1984): 565-67.

Madaus, George F. "Test Scores as Administrative Mechanisms in Educational Policy." Phi Delta Kappan 66 (1985): 611-17.

Popham, James W. "The Merits of Measurement-Driven Instruction." Phi Delta Kappan 68 (1987): 679-82.

Salganik, Laura Hersh. "Why Testing Reforms Are So Popular and How They Are Changing

James 14

Education." <u>Phi Delta Kappan</u> 66 (1985):
607-10.

Strenio, Andrew J., Jr. <u>The Testing Trap</u>. New
York: Ransom, 1981.

Suhor, Charles. "Objective Tests and Writing
Samples: How Do They Affect Instruction in
Composition?" <u>Phi Delta Kappan</u> 66 (1985):
635-39.

PREVIEWING THE RESEARCH PAPER PROCESS

You already know what a good thesis looks like—a precise opinion about a limited topic. Research papers, too, require a good thesis, but because the research paper is longer and uses other people's ideas, we might call the thesis a thoughtful assertion about the limited topic. That means the research thesis is more than just an opinion: it's opinion supported by facts, ideas, and words of other authorities. To help you devise a good thesis, we'll preview the research process here.

Although you might be an intuitive writer and settle immediately on the exact thesis statement you'll use in writing your paper, that would be very unusual. If you're an ordinary mortal like most of us, this will be more common: You pick a topic, narrow it enough to make the scale of research reasonable, and move slowly toward the final thesis statement as your research goes along. For example, the writer of the sample paper began with *testing,* narrowed that to *minimum competency testing* after beginning her research, and finally settled on *the negative impact of minimum competency testing on the quality of education* as the basis for her thesis statement.

In the next six chapters we'll go into more detail, but here's the research paper procedure we recommend to start you on your way:

- *Select a general topic* that interests you.
- *Do some preliminary reading* in handy, reliable sources to find out whether your topic and your ideas about it seem to be based on accurate assumptions and whether reliable, relevant sources appear to be available. If you're unhappy about your topic at this point, choose something else.
- *Develop a working thesis statement* to set a reasonable scope for research. As you find sources and think about what you've learned, constantly refine your working thesis by checking to see whether the subject is precise. Keep your mind open so that you can refine the working thesis when necessary.
- *Find supporting sources* that deal with your topic. You needn't limit your search to library sources, although the time available to work on your paper may prevent you from conducting interviews or tests. For this reason, most of our discussion about research papers focuses on library resources. Be sure to evaluate your sources for relevance and reliability rather than blindly trusting what you read and hear. And be sure to keep accurate records about your sources; you'll need information about them when you document your paper.
- *Gather supporting facts and opinions* from your sources. You won't be able to remember every detail, and you'll need some sort of system to match information with sources so you'll be able to document what you borrow. (We'll discuss two very different ways of accomplishing these objectives.)
- *Organize your thoughts and support.* You should develop working outlines as you conduct your research; they help you see where you're going with your investigation—especially where you need more material. Before you draft your paper, however, you'll need to develop some sort of final outline to guide your writing. Moreover, many instructors require their students to submit formal outlines either before they begin writing or with the final paper.

- *Write a first draft.* The writing step is much like you've done for shorter papers, but you'll also be incorporating borrowed material from your research. As you write, you can insert the appropriate parenthetical references in the text for part of the documentation process. You'll also write and organize Works Cited entries for the listing that ends your research paper.
- *Revise the draft*—as many times as necessary to get the paper right.
- *Prepare the final version of your paper to hand in.*

POSSIBLE TOPICS

Now we'll look at some topics that may stir your imagination. Any of these broad topics could lead to a good narrow topic and thesis, or they may suggest similar topics that interest you. All, however, need to be narrowed carefully. Moreover, you'll do yourself and your readers a real favor if you stay away from some kinds of topics. Avoid writing about contemporary politics or religion—such topics often are too personal to write a research paper about. Thus, they are frequently ineffective from the beginning.

Remember, the topics that follow all need deliberate limiting. And, of course, before you can develop a thesis, each needs a thoughtful assertion—a precise opinion—made about it.

Acid Rain	Espionage	Refugees
Adoption	Flemish Painting	Reunification of
AIDS Research	Gambling	Germany
Airline Deregulation	Hazardous Wastes	Savings and Loan
Auto Safety	Hospices	Banks
Ballet	Insulation	Speech Disorders
Bicycling	International Terrorism	Strip-mining
Cable Television	Iraq's Invasion of	Tax Reform
Censorship	Kuwait	Teen Alcoholism
Changes in Europe	Islamic Movement	Trojan War
Chemical Fertilizers	Junk Bonds	Urban Transportation
Child Abuse	Learning Disorders	Vegetarianism
Child Custody	Midwives	Volcanoes
Commercial Satellites	Minoans	Worker Productivity
Digital Technology	Missing Children	Yoga
Drugs in Sport	Organ Donation	
Drug Testing	Panama Canal	
Endangered Species	Pollution	
Environmental	Prison Overcrowding	
Legislation	Rain Forests	

Chapter 20

Finding Support

Sometimes when you have to write a research paper you won't know much about the subject, so you won't know what you want to say until you've studied the subject enough to narrow it to a manageable size, to a thesis. For example, from the broad subject of *pollution,* you might narrow to *pollution from plastics* and even further to the narrower thesis that *Fast food restaurants are the primary source of polluting plastics in North America.*

WHERE TO BEGIN

One way both to narrow your topic and to get a lead on information you need is to do some preliminary research in general reference tools such as encyclopedias. Even here, keep an informal record of your research by listing briefly the title and headings or subjects you looked under. This step is especially important if later you want to return to pick up the bit of information you remember reading but neglected to write down.

You may be in for some surprises as you continue working on your subject; what you find may take you in unexpected directions. Despite your initial belief, you might find, for example, that two of the fast food chains have stopped using plastics and are active in research to prevent their products from contributing to pollution. When such a change happens, you must revise your thesis. In this case, you might say something like "Although many people think fast food chains are destructive polluters, they are actually working hard to prevent pollution caused by their products."

Once you have a working thesis, you're ready to begin the more formal research process. The problem is to know where to begin among all the resources available.

You may want to conduct a survey or series of experiments. Your research could involve audio or video tapes or viewing a series of television programs. Or perhaps you'll want to interview participants in a relatively recent event of some importance—or business executives involved in an ongoing project. Finding sources for a research paper can include any search for information relevant to a topic and thesis.

Most college research paper projects, however, involve library research and are usually limited to the books and articles that are readily available in the college library. The limitation is the time you have available to conduct your research and prepare your paper. For this very practical reason, our discussion of sources focuses on the college library. Fortunately, though, the things you're learning about conducting research and writing a research paper apply just as well to other types of research you might conduct if you had more time available.

BOOKS

The Catalog

Traditionally, the primary guide to a library's book collection has been called the "card catalog," because all the library's books were listed on index cards filed in long, narrow drawers. Today you library may not have such cards, but it will have a catalog of some sort—in microform or in a computer file—perhaps called "catalog of books," "catalog of documents," or merely "catalog." Whatever the form and name, however, it will provide essentially the same information as the traditional card catalog. Since greater numbers of colleges now have computerized catalogs, let's deal with those first.

The Computerized List

To begin using your library's computerized list of books, you'll need to follow the directions either near the computer or on the screen. The directions can lead you in several ways to find books you need for your research. Generally, those directions tell you to enter an author's name, a book's title, or the subject you're interested in. Here's a sample first screen from one library:

```
What type of search do you wish to do?

       1.  TIL - Title, journal title, series title, etc.

       2.  AUT - Author, illustrator, editor, organization, etc.

       3.  A-T - Combination of author and title.

       4.  SUB - Subject heading assigned by library.

       5.  NUM - Call number, ISBN, ISSN, etc.

       6.  KEY - One word taken from a title, author or subject.

Enter number or code, then press CARRIAGE RETURN.
```

You can see that this list also includes the combination of author and title, the call number (the number the library files the book under in the book stacks), or a key word search. If you're looking for books by one author, naturally you'd try an author search. If you know a book's title, you can ask the computer to get the call number you need.

But the computer can help you in other ways by searching the index for you. You could ask for a subject or a key word search. Let's say you decide to ask for a key word search for *pollution.* Here's what you'd get:

```
                                                    LIB *TIL KEYWORD SEARCH

Your Title Keyword: POLLUTION                          Matches 385 titles

                                           No. of citations    Your
                                            in entire catalog   Lib
  1  2nd Soviet-Swedish Symposium on the Pollution of the Baltic>     1     1
  2  Acid rain and emissions trading : implementing a market appr>    1     1
  3  Aerophysics of air pollution /                                   1     1
  4  Against pollution and hunger; [proceedings]                      1     1
  5  Air pollution.                                                   9     9
  6  AIR POLLUTION–1970                                               5     5
  7  Air pollution and acid rain : the biological impact /            1     1
  8  Air pollution, acid rain, and the future of forests /            1     1
  9  Air pollution and athletic performance /                         1     1
 10  Air pollution, the automobile, and public health /               1     1
 11  Air pollution control /                                          4     4

Type a number to see more information -OR-
   FOR - move forward in this list        CAT - begin a new search
   CMD - see additional commands
```

With 385 titles that include your key word, you might have more information than you can use. So, let's go back to the computer to look at a subject search for *pollution.* This search lists all titles that the library has filed under that subject. With this search you get 86 entries:

```
                                              No. of citations    Your
                                               in entire catalog   Lib
  1  Pollution.                                      91              86
  2  Pollution Abstracts Periodicals.                 1
  3  Pollution Addresses, Essays, Lectures.           2               2
  4  Pollution Bibliography.                          4               4
  5  Pollution Bibliography Periodicals.              1               1
  6  Pollution British Columbia Congresses.           1               1
  7  Pollution Congresses.                           13              13
  8  Pollution Control Equipment.                     3               3
  9  Pollution Control Equipment Handbooks, Manuals, etc.   1         1
 10  Pollution Control Equipment Linings.             1               1
 11  Pollution Control Equipment Maintenance and Repair.    1         1
```

If you then ask for a listing of number 4 above, "Pollution Bibliography," you see a short title list of the four entries cataloged under that subject heading:

```
                                             matches    4 citations
                                                    (All in this library)
     Ref  #  Author            Title                             Date

         1  Burk, Janet L.      Environmental concerns : a bibliogr  >   1975
         2  Kiraldi, Louis, 1911-  Pollution: a selected bibliography   >   1971
         3  McDonald, Rita,     Guide to literature on environmenta  >   1970
         4  Rehfus, Ruth.       Mercury contamination in the natura>   1970
```

If we want to see more about a source on air pollution, different keystrokes give a short entry for one of the books identified in our earlier search. This short entry gives the author, title, and call number and indicates that the book is in the library— all important bits of information.

```
     AUTHOR:    Lynn, David A.
     TITLE:     Air pollution, threat and response / David A. Lynn.
     IMPRINT:   Reading, Mass. : Addison-Wesley Pub. Co., c1976.

                      Loan            Cpy
     Location         Type            #          Status

       BKSTAX         BOOK            1          In Library
     Call Number:  TD 883 .L96
```

But just being in the library isn't quite enough (either for you or for the book); you need more information. One more keystroke gives a full entry, one that tells how big the book is, whether it has a more detailed bibliography, and another subject ("air pollution") you might search for.

```
     AUTHOR:    Lynn, David A.
     TITLE:     Air pollution, threat and response / David A. Lynn.
     IMPRINT:   Reading, Mass. : Addison-Wesley Pub. Co., c1976.
     PHYSICAL FEATURES:  x, 388 p. : ill. ; 24 cm.
     NOTES:     CALL NO.: TD 883 .L96 * Includes index. * Bibliography: p. 349–364.
     SUBJECTS: Air — Pollution.
     CALL NUMBER: TD 883 .L96 * TD 883 .L96
```

Without leaving the computer terminal, then, you can get a list of the books the library has on your subject, their call numbers, and other detailed information about them. Unlike the card catalog, this computer catalog even tells whether the book is available for checkout.

The important points about computer searches are these:

- They save time.
- They reveal useful information about potential sources.
- They are fun to do.

Quick Tips for Using the Computerized List of Books

- Decide on your subject.
- Do the computer search.
- Jot down the call numbers for the books you find or print the computer list.
- Find the books you need in the library's stacks.

The Card Catalog

Your library may have the traditional card catalog. Cards come in three kinds: author, title, and subject. If you know a book's author or title, look for one of those. But as you look for support for your research paper, you may know only a general subject, say *architecture*. Then you can look at cards filed under that heading.

The information on the card catalog cards, like that in the computerized catalog, will save you time. All three kinds of cards start as author cards. A title card has the title typed across the top so it can be alphabetized by title easily, and a subject card has the subject typed on top so it can be alphabetized by subject. Beyond that top line, however, the contents of the cards are the same.

If you were trying to find out something about building styles of ancient civilizations, you could look for books on architecture, specifically on the history of architecture. In the card catalog under the subject heading "Architecture—History" you might find this card:

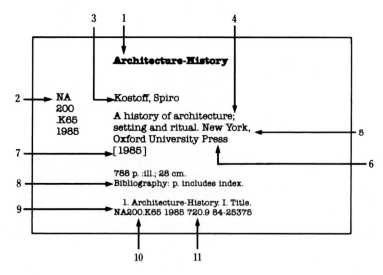

1. Subject heading. A title card would have the book's title instead. The basic author card would have nothing in this position.
2. Call number. The library where we found this card uses the Library of Congress classification system for filing its books. If it had used the Dewey decimal classification system, "720.9" would have appeared in this position.
3. Author's name.
4. Title.
5. Place of publication.
6. Publisher.
7. Publication date.
8. Notes on special contents. The book is illustrated, has a bibliography, and is indexed. Information about the number of pages may prove useful in evaluating the potential value of the book. The bibliography is especially important, for it can lead to other related books.
9. Recommended subject headings.
10. Recommended Library of Congress number.
11. Recommended Dewey decimal number.

Besides finding this card under "Architecture—History," you would find it under the author's name and the book's title. Depending on how a library files its cards, the three card types may be integrated in the same catalog or filed separately.

PERIODICALS

The library catalog, regardless of its form, isn't the only way to find support you need for your research. Periodicals, which include popular magazines and professional journals, are also basic sources, sometimes the most important sources. Even the most recent book is at least a year out of date by the time it appears, and the information in it may be several years old. If you are writing on the battle of Hastings in 1066, books could be your principal sources. But if your topic requires last-minute, up-to-date information, you will need to use some periodicals.

How do you find what you need? You could, of course, go to the library stacks and start leafing through all the bound volumes of *Newsweek* or *Runner's World* in hope you'd find the article you need. But even just looking at the table of contents in each issue would take more time than you can afford. So what do you do? Find a shortcut to get to the information quickly. That's where reference tools come in. They help you find the right article the way the catalog helped you find the right book. The problem is that there is more than one catalog for periodicals.

Indexes

Suppose you need to write about *censorship*. But you know that that's too big a topic, so you narrow it to *censorship in education*, which is still pretty broad. You go further to decide on the more limited topic of *censorship in school newspapers*. That still may need more limiting and the sharper focus of a thesis, but *censorship in school newspapers* is narrow enough to set reasonable bounds on research. After checking the card catalog for books, you decide to try the periodicals. You check one of the most widely known periodical indexes, the *Readers' Guide to Periodical Literature.* On page 368 of the 1989 volume, under the heading of *Censorship,* you find this:

CENSORSHIP

See also

Art—Censorship
Banned Books Week
Freedom of information
Freedom of the press
Government and the press
Humor—Censorship
Motion pictures—Censorship
Obscenity (Law)
Photography—Censorship
Television broadcasting—Censorship
Textbooks—Censorship

Bad Astra: the other side of the Spectrum [court rules against predistribution review policy in case of high school underground newspaper in Renton, Wash.] P. A. Zirkel. bibl f il *Phi Delta Kappan* 70:734-5+ My '89

A boy sides with Dr. Seuss's Lorax, and puts a town at loggerheads [parents of S. Bailey call for removal of title from school reading list in Laytonville, Calif.] R. Arias. il pors *People Weekly* 32: 67-8 O 23 '89

Combating censorship in the U.S. H. F. Pilpel. il *USA Today (Periodical)* 117:84-6 Ja '89

Comedy of errors? [discussion of October 2, 1989 article, 'A gangsterdom of the spirit'] *The Nation* 249:406 O 16 '89

For goodness sake? [S. King's books banned in public school libraries] H. Wornom. por *Omni (New York, N.Y.)* 12:16+ D '89

'A gangsterdom of the spirit' [E. L. Doctorow's controversial commencement speech at Brandeis University] *The Nation* 249:348 O 2 '89

Have Christian books been censored? [rejection by book reviewers] S. Charles. il *Publishers Weekly* 235:58 Mr 3 '89

What do these entries tell you? First, under *See also* are other headings you might consult for more information. Then under the first entry, you see the title of the article, with a brief summary in brackets. Summaries like this help you find useful articles when the title doesn't give you much help.

You also can see that most of the articles appear in magazines that are generally available in public or university libraries. Note that each entry gives a volume or issue number, followed after the colon by the page numbers and the abbreviated date. Despite the summaries, of course, you can't be sure these articles will be useful until you read them.

The *Readers' Guide* covers some 180 magazines and journals considered to contain articles of general (or "popular") interest: *Time, Newsweek, U.S. News and World Report, Jet, Good Housekeeping, Popular Mechanics,* and the like. Since it doesn't cover professional or scholarly journals, it may not help much with scholarly topics, but as the sample shows, it's certainly worth checking if you're working on a topic that would be covered by general-interest magazines.

Don't stop here. Try another index. The *Social Sciences Index* is like the *Readers' Guide,* but it may be more helpful because it covers some 400 periodicals, as well as some books and government documents. Here's an excerpt from Volume 15 (April 1988-March 1989) under the major heading *Censorship:*

Censorship
> *See also*
> Freedom of information
> Freedom of speech
> Freedom of the press
> Motion pictures—Censorship
> Television programs—Censorship
> Textbooks—Censorship

International aspects
The gag around the world's mouth. *Economics* 307:42+ My 21 '88

Hong Kong
Censorship: opening up, clamping down. C. Pomery. *Far East Econ Rev* 140: 79-81 Ap 7 '88

India
India bans a novel of the sacred and profane [Salman Rushdie's Satanic verses] J. Bhatia. *Far East Econ Rev* 142:50-1 O 27 '88

Salman Rushdie and India: Satanic reverses [review article] *Economist* 309:101 O 22 '88

Japan
Japanese film censorship; scissors and woodblocks. *Economist* 306:91-2 Mr 5 '88

Korea (South)
A funny thing happened on the way to democracy. M. Clifford. *Far East Econ Rev* 140:52-3 My 26 '88

South Africa
South Africa's press restrictions: effects on press coverage and public opinion toward South Africa. E. Singer and J. Ludwig. bibl *Public Opin Q* 51:315-34 Fall '87

Soviet Union
Solzhenitsyn's Nobel prize. L. Labedz. *Survey* 30:3-11 Mr '88

United States
Censoring rock lyrics: a historical analysis of the debate. J. R. McDonald. bibl *Youth Soc* 19:294-313 Mr '88

The censorship of pornography: catharsis or learning? T. McCormack. bibl *Am J Orthopsychiatry* 58:492-504 O '88

School officials get clearance to censor student newspapers; appeals court reversed [Hazelwood High School case] N. Cohodas. *Congr Q Wkly Rep* 46:133 Ja 16 '88

The format of the entries is similar to that in the *Readers' Guide.* Again there's a brief summary of the article if the title isn't self-explanatory. But you also can see that the focus is more international and political than that of the *Readers' Guide.*

You probably recognize almost all the magazine titles in the extract from the *Readers' Guide,* but probably few if any in the extract from the *Social Sciences Index.* Right? This fact is a reflection of our exposure to popular magazines, of course, but it also reflects the relative availability of the publications in libraries. Large public libraries will have many of the magazines indexed in the *Readers' Guide* but only a few in the *Social Sciences Index.* Your college library will have a mixture of popular magazines (particularly the news magazines) and professional and scholarly journals.

How can you tell what a library holds? Usually a library has a list of all the periodicals available there. It could be a short list posted on a wall. Often, though, it is a large computer listing lying conspicuously on a table in the reference area (where the indexes are kept) or near the periodical shelves. Check this list for the periodical title you need and for the volumes or issues the library holds.

Abstracts

As useful as the *Readers' Guide,* the *Social Sciences Index*, and other indexes can be, they cover only about two percent of published articles. Another kind of reference tool, an abstract, also may help. There are hundreds of abstracts to cover thousands of topics. You must consult the specialized index for abstracts for your subject: *Psychological Abstracts, Biological Abstracts,* or *Chemical Abstracts,* for example. An abstract summarizes the contents of a technical or scholarly article, but the abstract is much longer than the brief summaries you saw in the *Readers' Guide* and the *Social Sciences Index.*

Let's say you become interested in the psychological aspects of drunk driving. You might, therefore, find *Psychological Abstracts* useful. On page 831 of the volume for 1989, you find this abstract:

> 8866. **Beck, Kenneth H. & Summons, Terry G.** (U Maryland, Safety Education Ctr, College Park) **Adolescent gender differences in alcohol beliefs and behaviors.** *Journal of Alcohol & Drug Education,* 1987(Fal), Vol 33(1), 31-44. —2,313 male and female high school students were surveyed with an anonymous questionnaire to determine measures of alcohol consumption, abuse (drunkenness and drunk driving), beliefs about drunk driving and drinking in general, and sources of information they use about alcohol. Males drank beer, wine, and liquor more frequently and in greater quantities than females; reported more frequent instances of drunkenness and drunk driving; believed the risks associated with drunk driving were less serious and likely to occur and their own effectiveness at controlling the risks were greater than females; and reported their own experience as their best source of information about alcohol more often than did females.

Like the periodical indexes, the abstract provides bibliographic information that you'll need to find the work the abstract covers. But unlike the indexes, abstracts are numbered for reference and provide extended summaries that help you decide if you need to see the full article. Again, check your library's list of periodical holdings to see if the journal and issue are available.

Remember that the abstract is not an article, but a summary only. It's like a metal detector; it can tell only that something is there, not how valuable it is. To use the article, you must read it. The abstract number can make it easier if you have time for the librarian to order a copy of the original. As a general rule, however, don't cite abstracts in your parenthetical references or Works Cited listing. Go to the original.

OTHER SOURCE LISTINGS

What happens if you've been to all these library resources and still haven't found what you want? Don't give up, for now the real challenge of research begins. Your library will have many more research tools to help you get your paper written.

Among the more common reference tools, besides those we've already mentioned, you might find these in your library:

- *Annual Bibliography of English Language and Literature:* indexes articles and books about authors and literature written in English.

- *Biography Index:* an index to biographical material on living and historical figures.

- *Biological Abstracts:* abstracts covering articles on biosciences published in professional journals worldwide.

- *Book Review Digest:* a summary of book reviews for modern literature; useful for finding out how a book was received.

- *Business Periodicals Digest:* as the title indicates, index of business and economics articles.

- *Chemical Abstracts:* abstracts of research articles in chemistry.

- *Economic Books: Current Selections:* contains descriptive annotations.

- *Education Index:* for articles dealing with education research and development.

- *MLA International Bibliography:* published annually by the Modern Language Association; covers scholarly journals and books about language and literature in English and other languages.

- *New York Times Index:* a key, comprehensive index to all news events in the *New York Times;* a basic tool, good for almost any topic including books reviewed in the *New York Review of Books.*

- *Social Sciences, Humanities, and General Sciences Indexes:* a family of indexes covering scholarly and professional journals on these subjects. (The *International Index,* published 1907-65, became the *Social Sciences and Humanities Index,* which split in 1974 into the *Social Sciences Index* and the *Humanities Index;* the *General Sciences Index* joined the family in 1978.)

Other good sources of help are subject bibliographies. They list all the books and articles on a limited subject, such as Vincent Van Gogh, the Arab-Israeli war, novels in early America, or the refugee problem. Consult an experienced librarian for help finding a bibliography in your subject.

Computer Listings

If you are lucky, your library also may have access to on-line computer services or to indexes stored on computer disks. For example, the *PAIS (Public Affairs Information Service) Bulletin* indexes about 1,300 periodicals. In January 1991, the *PAIS Bulletin* merged with the *PAIS Foreign Language Index* and became *PAIS International in Print.* The PAIS index is available on CD-ROM in many libraries. Updated regularly, it allows for a quick search for articles and books. Here is a partial listing of brief citations under the heading *Censorship:*

```
IMMMMMMMMMBriefMCitationsMMMMMMMTotalMcitations:M200M MMMMMMMMMI
: Date Author            Title                                  :
: DDD   DDDDDDDDDDDDDDD      DDDDDDDDDDDDDDDDDDDDDDDDDDDDDDDDDDDDDDDDDDDD :
: 1990 Merrett, Christopher In a state of emergency: libraries and govern :
: 1989 American Lib. Assn.  Intellectual freedom manual.          :
: 1989                      Bibliographie der Buch—und Bibliotheksgeschi: :
: 1989 Bothmer, Michael.    Den Zensor im Nacken.                 :
: 1989 Buchan, Norman and T Glasnost in Britain? against censorship and i :
: 1989 Doornaert, Mia and S Inghilterra: attacco alla liberta di stampa: :
: 1989 Gartner, Michael G.  Advertising and the First Amendment.  :
: 1989 Glade, Henry and Dor Sowjetische Verstosse gegen das Welturheberre :
: 1989 Observatoire de L'in L'information dans le monde: 206 pays au micro :
: 1989 Remmer, Alexander.   A note on post—publication censorship in Poland :
: 1989 Riddle, Charles.     A profile of Namibian media: the censored :
: 1989 Savage, James G.     The politics of international telecommunication :
HMMMMMMMMMMMMMMMMMMMMMMMMMMMMMMMMMMMMMMMMMMMMMMMMMMMMMMMMMMMMMMMMMMH
    ENTER = Select an item          ESC   = View previous screen
    Del  = Unselect an item         F7    = Function keys explained
    F10  = View full citations      CTRL-X = Select all items on this screen
    F5   = Print selected item
```

Although you may not want the foreign-language entries, the advantage of the CD-ROM version is that you can find more information more quickly than by looking in the printed version. For example, here is the complete entry for one of the citations above:

```
American Lib. Assn. Office for Intellectual Freedom.
   Intellectual freedom manual. 1989 3d ed xxxiii+230p
   bibl il (LC 88-39674) (ISBN 0-8389-3368-8) pa
   $17.50--Am Lib Assn.

   Designed to answer practical questions that
confront librarians in applying the principles of
intellectual freedom to library service.

Subject headings:  1. Freedom of information.  2.
Libraries - Censorship.  3. Intellectual liberty. 4.
United States.

Language: English
Document type: Monograph
```

You can see that this looks a lot like a library catalog entry, either on computer or card. However, it doesn't have a call number, nor does it tell whether your library owns the document. But the entry does show other subject headings you might use to find more information.

Because libraries differ greatly in size and resources, you may want to talk to your own reference librarian for help for your library. One of your goals, however, should be to become self-sufficient in library research so you can move quickly and surely to solve problems for yourself.

EVALUATING YOUR SOURCES

Some sources are more valuable than others. Understanding the differences between *primary sources* and *secondary sources* can help you evaluate the material you find and determine how to use it in supporting your own points.

Primary Sources

A primary source is an original source of basic facts or opinions on your subject: eyewitness accounts, official investigations, newspaper articles of the time. If you conduct original research—personal interviews, for example—the material you gather falls in the primary source category.

The following is an excerpt from page 443 of Volume 1 of the *Personal Memoirs of U. S. Grant* (published by Charles L. Webster & Company of New York in 1885); here Ulysses S. Grant is explaining why he risked operations against Vicksburg without first setting up a protected logistics base:

> Marching across this country in the face of an enemy was impossible; navigating it proved equally impracticable. The strategical way according to the rule, therefore, would have been to go back to Memphis; establish that as a base of supplies; fortify it so that the storehouses could be held by a small garrison, and move from there along the line of railroad, repairing as we advanced, to the Yallabusha, or to Jackson, Mississippi. At this time the North had become very much discouraged. Many strong Union men believed that the war must prove a failure. The elections of 1862 had gone against the party which was for the prosecution of the war to save the Union if it took the last man and last dollar. Voluntary enlistments had ceased throughout the greater part of the North, and the draft had been resorted to to fill up our ranks. It was my judgment at the time that to make a backward movement as long as that from Vicksburg to Memphis, would be interpreted, by many of those yet full of hope for the preservation of the Union, as a defeat, and that the draft would be resisted, desertions ensue and the power to capture and punish deserters lost. There was nothing left to be done but to *go forward to a decisive victory.* This was in my mind from the moment I took command in person at Young's Point.

If you're writing a paper about the Battle of Vicksburg, or perhaps about General Grant's strategic planning of Civil War campaigns, then Grant's own words showing his thoughts about the Vicksburg campaign are particularly important. Other writers might tell you what Grant probably was thinking, but Grant on Grant's thinking provides one of the best sources. Primary sources are not always easy to find, but they're worth looking for.

Secondary Sources

A secondary source is secondhand, removed at least one step from primary sources. It uses primary sources or other secondary sources as its basis. Thus a 1991 article about Grant's Vicksburg campaign would be a secondary source, drawing perhaps from Grant's *Memoirs* but also from the writing of other people who were at Vicksburg and from other books and articles analyzing the Vicksburg operations.

Compare these two lists:

Primary Source	**Secondary Source**
• The Panama Canal Treaty printed in the *Congressional Record*	• An article about the Panama Canal Treaty in *Time*
• Shakespeare's Sonnet 73	• A critical analysis of Shakespeare's sonnets
• The transcript of a trial	• An article in *Newsweek* about that trial
• An 1865 newspaper article about Lincoln's assassination	• A 1990 book about Lincoln's assassination

The distinction isn't always clear-cut. The last primary source might have been considered a secondary source in 1865, if the writer wasn't present at the assassination. Today we'd call it a primary source because a journalist in 1865 had greater opportunities for investigating true primary sources (such as eyewitnesses) and also could capture the feelings of the time.

Secondary sources select, filter, evaluate, and analyze material from primary sources (as well as other secondary sources). That is both their value and their weakness. Primary sources are more likely to provide "unfiltered truth," but primary sources generally lack the scope provided by secondary sources, which draw on multiple primary and secondary sources. That is, secondary sources are valuable because their writers already have done a lot of work for you, but at the same time you have to be cautious and guard against the biases of the writers who selected and filtered truth for you.

So which source type should you look for? Both. Try to find as many primary sources as you can. If you're writing about a topic for which witnesses are available near you, try to arrange an interview. And look into old newspaper files if they're available.

But look for secondary sources, too. Each type of source—primary and secondary—has its own strengths and weaknesses. And each type can help you evaluate the other. Details from primary sources can help you determine the validity of the conclusions in secondary sources; secondary sources, on the other hand, can help you understand the primary sources by telling you what to look for.

No matter what type of source you find, you need to decide whether it is *relevant* (of value for your treatment of your topic) and *reliable*.

Relevant Material

What you find about a potential source in a catalog, index, or abstract can suggest that a source will have information important for your thesis, but you'll have to get the work in hand before you can be sure. Here are things to check:

In a book
- the table of contents
- the index
- the preface, foreword, or author's introduction (if the book has these)

In an article
- skim the headings (if the article has them) and starts of paragraphs

Let's consider the third item under books for a moment. Students often overlook prefaces, forewords, and introductions, but these can be valuable indicators of relevance. Frequently they discuss the range of material in a book and the author's intentions in writing it. Scope and intentions also can help you judge the source's reliability.

Reliable Material

You always have to ask yourself, "Can I trust what I'm reading?" Just because something is printed doesn't make it so.

How do you know when to be suspicious? You always should be a little wary, but be especially so if the tone of a source—the personality an author projects—raises questions. Forewords and the like can be particularly important for evaluating an author's objectivity.

For example, consider the problem with sources about the battle of the Alamo, when a group of Texans stood up against a larger, better armed Mexican force. Most of us know stories about the battle and its heroes—and that's part of the problem with source reliability. The event is surrounded with numerous legends, a scarcity of eyewitness reports, self-serving accounts from some individuals associated with the event, and numerous secondary source evaluations that treat the people and related events from various perspectives.

In one book about the Alamo, for example, we find a foreword in which the book's author touts the noble motives of the Texans and the glory they deserve. In the foreword to another book we find an author commenting on the difficulty of gathering trustworthy material about the event. Do these forewords prove anything about the books? No, but we could be more comfortable at the outset about the objectivity of the author of the second book. Of course, we still would have to evaluate the reliability of the information as we read.

Date of publication can be helpful in evaluating the reliability of information. It's not as simple, though, as believing that newer sources are more reliable than older ones. But, for example, a book or article published shortly after the Soviet reactor failure at Chernobyl is less likely to be accurate about the long-term effects of that disaster than one written in 1990. (And one in 2050 will have a greater advantage on this same point.) So don't exclude older sources, but look for recent ones when the data you want is recent.

Finally, as you widen your research, you'll find that the best help in evaluating the reliability of sources comes from the data in other sources. Look for overlapping information—and be skeptical about information that varies significantly from the norm. The exceptions could be extremely reliable and important, of course, but they merit careful examination.

EXERCISES

A. A mid-1990 issue of *Time* magazine ran an article by Dick Thompson about AIDS.

1. What is the title of the article?

2. What is the full date of the *Time* issue that includes the article?

3. On what pages does the article appear?

4. A chart in the article shows the percentage of reported AIDS cases among heterosexuals rising from 0.5 percent in 1981 to what percent in 1989?

5. What reference work did you use to find the article?

6. What subject heading is the article listed under in the reference work?

B. In December 1989, the *New York Times* reported that deposed Romanian (or Rumanian) leader Nicolae Ceausescu had been held captive in a moving armored vehicle for several days prior to his trial and execution. Use library resources to answer the following:

1. How many days was he imprisoned in the moving armored car?

2. Who was held prisoner with him?

3. What issue of the *New York Times* carried the article?

4. In what section and on what page did the article appear?

5. What library resource did you use to answer these questions?

C. In November 1989, the Berlin Wall fell. Portions were broken down and check-points were opened for free passage—all marking the end of the Cold War. Use library reference tools to do the following:

1. List three different periodical articles that deal with the opening of the Berlin Wall or the end of the Cold War. Use at least two different reference tools to find these articles. With each article title, provide the name of the reference work where you found the article listed.

2. List the name, date, and page number of a national newspaper article that treated these events. Also name the reference work in which you found the listing.

3. List the name, date, and page number of a local newspaper article that treated the events. How did you find this article?

D. In 1989, *Defense and Foreign Affairs* published an article by Carleton A. Conant about Libyan chemical weapon developments.

1. What was the name of the article?

2. Which national government was alleging that the Libyans were developing a chemical weapons manufacturing capability?

3. In what issue did the article appear, and on what pages?

4. What reference work did you use to find the article?

5. Under what heading did the information appear in that reference work?

E. In 1988, John Wilson Lewis published a book entitled *China Builds the Bomb*.

1. Who was his coauthor?

2. Who published the book?

3. How many pages does the book have?

4. Where did you find the answers to these questions?

Chapter 21

Taking and Organizing Notes

Let's review for a moment. You settle on a general topic and narrow it as much as you reasonably can. Your preliminary reading helps you focus the topic and at the same time reassures you that sources appear to be available for you to draw on for support material. For example, let's say you're interested in those prehistoric people who left their homes on the Asian continent and for some reason found their way to the American continent and developed new lives here. You realize that *prehistoric Indians* is too large a topic, so you reduce it to *prehistoric Indians in North America,* to *the new way of life in America.* That, you decide, is still too broad, but it's a place to start with your preliminary reading. This preliminary exploration of the topic leads you to a new, interesting idea: contrary to the popular belief you've heard for years that the prehistoric Indians wandered across the American continent struggling to survive, there is relatively recent evidence that the prehistoric Indians adapted well and produced sophisticated cultures.

Using your library's computerized listing of books and the indexes and bibliographies of your library's reference section, you find that available sources appear to be adequate to support your research. You have in hand a list of books and periodical articles that look promising. Now what? Here's where the work begins.

You obviously can't remember every fact or idea you find as you read those sources. You could keep all the books and magazines piled up around you and then flip through them to find a bit of support when you need it. But that's the hard way. Therefore, most researchers develop some systematic way to organize their research reading. This organization is not the same as ordering ideas and their support for writing your paper. The organization here involves keeping track of the research information you find as you work through your potential sources.

This chapter shows you two methods for noting specific ideas and facts and keeping them organized. The most commonly taught system for keeping track of research information involves taking notes on note cards. This system, which we'll call "the traditional system," has proved its value to thousands of researchers. The second system we'll call "the copying machine system" because it relies heavily on a stack of coins and a copying machine. It offers a shortcut in the notetaking process by eliminating the need to write down notes.

THE TRADITIONAL SYSTEM

Both the traditional and the copying machine systems involve keeping track of *two* kinds of information. The first kind is information about the sources you use; the second kind is the information you find in those sources.

The traditional system employs two sets of index cards—one set for each kind of information. Some researchers prefer two sizes of index cards (for example, 3 × 5 cards for sources and 4 × 6 or 5 × 8 cards for notes from the sources); others use the same size cards for both kinds of information. No matter what size of index cards you choose, here's the traditional notetaking process.

Bibliography Cards

For Books

Pick the most likely-looking book and check the table of contents or index to see which parts of the book apply. (It's just not sensible to read the entire book if only Chapter 2 deals with prehistoric American Indians.)

If the book has nothing useful, put it aside to return to the library as soon as you can. Someone else may need it.

When you find a book that has information you think you might use, make out a *bibliography card.* Record only one book on each card and be careful to include all the necessary data about the book. Chapter 25, "Works Cited," explains in detail the information you'll need and shows the various formats for presenting that information for your final paper. For now, be sure your bibliography card has all the following items that apply to the book you're recording:

- author(s) or group responsible
- title and subtitle of book (and volume title if part of a multivolume set)
- title of part of the book (if you're using only a piece of the book, such as an essay in a collection)
- translator(s)
- editor(s)
- edition (don't worry about the number of "printings," but do note the edition if the book is other than the first edition)
- volume number and number of volumes in a multivolume set
- series (if the work is part of a series, such as "Studies in Anthropology, No. 5")
- place of publication (the first one listed if there are several)
- publisher
- date of publication (latest copyright date, not date of printing)

- inclusive page numbers of a part of the book (if you're using only a piece of the book, such as an essay in a collection)

You can save yourself time later by putting all the items in correct bibliographic format for your paper's Works Cited pages (Chapter 25 shows formats). Here's a sample bibliography card with the necessary information in the form required for its Works Cited entry:

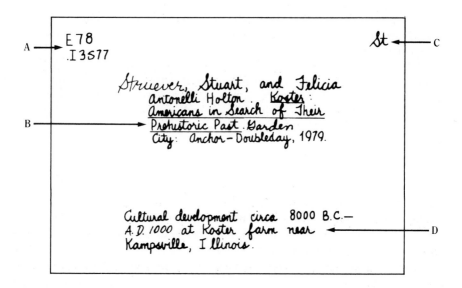

Note these things about the bibliography card:

A. Always include the *library call number* for books; it will save you time if you have to go back to recheck a quotation or find information you forgot to copy down.

B. Include all the applicable information (author, title, etc.) from the list above.

C. Add your own *bibliography code*. We use the first two letters of the first author's last name. But you may use any consistent system—numbering, small letters, Roman numerals. The coding system will save you time as you take notes and as you write drafts of your paper.

D. *Optional.* As a reminder, add a brief note about what the book contains.

With your first bibliography card, you've begun to compile your paper's working bibliography. As you consult the books and articles you've found, prepare a separate card for each one.

For Articles in Periodicals

For magazines, journals, and newspapers, be sure your bibliography card has all the following items that apply to the article you're recording:

- author(s) (articles may be unsigned, and sometimes you'll find only initials for the author)
- title of article
- type of article (for letters to the editor and reviews)
- name of periodical
- series number (such as "old" or "new")
- newspaper edition (if the newspaper publishes more than one edition per day)
- volume and/or issue number(s)
- date of publication
- inclusive page numbers for the article

Also note whether the periodical is paginated continuously throughout a volume or independently by issue. For example, if issue 2 of a volume ends with page 563 and issue 3 of the same volume begins with page 564, the publication paginates continuously throughout a volume. If each issue starts with page 1, then the issues are paginated independently. This distinction won't matter for your research, but it will help you decide which format to use when you write your entries for the Works Cited pages of your final paper.

For Other Source Types

Besides books and articles in periodicals, your sources may include speeches; lectures; class handouts; reference works, such as encyclopedias or *Who's Who*; computer software; material from computer or information services; unpublished theses, dissertations, or letters; interviews; films, filmstrips, slide programs, or video-cassettes; radio or television programs; records or tapes; or legal records or documents. The bits of information you'll need to record now so you can document these varied source types later differ greatly from type to type. Check the Works Cited formats in Chapter 25 to see what data you need to keep track of.

Note Cards

When you come across a fact or idea you think you can use, make a *note card*. Put only one fact or idea on each card. When you are ready to use the information for your draft, you can move the information more freely if you have only one idea on each card.

Now read the following passage from page 244 of the Struever and Holton book about the archaeological diggings at the Koster farm near Kampsville, Illinois. ("Horizon 11" is the designation for a level of human occupation dating to about 6400 B.C.)

> Traditionally, archaeologists have assumed that Archaic people went through a long, slow, gradual process in learning how to cope with their environment and how to extract a decent living from it. They thought it took the aborigines several thousand years, from Paleo-Indian times (circa 12,000–8000 B.C.) to 2500 B.C., to learn about various foods in eastern North America and how to exploit them.
>
> This is simply not true. The Koster people knew their food resources intimately and did a superb job of feeding their communities. During the occupation of Horizon 11, Early

Archaic people had developed a highly selective exploitation pattern of subsistence. They were not just taking foods randomly from the landscape. Rather, they calculated how to provide the community with the most nutritious foods possible while expending the least effort. In addition to deer and smaller mammals, they ate large quantities of fish, freshwater mussels, and nuts. Fish and nuts—in addition to being available each year, and easy to take in large quantities—are highly complementary components of a nutritious diet. Nuts contain fat for high energy, which many freshwater fish lack. The kind of input-output analysis which was taking place was worthy of the most sophisticated culture.

Quotation Note Cards

Here's a sample note card for a *quotation* of an important portion of that passage:

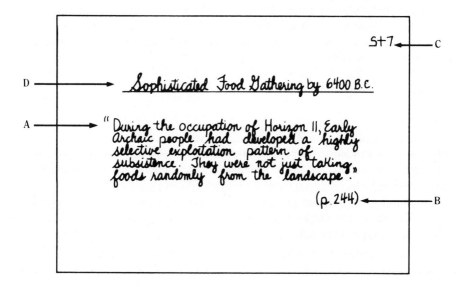

What to include on a quotation note card:

A. Put *quotation marks* around quoted material.

B. Put the *page number* (here, p. 244) in parentheses. If you are using a book that is part of a multivolume set but that doesn't have a separate title, include the volume number and then the page number like this: (3:172).

C. The *code number* shows that this is the seventh card made from the Struever and Holton book. Using the bibliography code (St) from the bibliography card makes it unnecessary to put complete bibliographic information on each note card, and the number added (to make St7) provides a code that distinguishes this note card from others from the same book. In Chapter 22 we'll show you another way to use the code number. For now, keep all note cards from the same work together.

D. *Optional.* Use key word headings that might help you later to arrange the facts and ideas and to make sure you have enough support.

Summary Note Cards

If you had *summarized* the entire passage, condensing the original material into a shorter version in your own words, the card would look like this:

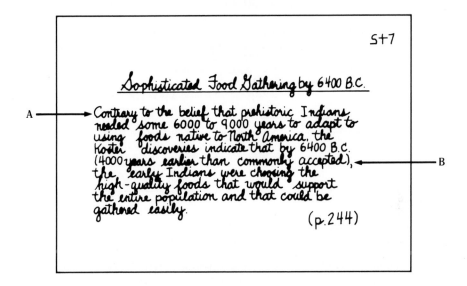

A ───

B ───

What's different about a summary note card?

A. *No quotation marks.* Of course, even though you don't borrow the exact words, you do borrow the idea, and you must give credit for it (more about this in Chapter 23).

B. *Your own words but the author's ideas.* More important than reducing the length of the original, with a summary you mentally "process" the material, capturing the idea or facts and making yourself more knowledgeable about your topic. Notice that the comment in parentheses within the summary above is an *interpretation* of the evidence in the original, demonstrating that the writer of the note card has processed the passage.

Paraphrase Note Cards

A *paraphrase,* too, is a retelling of the original in your own words. But a paraphrase is different from a summary: the paraphrase tends to follow the sentence-by-sentence pattern of the original more closely and also is about the same length as the original. Use paraphrase note cards sparingly. If you're going to take notes that closely follow the original, why not quote instead? Then you'll have the exact words in case you decide to quote all or part of the passage in your paper. Still, a paraphrase is useful when the original is technical or complex or when it isn't worded well—then the paraphrase can help simplify or "interpret" the original. If we paraphrase the two sentences quoted in the sample quotation note card on page 216, the paraphrase would look like this:

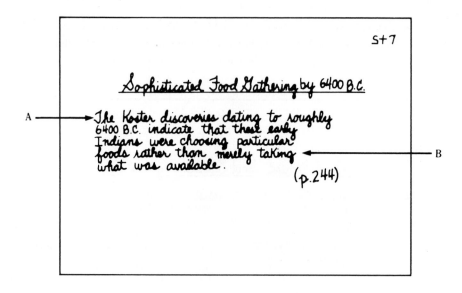

What's special about the paraphrase note card?

A. *Your own words,* so there are no quotation marks. Of course, a paraphrase (or a summary) could include *some* exact words from the original, and those words would go in quotation marks. Yet, the paraphrase as a whole is not a quotation. But it is a borrowing that requires your giving credit for it (more on that in Chapter 23).

B. *An interpretation of the original,* especially complex or technical wording. "During the occupation of Horizon 11" has become "dating roughly to 6400 B.C.," and "highly selective exploitation pattern of subsistence" has been simplified to "choosing particular foods."

How To Go Wrong

Most of the problems with taking notes come with paraphrases and summaries. If you're putting the original into your own words and you want to retain wording from the original, you must use quotation marks. What if you had written something like this?

> For many years archaeologists have assumed that the prehistoric Indians needed several thousand years to discover how to exploit the various foods in eastern North America, but the Koster Indians had learned to be highly selective in their food choices rather than just taking foods randomly from the landscape.

This looks like a paraphrase or summary, right? Right. It *looks* like one, but it's an unacknowledged, loose quotation. It should have looked like this:

> For many years "archaeologists have assumed" that the prehistoric Indians needed "several thousand years" to discover "how to exploit" the "various foods in eastern North America," but the Koster Indians had learned to be "highly selective" in their food choices rather than "just taking foods randomly from the landscape."

Of course, that looks peculiar. No thought has been given to choosing effective portions of the original for a quotation—rather, the use of key words from the original appears to be accidental.

You *can* mix quotation with summary or paraphrase, but be selective in the quotation part. And keep this rule in mind: *Whenever you use another author's words, put them in quotation marks.* Failure to do so is dishonest.

THE COPYING MACHINE SYSTEM

As you can see, the traditional system requires considerable writing, and that can slow you down, interrupting your train of thought during research. The copying machine system offers an alternative.

- Use a copying machine to make a copy when you find a portion of a book or an article that looks worthwhile.
- Write the complete bibliographic information on the copy (just as you would on a bibliography card in the traditional system).
- Use a *highlighting* pen to mark anything you want to be able to refer to later (the equivalent of writing down quotations in the traditional system). Please do not highlight material in library copies of books and periodicals.

WHICH SYSTEM SHOULD YOU USE?

The traditional system takes time but offers two distinct advantages:

- As you take notes, you are actively involved with the material, so you will understand it better than if you had only glanced through it.
- Note cards offer flexibility: you can rearrange them to match your outline or even place them in the rough draft to save time during the writing stage.

At the same time, though, the traditional system can be tedious. Nevertheless, for many researchers the benefits of the painstaking process outweigh the cost.

For others, the pain of notetaking outweighs the benefits. If you are one of these, consider the copying machine system. You won't be able to shuffle note cards. Moreover, you'll still have to spend time processing the material you've highlighted on the copies—turning the original material from your sources into quotations, summaries, and paraphrases to integrate with your own writing. However, you'll do that processing as you write the draft of your paper, so you'll choose the form for presentation to fit your needs as you write. That offers flexibility not possible with the traditional system.

Choose the system that fits your personality. Either system can work well. What won't work is having no system at all: random reading combined with mistaken confidence in your ability to remember details from research when the time comes to write your paper.

EXERCISES

A. The passage below is from page 219 of the revised second edition of *Man's Rise to Civilization: Cultural Assent of the Indians of North America,* by Peter Farb. This edition was published in 1978 by E.P. Dutton of New York, New York. In the library it has call number E77.F36 1978.

> A number of Indian groups did develop pictographs and other mnemonic devices for recalling important events. Wampum, which Whites nowadays often suppose to be the Indian form of money, was originally such a memory device. Beads from white and purple shells were woven into belts by both the Iroquois and the Algonkian tribes of the Northeast (from whose language the word itself comes). The designs recorded treaties and agreements, other important events, and public accounts. Among the Iroquois, one sachem was in charge of keeping the wampum belts and of remembering what the symbols meant, so that he could interpret them when the occasion arose. But this original purpose was corrupted by Europeans, who used the belts as a sort of money and then flooded the market with imitations manufactured in Europe.

1. Make a bibliography card for the book.

2. Select a significant point from the passage and prepare a note card quoting directly from it.

3. Now prepare another note card paraphrasing the lines you quoted in Exercise A2.

4. Prepare a note card summarizing the entire paragraph; use no more than two sentences of our own words for the summary.

5. A final check:
   - Did you put a bibliography code on the bibliography card?
   - Did you use that code on the note cards?
   - Is the library call number on the bibliography card?
   - Did you use quotation marks where needed?

B. In the periodicals in the library you find an article in *MacUser* about erasable optical storage devices. *MacUser* is a monthly magazine that paginates each monthly issue individually. The article, by John Rizzo and others, is entitled "Maximum Movable Megabytes: Erasable Optical Drives." It appears on pages 102 to 130 of the November 1990 issue (volume 6, number 11) of *MacUser*. The following passage is from page 104:

> For those of you who blinked and missed the advent of this new technology, an erasable optical drive holds between 600 megabytes and a gigabyte (1,000 mega-bytes) of data on a 5.25-inch disc contained within a removable cartridge. Unlike other types of optical drives, such as CD-ROM (compact disc, read-only memory) and WORM (write once, read many), erasable optical drives let you write data as well as read it, as with a magnetic hard disk. But unlike hard disks, erasable optical cartridges are impervious to magnetic fields and can hold data for at least ten years—and probably dozens more.
>
> The cost per megabyte of erasable optical cartridges compares well with that of comparably sized hard disks. . . . In drives with a capacity of more than 600 mega-bytes, a megabyte of removable, erasable optical storage is cheaper than hard-disk storage. This break-even capacity is about the same as it was a year ago—retail prices for some erasable optical drives have dropped below $4,000, but hard-disk-drive prices have also been falling.
>
> The bad news is that optical drives are still slower than hard-disk drives, which will frustrate power users. The fastest optical drives are about as fast as the slowest hard drives. Even so, those of you who have fallen asleep while your CD-ROM drive accesses data shouldn't worry: Erasable optical drives are several times faster than their read-only cousins.

1. Make a bibliography card for the article.

2. Select a significant point from the passage and prepare a note card quoting directly from it.

3. Now prepare another note card paraphrasing the lines you quoted in Exercise B2.

4. Prepare a note card summarizing the entire passage; use no more than three sentences of your own words for the summary.

5. A final check:
   - Did you put a bibliography code on the bibliography card?
   - Did you use that number on the note cards?
   - Did you use quotation marks where needed?

Chapter 22

Organizing Your
Thoughts and Support

In the last chapter we discussed organizing your research material so you know which supporting ideas and facts are from which sources. Now we need to look at organization in a different way—this time ordering ideas and their support so you can write your paper.

OUTLINING

Of course, you don't need to wait until you've finished taking notes to begin organizing that new knowledge. You'll do well to develop an outline early and revise and expand it as you learn more. A working outline helps you discover gaps in your support, thereby suggesting areas for continued research. In other words, you need to work back and forth between notetaking and outlining—each influences the other.

A Working Outline

How do you begin organizing support material? By thinking. Jot down the *key* ideas you've discovered about your topic—just the key words. Now look for patterns:

- Do certain ideas seem to fall logically into clusters? Look for points that fit into groups with other points.
- Do you see a pattern of thought that relates those clusters of ideas to each other? Would chronological order work? How about cause and effect or one of the other patterns of development you studied in Part Four?

Once you recognize the basic arrangement that will work to bring order to the ideas and supporting facts for your topic, fill in a simple working outline.

Basic Working Outline

Introduction—working thesis

I. First major topic:

    A. Support idea:

    B. Support idea:

    C. Support idea:

II. Second major topic:

    A. Support idea:

    B. Support idea:

    C. Support idea:

III. Third major topic:

    A. Support idea:

    B. Support idea:

    C. Support idea:

Conclusion—restated working thesis

Does the working outline form look familiar? It should. It's the same basic pattern you've been working with from the beginning of this book, expanded to handle more ideas than you needed for shorter papers. Of course, you may not need exactly three major topics with three support ideas for each. This is just a model.

An outline reduces a large quantity of information to its bare skeleton—just the main ideas and key support. It's a tool to show logically and clearly the relationships among the main points of your paper.

As you conduct your research, the working outline can help you see gaps in your support. Moreover, trying to fit the pieces together as you go along can help you discover new areas you may want to examine—new directions for your research.

A Final Outline

When you've worked out fully the major ideas, supporting ideas, *and* specific support for your paper, you'll have its complete skeletal organization. That skeleton provides the framework for your writing. It ensures that you follow a logical structure as you write.

Outline Numbering and Lettering Scheme

I.

II.

    A.

    B.

       1.

       2.

          a.

          b.

             (1)

             (2)

                (a)

                (b)

III.

- If you have a *I*, there should be a *II;* if you have an *A*, there should be a *B;* and so on.
- Normally you should not need to go beyond the fourth level—the *a.* and *b.*

The final outline you prepare to guide your writing could be a topic outline or a sentence outline.

A *topic outline* lists key points as ideas but does not show complete thoughts. Each entry begins with a capital letter, but the entry has no punctuation at the end since it isn't a complete sentence.

Partial Topic Outline

Here's a topic outline for the first major idea of the sample research paper in Chapter 19:

I. Why minimum competency tests were adopted

   A. Public perception of inadequacy in education

      1. Employers' view of high school diplomas

  2. Decline in SAT scores

  3. Perception of costs versus quality

B. Standardized testing of minimum skills as simple proof

  1. Failure of complex reporting to parents

  2. Seemingly scientific basis of standardized tests

  3. Appeal to decision makers

The key points of a topic outline are adequate for someone familiar with the material summarized in the topic entries. Thus, a topic outline can work well as a guide for writing. It may be all you need to prepare before you begin writing the first draft of your research paper.

However, because the entries in the topic outline don't provide complete thoughts, the outline usually doesn't communicate well to anyone besides the person who wrote it. In particular, the unity and coherence of the points within the topic blocks may not be obvious in a topic outline.

For this reason, many instructors require their students to submit sentence outlines for their research papers—either before writing a draft or with the final paper. A sentence outline more clearly demonstrates the links among points within the outline—so unity and coherence become more clear. As a practical matter, the sentence outline is the outline type that someone besides the writer—such as an instructor—can read and understand.

In a *sentence outline* each entry begins with a capital letter and ends with the punctuation appropriate for the sentence. Following is the sentence outline for the sample research paper in Chapter 19. It's formatted to be handed in with the research paper; for that reason its pagination begins with the page number following the Works Cited page of the sample paper. If your instructor wants the outline to come at the beginning, use the same format but change the page numbers to lowercase Roman numerals (i, ii, etc.—*James i,* for example).

James 15

Thesis: Minimum competency tests are of
questionable value for students; they hold at
risk the quality of education of all students--
not just those who fail one or more times--
making them hostages to the testing system.

I.   Minimum competency tests should be viewed
      against the background that led to their
      creation: the need for simple measures of
      quality that would restore public
      confidence in American education and the
      standardized tests of minimum skills that
      resulted.
      A. In the 1960s and early 1970s, the
         American public felt that the quality of
         education was inadequate.
         1. Employers claimed high school
            diplomas were meaningless.
         2. The public interpreted the decline of
            Scholastic Aptitude Test scores as
            proof that secondary schools were
            failing.
         3. Meanwhile education costs rose,
            prompting calls for proof that tax
            dollars were buying quality in
            education.

James 16

B. The public desire for simple,
   easy-to-understand proof of quality led
   to standardized tests of minimum skills.

   1. After complex reporting to parents
      failed to restore public confidence in
      education, testing appealed for its
      simplicity.

   2. Standardized tests offer apparently
      scientific, unbiased measures of
      quality.

   3. Standardized tests offered decision
      makers a convenient, cost-effective
      way to both improve education and
      satisfy public demands.

II. The tests that resulted measure development
    of minimal skills, or minimum competency.

    A. Minimum competency tests are standardized
       examinations of development of minimal
       skills, primarily in reading, writing,
       and math.

    B. Usually the tests are connected to
       serious consequences, such as promotion
       to a higher grade or graduation from high
       school.

    C. By 1984, 40 states had adopted some type
       of minimum competency testing, about half

connected to high school graduation.

III. Standardized testing of minimum
     competencies leads to three major drawbacks
     of mass testing: class time lost to
     coaching, narrowing of the curriculum, and
     deflection in the overall curriculum.

   A. Minimum competency tests result in
      significant amounts of time being
      devoted to coaching students for the
      test--time taken from other classroom
      activities.

      1. The New Jersey department of
         education admitted providing local
         districts with testing materials used
         for extensive coaching.

      2. Maryland's citizenship competency
         test can lead to a student's being
         taken out of regular social science
         classes for up to 15 weeks for
         remedial coaching.

   B. Minimum competency tests lead to
      narrowing, or trivialization, of the
      curriculum.

      1. Maryland's citizenship competency
         test reduces citizenship to a trivia
         test.

James 18

      2. Multiple-choice questions reduce
         writing to rules of grammar and
         punctuation.

      3. Testing science competency reduces
         science from a process of
         investigation to identification of
         basic facts.

   C. Minimum competency tests lead to
     deflection in the overall curriculum.

      1. Deflection results from emphasis on
         tested material rather than on other
         curriculum areas not tested.

      2. A survey of testing in Florida in 1977
         showed that emphasis on basic skills
         deflected from literature, language,
         and composition.

      3. Virginia's math competency testing of
         recognition of parallel lines resulted
         in reduced student ability to
         recognize perpendicular lines.

IV. The effects of minimum competency testing
    that are used as justification by advocates
    hold the educations of students at risk.

   A. Improvements in test scores are an overly
     simplistic measure of success.

      1. Minimum competency test scores for a

number of states show improvements.

2. Improvements in scores can be
   interpreted as a natural reaction to
   the high stakes connected to the
   tests.

B. Use of minimum competency tests to both
   determine curriculum and judge whether
   teachers comply holds students hostage.

1. Minimum competency testing can
   determine what and how teachers teach.

2. High-stakes testing to judge whether
   teachers are teaching as they are
   directed places students at risk.

C. Minimum competency tests have no
   demonstrated connection to success in
   life.

1. For students not attending college,
   two studies comparing test scores and
   earnings show no connection.

2. Research shows a significant
   connection between unemployment and
   lack of a high school diploma.

3. For most students attending college,
   tests of minimum competency are
   meaningless.

James 20

Conclusion: Although minimum competency testing appears to offer simple, satisfying statistical evidence of the usefulness of the tests, behind this evidence are serious impacts that hold hostage the quality of education of American students.

Outlining and the Computer

Computer programs can be a big help with outlining. With some programs, in fact, the outline on the computer serves as a direct step toward establishing headings within the paper that you write on the computer.

There are several computer programs whose primary purpose is to assist with organizing thinking. Their output, as you might expect, is an outline. These programs are intended to assist with brainstorming and to convert the disorganized results of brainstorming into the organized pattern of an outline. The programs allow rapid clustering of points and easy movement of blocks of material among the various subordination levels that make up the outline.

Some of the programs permit users to "hide" (save in a hidden mode) notes, paragraphs, and even graphics under an entry in the outline. With this type of capability you can write a rough version of a piece of your paper as you think about it while you're organizing your material. You then tuck it away behind its outline point. As you write your paper, you reveal the hidden text and incorporate it into your draft.

Many computer word processing programs have some of these same features for outlining. They have built-in formats that set up the standard letter-number system of an outline, and they allow you to move material easily from one level of subordination to another within the outline. If the word processing program operates with a split-screen or windows mode, you can review the outline on screen as you write the paper's draft in another part of the screen. Some word processing programs even are set up to convert parts of an outline into particular levels of headings in the text of a document.

HEADINGS FOR LARGE PAPERS

Just as the points in an outline guide you through the research paper, headings—which equate to major points in an outline for a paper—guide readers through the material they read. In Chapter 10 we showed you a good way to make headings—using initial capital letters and starting on the left margin. But because research papers can get fairly long, you may need more than one type of heading (to show more levels of subordination).

Here are two types we suggest:

Two Heading Styles

```
    XXXXXXXX XXXXX XXXXXXXXX XXXX XXXXXXXX XXXX XXXXX
XXXXXX XXXXX XXXX XXXXXXXXX XXXX XXXXXXXXXX XXXXXX


         THIS IS A MAJOR HEADING


    XXXXXXXX XXXXX XXXXXXXXX XXXX XXXXXXXX XXXXXXXX
XXXXXX XXXXX XXXX XXXXXXXXX XXXX XXXXXXXXXX XXXXXX XXXX
```

This Is a Minor Heading

xxxxxxxx xxxxx xxxxxxxxx xxxx xxxxxxxx xxxx xxxxxxxxxx
xxxxx xxxx xxxxxxxxx xxxx xxxxxxxxxx xxxxxx

This Is Another Minor Heading

xxxxxxxx xxxxx xxxxxxxxx xxxx xxxxxxxx xxxx xxxxxx xxx
xxxxx xxxx xxxxxxxxx xxxx xxxxxxxxxx xxxxxx

THIS IS ANOTHER MAJOR HEADING

xxxxxxxx xxxxx xxxxxxxxx xxxx xxxxxxxx xxxx xxxxxxxxxx
xxxxx xxxx xxxxxxxxx xxxx xxxxxxxxxx xxxxxx

If you have a computer, you can get much fancier, of course. In fact you could have headings in different sizes and type faces.

Here are two possibilities:

Headings Using a Computer

xxx xxxxxxxx xxxxx xxxxxxxxx xxxx xxxxxxxx xxxx xxxxxx xxxxx
xxxx xxxxxxxxx xxxx xxxxxxxxxx xxxxxx

THIS IS A MAJOR HEADING

xxx xxxxxxxx xxxxx xxxxxxxxx xxxx xxxxxxxx xxxx xxxxxx xxxxx
xxxx xxxxxxxxx xxxx xxxxxxxxxx xxxxxx

This Is a Minor Heading

xxx xxxxxxxx xxxxx xxxxxxxxx xxxx xxxxxxxx xxxx xxxxxx xxxxx
xxxx xxxxxxxxx xxxx xxxxxxxxxx xxxxxx

This is Another Minor Heading

xxx xxxxxxxx xxxxx xxxxxxxxx xxxx xxxxxxxx xxxx xxxxxx xxxxx
xxxx xxxxxxxxx xxxx xxxxxxxxxx xxxxxx

THIS IS ANOTHER MAJOR HEADING

xxx xxxxxxxx xxxxx xxxxxxxxx xxxx xxxxxxxx xxxx xxxxxx xxxxx
xxxx xxxxxxxxx xxxx xxxxxxxxxx xxxxxx

Whichever way you make headings, be sure the major heading stands out more on the page than the minor heading does.

A Practical Point About Outlines and Headings

We noted earlier that outlines rarely need to go beyond four levels of subordination. Well, headings shouldn't go even that far.

Levels of headings equate to outline levels, of course, but you have to be wary of the complexity you try to portray with levels of headings. For assignments the length of a research paper, two levels of headings will work well.

Even writers of books only occasionally go beyond two levels of headings. (You can find third- and even a few fourth-level headings in Chapter 25 of this book, for example, because the complex material there is easier to follow with the extra heading levels.)

Why not give headings to match every item in an outline? Writing with excessive headings appears choppy. Moreover, readers become confused when writers try to portray three and four levels of subordination throughout a document.

A smart writer, then, uses headings to highlight important points of a paper's organization—but only the most important points.

A TIMESAVER IN WRITING

Once you've prepared an outline, you're ready to assemble your detailed support. Arrange your notes (note cards or highlighted photocopy pages, depending on the research system you chose) to follow your outline. Use the floor, your desktop, your roommate's bed, whatever you need to spread the cards out so you can see how they fill out the outline's skeleton.

Don't let your outline keep you from moving notes around. That outline is not engraved in bronze; you can alter it as you need to. But laying out your notes will help you see where the outline may be incomplete or where you need more information. You may have more notes than you can use. Don't throw any away; you may find a place for them later.

When you are satisfied with the outline and its support, start writing. You may begin at the beginning with an introduction, then move on to the first major topic, then the second, and so on. Many writers do it this way, and it may work for you.

Or you may decide to start with the first major topic, go on to the next topics, and finish writing with the conclusion—and then the introduction. Many other writers do it this way.

The reason is simple: frequently you're not sure what you're going to say until you've said it. You actually discover that you think as you write because the ideas take over and lead you to new discoveries. If you have already written the introduction, you may find it has little relationship to what you finally say.

Regardless of where you start writing, you'll have to use some of your notes. If you're quoting—and if you've used the traditional system with note cards—here's a trick that can save you some work: In writing your draft, when you come to a place for a quotation, don't copy it again. Just paper-clip or tape the quotation note card in place—or leave room in your draft and write in the code number for the note card (remember the code number *St7* we used on page 216?). Doing it this way will save you writing and will keep the quotations accurate, no matter how many drafts you go through.

A caution: This trick isn't intended for use with summaries and paraphrases; those notes already are in your own words, and you should be weaving the ideas and facts into the fabric of your writing in the paper's draft.

Working those quotations, summaries, and paraphrases—the material you borrow from your sources—into your writing is one of the skills you need to develop for writing a research paper. And skillful use of borrowed material is the subject of the next chapter.

EXERCISE

The chapter provides a full sentence outline for the sample research paper in Chapter 19. It also shows a topic outline form of the first major idea block for the same paper. Using the format below, finish the topic outline for the sample research paper. We've supplied the major headings from the sample paper as the Roman-numeral-level entries in the outline.

II.   What minimum competency tests are

    A.

    B.

    C.

III.   Problems the tests generate for the classroom

    A.

        1.

        2.

    B.

        1.

        2.

        3.

    C.

        1.

2.

3.

IV. How minimum competency testing holds students at risk

A.

1.

2.

B.

1.

2.

C.

1.

2.

3.

Chapter 23

Using Borrowed Material in Your Paper

Skilled use of borrowed material is one mark of an accomplished writer. You can't expect just to sprinkle it on the paper in the hope it will magically create an argument for you. Good arguments with borrowed material supporting them don't just happen; they come from careful work. To make sure your borrowed material helps your argument, you must consider two key questions: whether to quote or not, and what to quote from. Answers to these questions are closely related and depend on the paper you're writing.

CHOOSING THE TYPE OF PRESENTATION

In Chapter 21 you studied three types of note cards: quotations, paraphrases, and summaries. Let's consider now why you might choose one of those types of presentation of borrowed material in preference to the others.

There are three basic reasons for choosing to quote from a source:

- A passage is worded particularly well, providing facts or opinions phrased effectively.
- A passage is written very clearly (so that paraphrasing or summarizing would provide a poor substitute).
- A passage provides the words of an authority (not necessarily someone famous, just someone in a position to know).

Paraphrases restate original source material in your own words. You interpret the technical or complex wording, but you retain the flow of the thought from the source. Thus, choose a paraphrase when the way a source presents an argument works well but the words themselves need adjustment for your purposes.

Summaries extract information from sources, capturing facts and opinions from the original but without either the original words or the original thought pattern. Choose a summary when you want only the data from a source.

We also can evaluate the three presentation types in relation to the two types of source material we discussed in Chapter 20—primary and secondary sources. Of course, there are reasons to choose a quotation, paraphrase, or summary with both primary and secondary sources. Yet, there is a difference worth noting.

Because a primary source is the origin of facts or opinions on your subject, material from it is likely to fit one or more of the criteria for quoting. For example, the excerpt from Grant's writing about the Vicksburg campaign (page 207) provides clear, effective wording. More important, it provides the words of an authority on Grant's thinking at the time of the campaign. If you were examining the successes and failures of military planners at Vicksburg, for instance, you'd be more likely to quote Grant than to paraphrase or summarize the passage.

Secondary sources select, filter, and analyze material from primary and other secondary sources. Therefore, the material itself already is pointed toward summaries. Material in secondary sources sometimes meets a criterion for quoting. As a general rule, though, you'll find fewer reasons to quote from secondary sources and more reasons to summarize or paraphrase. By no means is that an absolute rule, however.

But whether you use primary or secondary sources, whether you quote or summarize or paraphrase, you must follow three steps to use borrowed material effectively:

- *Introduce* the borrowed material.
- *Present* it.
- *Credit* the source.

INTRODUCING BORROWED MATERIAL

Perhaps the most neglected step in using borrowed material is the first one—introducing it. In this step you mention the author or title of the source before presenting the material, to signal to your readers that you are beginning the borrowed material. Here are some sample introductions:

```
As Grant explained in his Memoirs, . . . .

According to the press secretary, the President decided
that. . . .

Reverend Jackson was right when he said, . . . .

In his essay "Here's HUD in Your Eye," Larry McMurtry
reveals. . . .
```

The variety of introductions is almost endless, but all of them identify your source, often helping your readers judge whether the source you're citing is reputable. Without an introduction, the borrowed material seems just spliced in; look for such an example in the following paragraph:

> Washington's victory at Yorktown was precarious almost up to the moment of the British surrender. What really defeated the British was the inability of Lord Cornwallis to move his forces away from Yorktown. "The secret of the British failure there was either the ministry's neglect in immediately securing absolute naval supremacy on this coast . . . or the over-confidence or carelessness of the admirals in command. It is the British naval administration that is to be charged with the Yorktown catastrophe" (Johnston 101). The British under Cornwallis were occupying Yorktown because it was the best available naval station, and retreat by sea would have been possible had not the French fleet kept the British fleet away from the battle area.

Readers will recognize where the borrowing begins and ends because of the quotation marks, but they will wonder who Johnston is and where the quotation comes from. Annoying, isn't it? Don't annoy your readers; don't even leave them slightly frustrated from wondering about who said what. Introduce the material:

> Washington's victory at Yorktown was precarious almost up to the moment of the British surrender. What really defeated the British was the inability of Lord Cornwallis to move his forces away from Yorktown. In The Yorktown Campaign and the Surrender of Cornwallis, historian Henry P. Johnston blames the British navy: "The secret of the British failure there was either the ministry's neglect in immediately securing absolute naval supremacy on this coast . . . or the over-confidence or carelessness of the admirals in command. It is the British naval administration that is to be charged with the Yorktown catastrophe" (101). The British under Cornwallis were occupying Yorktown because it was the best available naval station, and retreat by sea would have been possible had not the French fleet kept the British fleet away from the battle area.

This way, your readers know who wrote what you've quoted and where you found it. The parenthetical documentation reference, used in conjunction with the research paper's Works Cited list, gives the complete data to find the book if your readers should want to.

An introduction is even more important for a summary or paraphrase than it is for a direct quotation. Quotation marks show where a quotation begins and ends. But where does the paraphrase begin here?

```
    Washington's victory at Yorktown was precarious
almost up to the moment of the British surrender. What
really defeated the British was the inability of Lord
Cornwallis to move his forces away from Yorktown. The
British failed because the navy did not control the
sea off the American coast or because the British
admirals blundered. The British navy should be blamed
for the Yorktown defeat (Johnston 101). The British
under Cornwallis were occupying Yorktown because it
was the best available naval station, and retreat by
sea would have been possible had not the French fleet
kept the British fleet away from the battle area.
```

How many of the ideas come from Johnston's book? Where does the paraphrase begin? At the first word of the paragraph? Or is it only the sentence ending with the parenthetical documentation reference? Who knows? But when you introduce the paraphrase, everyone will know:

```
    Washington's victory at Yorktown was precarious
almost up to the moment of the British surrender. What
really defeated the British was the inability of Lord
Cornwallis to move his forces away from Yorktown. In
The Yorktown Campaign and the Surrender of Cornwallis,
historian Henry P. Johnston asserts that the British
failed because the navy did not control the sea off
the American coast or because the British admirals
blundered. The British navy should be blamed for the
Yorktown defeat (101). The British under Cornwallis
were occupying Yorktown because it was the best
available naval station, and retreat by sea would have
been possible had not the French fleet kept the
British fleet away from the battle area.
```

With that simple introduction readers know where the paraphrasing begins. Be sure to introduce your summaries as well.

PRESENTING BORROWED MATERIAL

Paraphrases and summaries, no matter what their length, are fully integrated with your own writing. Introduce them, of course, and credit the source with a parenthetical reference, as we'll discuss later. But no special formatting is required for the presentation. Quotations require special presentation techniques.

Presenting Quotations in Your Final Paper

For a short quotation—*four or fewer lines of typing in your paper:*

- Type the quotation along with your own writing, without special indentation or spacing.
- Use double quotation marks (" ") to enclose your source's exact words and punctuation; if the quoted material itself includes quotation marks, use single quotation marks (' ') to enclose the interior quotation.
- Place a parenthetical reference, if required, after the quoted material and closing quotation mark but before the punctuation mark, if any, that ends the sentence, clause, or phrase with the material the reference documents. ("Placement in Text," in Chapter 24, provides a thorough explanation about placing parenthetical references in the text of your paper.)

For a long quotation—*more than four lines of typing*—in a paper with double-spaced text:

- Begin the quotation on a new line.
- Double-space before, within, and after the quotation.
- Do *not* use quotation marks for the quotation; however, if the quoted material itself includes quotation marks, use double quotation marks (" ") to enclose the interior quotation.
- Indent the quotation ten spaces from the left margin but retain the normal right margin. Indent an extra three spaces from the left for lines that begin paragraphs in the original.
- For the parenthetical reference, if required, skip two spaces after the punctuation that ends the quotation, provide the parenthetical reference, and put no punctuation after the closing parenthesis of the reference.

Here's a sample showing double-spaced text followed by a long quotation:

```
The integration of the Normans into the culture

of England was thorough but by no means smooth and

easy. In The History of England from the Accession of
```

James the Second, Lord Macaulay describes the degree

of control achieved by the Normans after the Battle of

Hastings and the opposition from Saxon rebels:

The Battle of Hastings, and the events

which followed it, not only placed a Duke of

Normandy on the English throne, but gave up

the whole population to the tyranny of the

Norman race. The subjugation of a nation by

a nation has seldom, even in Asia, been more

complete. The country was portioned out

among the captains of the invaders. Strong

military institutions, closely connected

with the institution of property, enabled

the foreign conquerors to oppress the

children of the soil. A cruel penal code,

cruelly enforced, guarded the privileges,

and even the sports, of the alien tyrants.

Yet the subject race, though beaten down and

trodden underfoot, still made its sting

felt. Some bold men, the favorite heroes of

our oldest ballads, betook themselves to the

woods, and there, in defiance of curfew laws

and forest laws, waged a predatory war

against their oppressors. Assassination was

an event of daily occurrence. Many Normans

suddenly disappeared, leaving no trace. The

corpses of many were found bearing the marks

of violence. Death by torture was denounced

against the murderers, and strict search was

made for them, but generally in vain; for

the whole nation was in a conspiracy to

screen them. (14-15)

In less than two centuries, these different people had

become indistinguishable for the most part.

Notice that the block indentation of the long quotation substitutes for quotation marks. The indentation indicates that you are quoting.

But remember, like a short quotation, the long one needs an introduction, too. In fact, the introduction to a long quotation often tells the readers what you expect them to notice about it, thus giving them the right perspective. In the introduction to the passage from Lord Macaulay's history, we told you to watch for Norman control and Saxon opposition.

SOME FINE POINTS IN QUOTING

Be careful to quote accurately. If you need to alter a quotation, there are special techniques to show the alteration.

Omitting Words

Sometimes you'll want to omit words from something you're quoting because they're irrelevant or awkward out of their original context. In addition, you may need to alter a passage so that the edited passage fits into the grammar and sense of your own writing. The device you use to show an omission is an ellipsis (. . .)—three spaced periods with a space at the beginning and the end.

When you quote only a word or phrase, you don't need to show that material has been left out before or after a quotation; the cutting is obvious. However, when your editing results in a complete sentence (or complete line of poetry), use the ellipsis to show that you've modified the original, no matter how minor the change. Of course, it's *never* acceptable to edit the original so that you change its meaning (for example, by leaving out *not* or *never*); omissions are acceptable only as a convenience to trim unnecessary words or to fit the quotation into the pattern of your writing.

When the omission occurs *inside a sentence (or line of poetry),* the remainder will look like this:

```
"Fish and nuts . . . are highly complementary
components of a nutritious diet."
```

If the omission occurs at the *end of a sentence,* use four spaced periods without a space in front of the first period (a period for the sentence plus the ellipsis):

```
"The Koster people knew their food resources
intimately. . . . They were not just taking foods
randomly from the landscape."
```

An ellipsis at the end of a sentence can represent an omission of the end of that sentence, one or more sentences, or one or more paragraphs. At the end of a line of poetry, it would indicate omission of one or more lines of poetry.

Except for a block-indented quotation, if an omission at the end of a sentence precedes a parenthetical documentation reference, show the ellipsis before the ending quotation mark and parentheses and provide the sentence punctuation after:

```
"The Koster people knew their food resources
intimately . . ." (Struever and Holton 244).
```

Notice that there is a space between *intimately* and the ellipsis but not between the ellipsis and the ending quotation mark.

If that same sentence ended a block-indented quotation (which would not have quotation marks), it would look like this:

```
The Koster people knew their food resources
intimately. . . .  (Struever and Holton 244)
```

Now there is no space after *intimately* but there are two spaces between the final period and the opening parenthesis of the parenthetical reference.

Adding Words

If you need to add an explanation within a quotation so that the quotation will make sense in the context of your writing, use square brackets to separate your words from those you're quoting:

> "During the occupation of Horizon 11 [circa 6400
> B.C.], Early Archaic people had developed a highly
> selective exploitation pattern of subsistence."

Don't use parentheses instead of square brackets. If your typewriter can't make
brackets, draw them neatly by hand, using black ink or pencil.

Adding Emphasis

You can emphasize a portion of a quotation by underlining (or italicizing) it. However, to ensure that readers can tell who added the emphasis, provide an explanation
at the end of the quotation if the emphasis is yours (no explanation is required if the
emphasis is part of the original):

> "The kind of input-output analysis which was taking
> place was <u>worthy of the most sophisticated culture</u>"
> (emphasis added).

Verifying Quotation Accuracy

If you find an error, or material that may seem to be peculiar, in the quotation you
want to use, add "sic" to the quotation—in square brackets if inside the quotation or
in parentheses if outside. The word *sic* (Latin for "thus") tells readers you have
rendered the quotation faithfully:

> "When the Imperial Air Forces of Japan attacked Pearl
> Harbor on 7 December 1940 [sic], they demonstrated how
> vulnerable ships were to surprise air attack."

Altering Final Punctuation

Within a quotation, punctuation must appear as in the original, unless properly
modified through use of an ellipsis or an addition in square brackets. Final punctuation, however, will depend on how you integrate the quotation into your own writing.
This quotation ends in a period:

> "They were not just taking foods randomly from the
> landscape."

However, you might change that period to a comma if the quotation became an
internal clause in your writing:

> "They were not just taking foods randomly from the
> landscape," according to authorities Stuart Struever
> and Felicia Holton.

CREDITING YOUR SOURCE

Whenever you use borrowed material, the third step also is essential: crediting your source. You must identify the printed or spoken source of your information.

Failure to credit your source is dishonest, a form of cheating called *plagiarism.* Plagiarism is presenting someone else's words or ideas without giving credit. You avoid plagiarism by documenting the words and ideas of others when you use them in your writing. Chapters 24 and 25 show you in detail the mechanics of documenting; here we're concerned with the concept of properly presenting research material in the text of your paper. The following are forms of plagiarism:

- Presenting someone else's idea but not documenting it (so the idea seems to be yours).
- Presenting someone else's words without documenting them (so they seem to be part of your writing).
- Quoting someone else's words—perhaps even documenting them—but failing to use quotation marks. This problem is most likely to arise if your paraphrases or summaries result in the type of unacknowledged, loose quotation you studied in Chapter 21. Also, you may want to look again at the special techniques used to alter quotations.

Together, the next two chapters cover documentation. Chapter 24 explains the parenthetical references that you'll place in the text of your paper. Chapter 25 tells you how to prepare the Works Cited pages, the list of sources for your research paper. In combination these in-text parenthetical references and the Works Cited list make up the parenthetical documentation system.

EXERCISES

A. In Volume 2 of his memoirs (*Personal Memoirs of U.S. Grant,* published by Charles L. Webster & Company of New York in 1885), Ulysses S. Grant describes fears in the North about Sherman's army being cut off during its famous march to the sea from Atlanta and Grant's assurances to President Lincoln:

> The Southern papers in commenting upon Sherman's movements pictured him as in the most deplorable condition: stating that his men were starving, that they were demoralized and wandering about almost without object, aiming only to reach the sea coast and get under the protection of our navy. These papers got to the North and had more or less effect upon the minds of the people, causing much distress to all loyal persons—particularly to those who had husbands, sons or brothers with Sherman. Mr. Lincoln seeing these accounts, had a letter written asking me if I could give him anything that he could say to the loyal people that would comfort them. I told him there was not the slightest occasion for alarm; that with 60,000 such men as Sherman had with him, such a commanding officer as he was could not be cut off in the open country. He might possibly be prevented from reaching the point he had started out to reach, but he would get through somewhere and would finally get to his chosen destination: and even if worst came to worst he could return North. I heard afterwards

of Mr. Lincoln's saying, to those who would inquire of him as to what he thought about the safety of Sherman's army, that Sherman was all right: "Grant says they are safe with such a general, and that if they cannot get out where they want to, they can crawl back by the hole they went in at."

1. Does this material represent primary or secondary source material?

2. What would be the advantages or disadvantages of quoting part or all of this material in a research paper about Sherman's march to the sea?

3. Quote at least two sentences from Grant and provide an introduction for the quotation. Be sure to quote accurately; if you alter the original material in any way, use the techniques in the chapter to show the alteration. Use (2:366–67) for the parenthetical documentation reference if your introduction contains the name of the author or (Grant 2:366–67) if it doesn't.

B. In *WWII: Time-Life Books History of the Second World War* (New York: Prentice, 1989), the editors of Time-Life Books provide a description of what they label the "unimaginable force" of the nuclear bombs dropped on Japan:

> In an effort to calculate the dimensions of the bombs' power, a group of Japanese scientists probed through the ruins for days afterward. They discovered that the air bursts had produced pressures that matched the sustained thrust of a tidal wave, knocking down all but the strongest buildings of concrete and steel. Heat, measured in thousands of degrees Fahrenheit and traveling at the speed of light, had set fire to wooden structures that were more than a mile from Ground Zero, the hypocenter above which each bomb exploded. At twice that distance, infrared rays had charred telephone poles and burned human skin.
>
> In Hiroshima, a thermal wave swept out over the city, setting alight the homes in its path. Into the vacuum created by its passing roared hurricane-like winds, fanning a fire storm that raged for hours. In all, 62,000 of Hiroshima's 90,000 buildings were destroyed.
>
> In Nagasaki, hills separating its industrial quarter from the rest of the city blocked the thermal wave, and no fire storm followed. Even so, the wave of heat instantly ignited wooden buildings within two miles of the hypocenter, and 11,500 of the city's 52,000 residences burned to the ground.

1. Does this material represent primary or secondary source material?

2. Would you be more likely to quote, summarize, or paraphrase material from this passage in a research paper about the effects of nuclear weapons? Why?

3. Write a short paragraph of your own in which you summarize or paraphrase material from this passage. Be sure to introduce the borrowing. For the parenthetical documentation reference, use (Editors of Time-Life Books 434) or (434), depending on how you write the introduction to the borrowing.

Chapter 24

Parenthetical Documentation

Whether you use quotations, paraphrases, or summaries, you must document the sources of your information. In Part Three you learned a preliminary documentation system that let readers know whenever you were using outside sources for support. This chapter introduces a better system, one that not only tells readers that you are using borrowed material, but also gives them enough information to find the source.

The formats for documentation in this chapter and the next generally follow the third edition of the *MLA Handbook for Writers of Research Papers,* published by the Modern Language Association of America. This handbook is an accepted standard for documentation in many academic fields, especially the humanities. Other style guides also exist, of course, and there are differences in specific entry and presentation formats from one manual to another. We've chosen to follow MLA on most points because the guidance is thorough, reasonable, and widely accepted.

Differences Among Documentation Style Manuals

Don't be too concerned about these differences. Most of them exist to accommodate the varied needs of differing academic fields. More important, however, most documentation guides differ little on what should go into a specific documentation entry for an article or book. In practical terms, then, if you learn one system well—the one in this book, for example—you can adapt easily to the particular style in another place at another time. You'll know basically what should be included in documentation entries by anybody's standard, so you'll be able to see quickly the peculiarities of any other system you're required to follow.

PARENTHETICAL DOCUMENTATION SYSTEM

The parenthetical documentation system depends on the interaction of material you place in two portions of your research paper:

- *General source listing.* At the end of your research paper you provide an alphabetized listing, called Works Cited, with full bibliographic information about each source document you used. The list provides a general reference to your sources but, of course, doesn't identify the specific portions you used for the quotations, summaries, and paraphrases in the body of the paper.
- *Specific portion reference.* Within the body of your paper, along with each presentation of material borrowed from your sources, you include in parentheses a documentation reference to the specific portion(s) of the source or sources supporting your text. This parenthetical information provides a reference to the data in the Works Cited listing so readers can connect the general and specific documentation portions.

Interaction of References in Text and Works Cited

When readers combine the information in parentheses in the body of your paper with the full bibliographic information in your Works Cited listing, they have the data they need to locate each source and to find the specific portion you used.

Let's say this is a portion of your paper:

In the Indian pottery canteen, form and function came together. Art historians have noted the usefulness of the canteen's shape and the way it was fired. The shape of the canteen allowed it to be carried by a rider on a horse. Because of the way the pottery was fired, it was somewhat porous; as a result, the action of water seeping through to the outside, where it evaporated, cooled and sweetened the water remaining in the canteen (Clark and Ingram 47).

The *specific portion reference* is (*Clark and Ingram 47*).

- *Clark and Ingram* tells readers to look for an entry in the Works Cited listing with those names.
- The *47* indicates that the information came from that specific portion of the work.

In the Works Cited pages—the *general source listing*—readers would find this entry, alphabetized under *Clark:*

Clark, Karen, and Fred Ingram. *Acoma Canteens and Other Pottery Designs.* Washington: Steinman, 1989.

Clearly, then, you want to learn the conventions for both the general source and specific reference portions of the parenthetical documentation system. The next chapter focuses on format conventions for the Works Cited listing (the general source portion of the parenthetical documentation). The rest of this chapter treats the specific portion references that give the system its name: the parenthetical references.

PARENTHETICAL REFERENCES

Basic Content

Parenthetical references in the text of your paper should give your readers the following information:

- *A reference to the opening of the corresponding entry in the Works Cited list.* If the Works Cited entry shows only one author, you'll give that author's last name. The reference also could be two or three last names, one person's name with "et al.," the name of a group, a shortened version of the title, or a name with the title, depending in every case on what information is necessary to identify clearly the *one* work in Works Cited that you are referring to. ("Basic Forms" below details the various possibilities.)

- *Identification of the location within that work of the material you're documenting.* Normally this will be a reference to a single page or several pages. However, when your Works Cited listing gives a multivolume work, the parenthetical reference will require a volume number with the page(s). If the reference is to a one-page article, to an article in an encyclopedia that alphabetizes its articles, or to a source that has no pagination (such as a film or videocassette), there will be no place reference.

Basic Forms

The material required for the parenthetical reference varies somewhat with the nature of the work you refer to from your Works Cited list and how much of it you are citing. (For rules on showing inclusive page numbers, see page 277.)

Work With One Name Listed

When the Works Cited listing begins with only one person's name, use the last name and the page reference: (Brown 281) or (Brown 281–83). If the name has a qualifier such as "ed." or "trans.," you still use only the last name.

Work With Two or Three Names Listed

If the Works Cited entry opens with two or three names, include those names in the parenthetical reference: (Wesson and Jones 117) or (Stockton, Avery, and Beal 63).

Work With One Name and "et al."

If the Works Cited entry begins with a name and "et al.," which means "and others," include the "et al." in your parenthetical reference: (Steinnem et al. 92–93).

Work With Group as Author

Treat the group just like another author: (President's Commission on Energy 315). A reference such as this, of course, could easily interrupt a reader's train of thought; we'll discuss later how to avoid that problem by streamlining the parenthetical references.

Work Listed by Title

If the Works Cited entry begins with a title, use the title, or a reasonable shortened version of it, in the parenthetical reference. Be careful in shortening the title, though, because readers must find the words you give in an alphabetized list; make sure the shortened title includes the word by which the work is alphabetized in your Works Cited listing. A reference to *A Short Study of Linguistics for Beginners* might look like this: (*Short Study of Linguistics* 53). Again, streamlining might be preferable.

Multivolume Work

In reference to a multivolume work, normally you'll give a volume number with the page reference: (Martin 2:65–66). This is a reference to pages 65 to 66 of volume 2 of a multivolume work alphabetized in Works Cited under "Martin." However, if the entry in Works Cited clearly identifies only a single volume of the multivolume work, then the parenthetical reference need not include the volume number.

Multiple Works Listed for the Same Name(s)

When two or more works are alphabetized in Works Cited for the same name(s), include in the parenthetical reference the title, or a shortened version of it, of the specific work you're referring to. If two books are listed for Brian Pierce, then a reference to one of them would look like this: (Pierce, *Amateur Golfing* 27). Here's another candidate for streamlining.

Citing an Entire Work

If you need to document a textual reference to an entire work, then a page reference is inappropriate, so the parentheses would contain only the author element: (Brown). Streamlining, however, will eliminate the need for any parenthetical reference.

Indirect Reference

Although you always should attempt to find the original source for a quotation, sometimes you'll have to quote information from a source that quotes the original. If you quote or paraphrase a quotation, add "qtd. in" (for "quoted in") or "paraphrased from" to the parenthetical reference, as here:

```
John Harris calls literary critic Edmund Wilson a
"pompous, close-minded reader" for his insistence that
detective fiction is not worth reading (qtd. in
Armstrong 13).
```

Multiple Works in a Reference

To include two or more works in a single parenthetical reference, list each as you would for itself and use semicolons to separate them: (Jackson 53–54; Morgan 15). Again, streamlining may help reduce the interruption, but if you need to show a long, disruptive list, consider using an actual footnote instead (see the section "Notes With Parenthetical Documentation" below).

Streamlining Parenthetical References

Several times we've mentioned the possibility of streamlining. The idea is to keep the information within the parentheses as short as possible so readers are not distracted. You accomplish this by giving part or all of the needed reference in the introduction to the borrowed material. If the introduction includes the name of a book's author, then the parentheses might contain only the page reference.

```
Brown notes General Grant's occasional impatience with
the progress of his attrition campaign in 1864 (281).
```

Because Brown's name is in the introduction to the material from his book, the parenthetical reference needs only the page reference.

Especially in the case where your Works Cited list has several works by the same author and you must refer to one of those works, streamlining lessens the interruption of the parenthetical reference. Without streamlining, a reference might look like this:

```
Although the Battle of the Crater, for which Union
coal miners tunneled under the Confederate
fortification lines near Petersburg, captures our
imagination today, it has been labeled a bloody
tactical blunder because of the cost in lives
(Winchester, Civil War After Gettysburg 314).
```

The version below streamlines that long parenthetical reference:

```
Although the Battle of the Crater, for which Union
coal miners tunneled under the Confederate
fortification lines near Petersburg, captures our
imagination today, in The Civil War After Gettysburg
Winchester labels it a bloody tactical blunder because
of the cost in lives (314).
```

Keep in mind that streamlining does not permit omission of required material, but it can reduce the interruption of parenthetical references.

Placement in Text

Place the parenthetical references in the text of your paper so that they interrupt the flow of thought as little as possible. Put the parentheses as close as reasonably possible after the end of the material you're documenting, but always at the end of a clause or phrase so the reference doesn't intrude. Normally, the parenthetical reference can be placed at the end of a sentence. Even with quotations, the reference doesn't have to come *immediately* after the quotation marks:

> Brown asserts that General Grant's "inability to remain patient with the pace of his attrition campaign" led to the horrendous Union losses in a mere half-hour at Cold Harbor, Virginia (281).

Of course, don't delay the parenthetical reference until the end of a sentence if readers could be confused about what material the reference documents:

> Although Brown notes Grant's occasional impatience with the progress of his attrition campaign in 1864 (281), the overall strategy of attrition--Grant against Lee's Army of Northern Virginia and Sherman against the Southern homeland supply base--brought the Union victory.

The reference here is in the middle of the sentence because only the first portion is attributable to the source. Note, however, that the parentheses do come at the end of the clause so the reference intrudes as little as possible.

Position Relative to Sentence Punctuation

Notice that the parenthetical reference in the first of the two samples above preceded the period at the end of the sentence, and the parentheses in the second sample came before the comma that ended the clause. Place your parenthetical reference before the punctuation mark, if any, that ends the sentence, clause, or phrase with the material you're documenting. If a quotation ends the sentence, clause, or phrase, normally you'll place the parenthetical reference between the ending quotation marks and the punctuation for the sentence, clause, or phrase:

> The Union losses at Cold Harbor, Virginia, can be attributed to General Grant's "inability to remain patient with the pace of his attrition campaign" (Brown 281).

The exception to this placement guidance is for a long quotation—one that is set off from the left margin of the rest of the paper with a block indentation. For this type of quotation, skip two spaces after the ending punctuation, provide the parenthetical reference, and put no punctuation after the closing parenthesis of the reference. Illustrations of this technique appear in the sample research paper (page 171) and in the illustrations for presenting borrowed material (page 243).

Notes With Parenthetical Documentation

Parenthetical references will take care of almost all documentation references, but they don't accommodate digressions from the text. Avoid long side arguments, but if you must add notes to support your text, use standard footnote or endnote entries: that is, use parenthetical references for your normal documentation, but also use notes for the explanatory digressions, like this one:

> [1]Smithson disagrees with Brown about Grant's blunder at Cold Harbor (224), but offers little support. See also Winchester 271; Souther 416-18; and Blake 76.

EXERCISES

A. Given the Works Cited entries below as the general source listing of a research paper, write the parenthetical references to show the specific portion references required for the numbered exercise items that follow. (Just show the parentheses and what would go in them; don't be concerned for this exercise with placing the references into textual passages.)

Bishop, Quinn T. "Progression in Regressive Pueblos in New Mexico and Colorado." *American Science* 43 (1990): 37–51.

Donovan, Janet. *Art of Southwest America.* New York: Shirlington, 1990.

Hill, Elliot F. *History and Art of the Mayans.* 3 vols. New York: Schocken, 1990.

Macy, Linda S. *Santa Clara Designs.* New York: Shirlington, 1988. Vol. 2 of *Pottery of the American Southwest.* 5 vols.

Moon, Calvin Roy, et al. *Mimbres Pottery, Decorations, and Symbology.* Albuquerque: La Madera, 1990.

1. Page 38 of the article in *American Science.*

2. Pages 76 to 77 of *Art of Southwest America.*

3. Page 64 of volume 2 of *History and Art of the Mayans.*

4. Pages 124 to 127 of *Santa Clara Designs.*

5. Page 231 of *Mimbres Pottery, Decorations, and Symbology.*

6. Page 50 of "Progression in Regressive Pueblos in New Mexico and Colorado" if another source by Quinn T. Bishop appeared in the same Works Cited listing.

7. A quotation from Albert Bicker's *Art of the San Juan Pueblo* that is quoted on page 93 of Janet Donovan's *Art of Southwest America.*

B. Rewrite the following passages to streamline their parenthetical references. In your revisions, be sure to modify the material inside the parentheses to account for information you incorporate into the introductions to the research material. And be sure you've followed the rules for punctuation relative to parenthetical references and quotation marks.

1. As one reviewer of software has written, "That famous old lady with the shoe house wouldn't have been so confused if she had used a personal computer and a file program to organize the health, school, and schedule information for each of her many children" (Byrd, "Getting Organized With a PC" 97).

2. It may be true that "Mother Hubbard's cupboard need not have been bare if she had managed her household inventories with a home computer" (Daniels, *Household Management and the Personal Computer* 34), yet she still might have had trouble stocking bones for her dog while she tried to pay for a computer and the software to run it.

Chapter 25

Works Cited

As you saw in Chapter 24, parenthetical references in the body of your research paper are possible because they refer to a *general source listing* at the end of the paper. This chapter focuses on that source listing—first on the format of the pages for the list as a whole, then on the formats of the entries that appear in that list, and finally on a few special format rules that affect the appearance of parts of some entries.

WORKS CITED PAGE FORMAT

The usual name for the listing of works at the end of the paper is *Works Cited*. This title assumes that the listing contains all (and only) the works you cite in the text of your paper; it does not include others that you read but that did not account for ideas or data in your paper. Your instructor might ask you to include the other works you read during research, in which case you could change the title to *Works Consulted*.

For the Works Cited page(s), start the list on a new page, numbering that page in sequence with the rest of your paper. Here's how the page should look:

- Use the same margins as for the rest of the pages of your research paper.
- Center the title one inch from the top of the page.
- Double-space after the title to find the line on which to begin the first entry.
- Double-space both within and between entries. (*Note:* Your instructor may prefer you to single-space within individual entries and double-space only between entries.)
- Begin the first line of each entry on the left margin, but for all subsequent lines of an entry indent five spaces.
- List entries in alphabetical order.

```
                                            Richards 9


                        Works Cited


Clark, Karen, and Fred Ingram. Acoma Canteens and

     Other Pottery Designs. Washington: Steinman,

     1989.

Donovan, Janet. Art of Southwest America. New

     York: Shirlington, 1990.

Macy, Linda S. Santa Clara Designs. New York:

     Shirlington, 1988. Vol. 2 of Pottery of the

     American Southwest. 5 vols.

Moon, Calvin Roy, et al. Mimbres Pottery,

     Decorations, and Symbology. Albuquerque:

     La Madera, 1990.
```

WHAT WORKS CITED ENTRIES CONTAIN

It has become commonplace to say that Works Cited documentation entries contain three basic parts: author, title, and publication information. And that's true enough for the most simple citations, which usually make up the majority of entries in a Works Cited list. Unfortunately, there are dozens of exceptions to that basic pattern. We believe that the following six basic groups more accurately describe a documentation entry and will better help you understand the job ahead:

1. Person(s) or group responsible for the piece of material you're documenting
2. The title(s)
3. Amplifying information, to help identify or describe the work precisely
4. Publishing information, or similar information that will help someone find the work
5. Identification of the portion you are citing

6. Supplemental bibliographic information (used with *multivolume book* citations only)

Here are those groups in a simple three-part citation:

```
            1                          2                      4
Donovan, Janet. Art of Southwest America. New York:

            Shirlington, 1990.
```

Group 3 is missing because no amplifying information is necessary to describe the book; group 5 is unnecessary because the entry is for the entire book, not a portion of it; and group 6 is unnecessary because the entry is not for a multivolume book.

An entry for an essay in a collection of essays published in one volume of a multivolume work, however, has all six basic groups:

```
                1                                  2
McKay, Felix Edgar. "Cocaine Cultivation in Peru." The

                                                      3
Illegal Drug Industry in Latin America. Vol. 3. Ed.

                  4                        5
Faith Dixon. New York: Schocken, 1989. 213-65.

                        6
4 vols. Gen. ed. Christopher N. Kennedy. 1987-90.
```

As you can see here, documentation entries can be quite complex. Yet, generally, despite complexities, the information falls into the six groups.

ENTRIES FOR BOOKS

General Form: Books

Divided here into the six basic groups are the fourteen elements you may need for a book citation. Few entries actually have all fourteen; the simple citation in the previous section has only five elements, while the sample complex citation has eleven. Obviously, you include only those elements that are appropriate for the book you're documenting.

(1) Person(s) or Group Responsible for the Piece of Material You're Documenting

- *Name(s) of individual(s) or group.*   Usually this is an author, but it can be an editor, translator, or organization. The key is identifying the people *directly responsible* for the particular piece of material you're documenting. Use names as they appear on the title page of the book. Do not include professional or educational titles, such as "M.S." or "Ph.D." If the entry is to begin with a person's name, reverse the name for alphabetizing (last-first-middle instead of first-middle-last).

(2) The Title(s)

- *Title of a part of a book.*   You'll need this when you're documenting an essay, a poem, a short story, and so forth, within an anthology, or when you cite a division of a book (such as the Introduction).

- *Title of the book.*   If a book has both a title and a subtitle, give both with a colon and a single space between them (omit the colon if the title itself ends with punctuation, such as a question mark). (Special rules beginning on page 275 give guidance for capitalization, quotation marks, and underlining in titles.)

(3) Amplifying Information, to Help Identify or Describe the Work Precisely

- *Translator(s).*   One translation is rarely like another, so it's necessary to show the translator(s) of the work.

- *Editor(s).*   The order of translator(s) and editor(s) can be reversed; show them in the order in which they appear on the book's title page.

- *Edition.*   Readers will assume you're citing the first edition, without revisions, unless you indicate otherwise. Portions of different editions of the same book will be different, so you need to show exactly which one you used.

- *Volume number or number of volumes.*   In a citation for a multivolume work, the number of the volume used or the number of volumes in the set can appear before the publication information, depending on how you refer to the material within your paper.

- *Series.*   If the work you're citing is part of a series, give the series name and the number of the work in the series (e.g., "Archaeological Studies, No. 12").

(4) Publishing Information, or Similar Information That Will Help Someone Find the Work

- *Place of publication.*   Look for the place of publication on the title or copyright page or at the back of the book, especially for a book published outside the United States. If several cities are listed, use the one listed first unless you have some reason for using a different one. Give the state or country along with the city if the city is not likely to be recognized or could be confused with another city with the same name.

- *Publisher.*   You need not name the publisher for a book printed before 1900. For books printed since 1900, use a shortened version of the publisher's name;

e.g., "Holt" rather than "Holt, Rinehart and Winston." (See pages 276–277 for special rules on dealing with publishers' names and special imprints.)

- *Date of publication.*   Again, look for the publication date on the title page, on the copyright page, or at the back of the book. If no publication date appears, give the latest copyright date. Ignore dates for multiple printings; however, if you are citing a work in other than its first edition, use the publication date for the edition you're using, not the original date. For example, if a book in its third edition shows dates of 1979, 1984, and 1987, use 1987.

(5) Identification of the Portion You Are Citing

You'll use this part of an entry only when you're citing a part of a book (e.g., an essay or Introduction).

- *Page numbers.*   Show the *inclusive* page numbers for the portion of the book you're citing. Don't be concerned if you refer to only one or a few of those pages in the text of your paper; those specific page references will be clear in your parenthetical references in the text. Here you must show the pagination for the entire piece. (See page 277 for special rules on showing inclusive page numbers.)

(6) Supplemental Bibliographic Information

You'll use this part of an entry only when your citation is for a multivolume work—and even then only part of the time, depending on the complexity of the bibliographic information and how you refer to the material within your paper.

- *Number of volumes.*   The number of volumes in a multivolume work will appear after publication and specific portion data when the earlier information in the citation is for a single volume of the set.

- *Information for the set of volumes.*   Data pertaining to the set of volumes—e.g. general editor and span of publication years for the set—may appear at the end of the citation for a multivolume work.

Sample Entries: Books

Following are samples illustrating recommended formats for citations for books. A word of caution: These samples were designed to illustrate particular portions of a book citation. They do not cover every variation you may run across. (A list of samples detailing all the variations would be unbelievably long.) If the book you're citing doesn't quite fit a sample, adapt the format to fit your needs, but be sure to include all the appropriate information you've just read about in the preceding section. *Note:* Since the samples have been listed to demonstrate points about formats, no attempt has been made to alphabetize them, except for entries under "Two or More Books by the Same 'Author(s).'" In your Works Cited pages, of course, you'll list all works in alphabetical order.

One Author

```
Donovan, Janet. Art of Southwest America. New York:
    Shirlington, 1990.
```

Two or Three Authors

Only the name of the person listed first is given out of normal order (last-first-middle rather than first-middle-last). Be sure to use authors' names as they appear on the book's title page. Do not include professional or educational titles, such as "M.S." or "Ph.D." Names of multiple authors may not be alphabetized on the title page; list them in the order in which they appear.

```
Clark, Karen, and Frank Ingram. Acoma Canteens and Other
    Pottery Designs. Washington: Steinman, 1989.
Hyson, Curtis F., G. Randolph Dill, and Jay H. Felmet,
    Jr. Magic, Mystery, and Medicine. Nashville:
    Vanderbilt UP, 1990.
```

More Than Three Authors

For more than three authors, give only the one listed first in the book and follow that with "et al." (for "and others").

```
Moon, Calvin Roy, et al. Mimbres Pottery, Decorations,
    and Symbology. Albuquerque, La Madera, 1990.
```

Group as Author

When a group or agency is responsible for a book, treat that group as the author and list its name first, even though the group's name may appear in the book's title or may appear again as publisher. List the group or agency name in normal order. ("GPO" in this entry is the accepted abbreviation for "Government Printing Office," which prints U.S. federal publications. Note that "DC" is omitted.)

```
National Commission on Aging. Report of the National
    Commission on Aging. Washington: GPO, 1988.
```

Government and International Body Publications

Many government agency publications are simple enough to be treated as books with groups as authors, with the responsible agency serving as author, as in the entry above. Occasionally government publications show a specific person as author; you can begin with that person (as in the second sample below), or you can show the individual author after the title (as in the first sample).

For the *Congressional Record,* you need show only the full date and the inclusive pages for the portion being cited. For other congressional documents, give the government and body, house, committee (if appropriate), document title, number and session of Congress, and type and number of publication, followed by standard publication data. Congressional documents include bills (S 16; HR 63), resolutions (S. Res. 16; H. Res. 63), reports (S. Rept. 16; H. Rept. 63), and documents (S. Doc. 16; H. Doc. 63).

There are also state and local government documents, foreign government documents, and those of international bodies (such as the United Nations). Begin these as you would a U.S. federal publication, naming first the government or international body (e.g., "Indiana. Dept. of Revenue" or "United Nations. Committee for Economic Development").

> United States. Dept. of State. <u>Islamic Developments in
>   Africa</u>. By Edan Irwin. Washington: GPO, 1989.
> Irwin, Edan. <u>Islamic Developments in Africa</u>. U.S. Dept.
>   of State. Washington: GPO, 1989.
> <u>Cong. Rec</u>. 21 Sep. 1990: 3143-45.
> United States. Cong. House. Permanent Select Committee on
>   Intelligence. <u>Technological Transfer Losses in the
>   1980s</u>. 101st Cong., 2nd sess. H. Rept. 1122.
>   Washington: GPO, 1990.
> United Nations. Committee for Economic Cooperation.
>   <u>Resource Development in West Africa</u>. Elmsford:
>   Pergamon, 1989.

Author Not Given

If no author is given in a book, begin the entry with the title. (When you alphabetize the entries for your Works Cited pages, you'll go by the first word in the title other than an article—that is, other than *A, An,* or *The.*) Of course, treat books with groups as authors or government and international body publications as indicated above, even though these books frequently show no individual as author.

> <u>A Collection of Slavic Stories and Rhymes</u>. Baltimore:
>   Court, 1990.

Editor(s)

If your use of an edited book, for the most part, is the text of the work itself, then the name(s) of the editor(s) ("ed." or "eds.") should appear after the title, as in the first sample below. However, if the work of the editor(s)—including introductory or other extratextual comments—is being cited, begin the entry with the editor(s), as in the second sample. Moreover, if you are citing an anthology or other collection—rather than a piece within the collection—use the second format below (for a piece in a collection, see "Part of a Collection" below).

> Kemp, Gilbert M. <u>Narcotics Trafficking and the Caribbean
>   Islands</u>. Ed. Pamela Hoffman. Madison: U of
>   Wisconsin, 1990.

Hoffman, Pamela, ed. <u>Narcotics Trafficking and the</u>
    <u>Caribbean Islands</u>. By Gilbert M. Kemp. Madison: U of
    Wisconsin, 1990.

Translator(s)

Normally you'll show the translator(s) of a book after the title, as in the first sample below. However, as with editors, if you are citing primarily commentary by the translator(s), then begin with the translator(s), as in the second sample. If the book has both a translator and an editor, show them in the order in which they appear on the book's title page.

Gatti, Carlo. <u>Cats of Venice</u>. Trans. Rachel Hipson.
    New York: Shirlington, 1989.
Hipson, Rachel, trans. <u>Cats of Venice</u>. By Carlo Gatti.
    New York: Shirlington, 1989.
Della Bella Mario. <u>The Shores of the Adriatic</u>. Trans.
    Carl Elliot. Ed. Malcom Hawk. Washington: Slay, 1990.

Two or More Books by the Same "Author(s)"

Sometimes two or more entries in your Works Cited listing have *exactly* the same names at the beginning for the person(s) or group responsible for the piece you're documenting. In such a case, give the name(s) only for the first entry; in the following entries type *three hyphens* and a period in place of the name(s). *The three hyphens signify the same name(s),* so if a person named is shown in the first entry as, say, an author and in the next as a translator, you should use the three hyphens for the name in the second entry, following the hyphens with a comma and "trans." (Notice, in the samples below, that the order is determined by the alphabetical order of the titles, since the author block is the same for each.)

Chin, Lee. <u>"Hong Kong Tea" and Other Stories</u>. Arlington:
    Burning Tree, 1990.
---, trans. <u>"The Lagoon" and More</u>. By Mario Della Bella.
    New York: Shirlington, 1989.
---. <u>Singapore Tales</u>. Arlington: Burning Tree, 1988.

However, if an entry with a single name is followed by an entry in which the first of multiple authors is that same name, do not use the three hyphens in the second entry. Three hyphens can stand for more than one name, but the name block in each case must be *exactly* the same.

Gatti, Carlo. <u>Cats of Venice</u>. Trans. Rachel Hipson.
    New York: Shirlington, 1989.
Gatti, Carlo, and Rachel Hipson, trans. <u>Carabinieri</u>
    <u>Parade</u>. By Luigi Mautone. Washington: Luke, 1990.

```
---, trans. Neapolitan Manners. By Rosa Valentino.
     New York: Shirlington, 1989.
```

Finally, the three hyphens also should be used when groups, governments, or international bodies serve as authors. And since government entries begin with the name of the government and the name of the body or agency sponsoring the work, you may need more than one set of three hyphens. The samples below illustrate the author blocks for several government publications.

```
Indiana. Dept. of Health.
---. Dept. of Revenue.
United States. Cong. House.
---. ---. Senate.
---. Dept. of Energy.
```

Extratextual Material

In citations for such extratextual material as an Introduction or Afterword, give the name of the author of that division of the book, followed by the name of the extratextual piece; the author of the work itself follows the book title. If the author of the extratextual material is also the author of the book, give only the last name after the book title, as in the second sample. Notice that both samples contain inclusive page numbers for the named extratextual section of the book.

```
Muñoz, Hector. Introduction. Protest in the Vietnam War
     Years. By David M. Ross. Washington: Luke, 1988.
     v-xxi.
Readman, Donna L. Afterword. Vienna Christmas. By
     Readman. Washington: Spinnaker, 1990. 224-32.
```

Part of a Collection

For parts of anthologies, collections of articles, and casebooks, the title of the piece precedes the title of the work. Normally the title of the piece will appear in quotation marks; however, if it was published originally as a book, underline (or italicize) it instead. Notice that as for an extratextual piece of a book discussed above, the inclusive pages for the piece of the collection end the citation.

```
Sacco, Franco. "Umberto Eco's Labyrinth." Contemporary
     European Fiction. Ed. Victoria Wood. Boston:
     Liberty, 1990. 175-98.
```

Cross-References

If you're documenting multiple pieces from the same collection, you have a choice. You can treat each piece as a part of a collection, giving full data for the collection itself each time. Or you can give one entry for the collection and then simplify the citations for the pieces by referring to the entry for the collection. Keep in mind, however, that each specific piece of the collection that you refer to in the text of your paper requires its own entry in the Works Cited section. Thus, with cross-referencing you save repeating some information in each of the citations for a piece of the collection, but you then must add an entry for the collection itself.

```
Fisher, Jill M. "Milan Kundera: Far From Unbearable."
    Wood 142-74.
Sacco, Franco. "Umberto Eco's Labyrinth." Wood 175-98.
Wood, Victoria, ed. Contemporary European Fiction.
    Boston: Liberty, 1990.
```

Republished Books
If you use a republished book (a new publication of an out-of-print book or a paperback version of a book originally published in hard cover), show the original publication date before the new publication information.

```
Roux, Elizabeth Greenleaf. Music for the Lute. 1954.
    Washington: Slay, 1990.
```

If the original book is republished under a new title, follow the original title and publication year with "Rpt. as" ("Reprinted as") and the new title. The full publication data, as in the citation above, is for the new publication.

```
Ferry, R. Michael. The Amazonia Rain Forest. 1973. Rpt.
    as Can We Save the Rain Forest? Albuquerque:
    La Madera, 1990.
```

Edition Other Than First
Readers will assume the book is a first edition unless you indicate otherwise, such as second edition ("2nd ed."), alternate edition ("Alt. ed."), revised edition ("Rev. ed."), and so on.

```
Doyle, Rachel Marie. Desktop Publishing Software. 2nd ed.
    New York: Schocken, 1990.
```

Series
If a book is part of a series, give the series name and the number of the work in the series.

```
Newberry, Susan G. Cliff Dwellings in Africa.
    Archaeological Studies, No. 12. Albuquerque:
    La Madera, 1989.
```

Multivolume Work
For a specific page reference to a multivolume work, the parenthetical reference in the text of your paper will include the volume number with the page reference if

you need to refer to more than one volume of the set (e.g., 2:111–12 for pages 111 to 112 of volume 2). However, if in your paper you never need to document material from more than one volume of the set, you can show the specific volume number in the Works Cited entry—as in the following sample—and give only the page reference in the text of your paper (e.g., 111–12 instead of 2:111–12). Notice that the sample ends with the total number of volumes in the multivolume set.

Hill, Elliot F. <u>History and Art of the Mayans</u>. Vol. 2.
    New York: Schocken, 1990. 3 vols.

If the single volume you cite for your paper has its own title, include the specific volume reference between the individual publication data and the multivolume title, as in the samples below. Again, references in the text of your paper would not include the volume number. Notice that the first sample ends with the number of volumes in the set; the second sample adds inclusive years of publication for the set because not all volumes were published in the same year.

Macy, Linda S. <u>Santa Clara Designs</u>. New York:
    Shirlington, 1988. Vol. 2 of <u>Pottery of the American</u>
    <u>Southwest</u>. 5 vols.
Moore, Donald. <u>Oriental Patterns in European Porcelains</u>.
    Bloomington: Indiana UP, 1988. Vol. 3 of <u>European</u>
    <u>Porcelain Manufacture</u>. 4 vols. 1985-90.

If your paper requires references to two or more volumes, then use the more general multivolume citation in your Works Cited listing (as below) and include the volume number with each parenthetical reference in the text of your paper.

Hill, Elliot F. <u>History and Art of the Mayans</u>. 3 vols.
    New York: Schocken, 1990.

If the multiple volumes of the set were published over a period of years, then the publication date portion shows the first and last years of the set:

Moore, Donald. <u>European Porcelain Manufacture</u>. 4 vols.
    Bloomington: Indiana UP, 1985-90.

If the multivolume set has not been completed, include "to date" with the number of volumes and follow the publication date of the first volume with a hyphen and a space before the ending period.

King, Chester N. <u>European Chamber Music and Its</u>
    <u>Composers</u>. 3 vols. to date. Baltimore: Court, 1987- .

When you cite a piece in a multivolume collection of pieces, show the volume number before the publication data and both the inclusive pages for the piece and the number of volumes in the set at the end of the entry.

```
Haynes, Clinton R. "Athapaskan Descendants." Indians of
     the Americas. Ed. Kimberly L. Dawson. Vol. 1.
     Austin: U of Texas P, 1989. 718-42. 3 vols.
```

Depending on the factors applicable to a multivolume work, the Works Cited entry can become quite complex. The following citation shows a piece in a volume of a multivolume set; the volume has one editor, while the multivolume set has a general editor; the volumes of the set were published over a period of years.

```
McKay, Felix Edgar. "Cocaine Cultivation in Peru." The
     Illegal Drug Industry in Latin America. Vol. 3. Ed.
     Faith Dixon. New York: Schocken, 1989. 213-65. 4
     vols. Gen ed. Christopher N. Kennedy. 1987-90.
```

Published Conference Proceedings

If the book title doesn't include information about the conference, provide amplifying information after the title.

```
Nature '89: Conserving the Earth's Bounty. Proc. of a
     Conference of the Environmental Conservancy
     Association. 19-21 Sep. 1990. Ann Arbor: U of
     Michigan P., 1990.
```

Pamphlet

Treat pamphlets as books.

```
Enos, Bernard B. Choosing a Hard Disk. Baltimore: Court,
     1990.
```

Missing Publishing or Pagination Data

Use the following abbreviations for missing publication or pagination information:

no place of publication: n. p.
no publisher: n. p.
no date: n. d.
no pagination: n. pag.

The abbreviations for "no place" and "no publisher" are the same, but their positions left or right of the colon will allow readers to tell the difference. When a book has no pagination indicated, your Works Cited entry needs to contain "N. pag." so that readers will understand why parenthetical references in the text of your paper do not show page numbers.

<u>Newsletter Design and Desktop Publishing</u>. N.p.: n.p.,
    1989. N. Pag.

ENTRIES FOR ARTICLES IN PERIODICALS

Periodicals are publications that are issued periodically on some sort of schedule—quarterly, bimonthly, weekly, daily, and so forth. Authorities group periodicals into three classes: journals, magazines, and newspapers. Newspapers are easy to recognize, but there isn't an absolute distinction between journals and magazines.

Many journals don't have the word *journal* in their titles, and not all periodicals with *journal* in their titles are considered journals for documentation. Nevertheless, some differentiation is necessary because the data required after the publisher in a Works Cited entry differ for the various types of periodicals. Fortunately, we don't need a scholarly distinction; instead we can make fairly simple divisions based on how the periodicals paginate their issues and on how frequently they publish issues. Therefore, the sample formats for periodicals can be distinguished on the following bases:

- *A periodical paged continuously throughout a volume is treated as a "journal, with continuous pagination."* (If, for example, the first issue of a particular volume ends with page 171 and the next issue begins with page 172, the periodical uses continuous pagination.)
- *When each issue of the periodical is paginated independently it is treated as a "journal, with issues paged independently" if it is published less frequently than once every two months.* (If each issue of a periodical begins with page 1, the issues are paginated independently.)
- *All other periodicals are distinguished by frequency of publication.*

General Form: Articles in Periodicals

(1) Person(s) or Group Responsible for the Piece of Material You're Documenting

- *Author(s).*   If an article is signed, the name(s) (sometimes only initials) will appear at either the beginning or the end of the article. Treat multiple authors as you would for book entries.

(2) The Title(s)

- *Title of article.*   (See pages 275–276 for guidance on capitalization, quotation marks, and underlining in titles.)

(3) Amplifying Information to Help Identify or Describe the Work Precisely

- *Type of article.*   You'll need this only for editorials, letters to the editor, and reviews.

(4) Publishing Information, or Similar Information That Will Help Someone Find the Work

- *Name of periodical.*   The name of the periodical itself is all the publishing information that is necessary. Drop any introductory article from the title. If readers aren't likely to recognize the title by itself, insert after the title the name of the institution or, particularly for newspapers, the city, enclosing the name in brackets.

(5) Identification of the Portion You Are Citing

- *Series number.*   If a journal has been published in more than one series (e.g., old and new), indicate the applicable one. Otherwise readers may have difficulty determining where to find the article you used.

- *Newspaper edition.*   If a newspaper has both morning and evening or special editions, you may need to show which you used; check the masthead of the newspaper when you read it. The same article often will appear in more than one edition, but not necessarily in the same place in each.

- *Volume and/or issue number(s).*   For *journals,* you'll include the volume and/or issue number for the issue you used.

- *Date.*   All entries will include at least the year, but whether year only, month and year, or complete date depends on the type of periodical.

- *Page number(s).*   (See page 277 for guidance on showing inclusive page numbers.)

Sample Entries: Articles in Periodicals

As with the samples for books, the following entries were designed to illustrate particular portions of documentation entries. You may need to adapt the formats to fit your needs, but be sure to include all pertinent information listed in the preceding discussion of general form. *Note:* The three-hyphen form for repeated authors (see "Two or More Books by the Same 'Author(s)'" on pages 263–264) applies to entries for articles in periodicals as well, but is not repeated below.

Journal, With Continuous Pagination
This type of entry includes the volume number followed by the year in parentheses, a colon, and then inclusive page numbers for the article.

```
Myers, Georgia. "Tellem Cliff Dwellings of Mali." African
     Studies 25 (1990): 373-92.
```

Journal, With Issues Paged Independently
After the volume number, add a period and the issue number.

Johnston, Lara M. "Owen Meany and the Angel of Death."
American Fiction 19:2 (1989): 45-59.

Journal, With Issue Numbers Only

If a journal does not use volume numbers, use the issue number as if it were a volume number.

Bishop, Quinn T. "Progression in Regressive Pueblos in
New Mexico and Colorado." American Science 43
(1990): 37-51.

Journal, With Series

If a journal has been published in more than one series, precede the volume number with the series. Use a numerical designator such as "4th ser." or "ns" and "os" for "new series" and "original series."

Lambert, Byron. "Draining the Aral Sea." World Science ns
12 (1988): 612-34.

Monthly or Bimonthly Periodical

Instead of volume and/or issue, use the month(s) and year.

Kinard, Mary Wayne. "Optical Disk Storage." Computers at
Home May 1990: 63-78.

Weekly or Biweekly Periodical

Whether a magazine or a newspaper, for a periodical published once a week or every two weeks, give the complete date rather than volume and issue numbers.

Mika, Marc. "Treasures of the Greco-Bactrian Period."
Museum News 23 Nov. 1990: 23-24.

Daily Newspaper

Show the newspaper's name as it appears at the top of the first page, omitting any beginning article (e.g., *The Washington Post* becomes *Washington Post*). If the newspaper title doesn't name the city, give the city and state in brackets after the title, as in the first sample below. The first sample also illustrates how to indicate the edition for a newspaper that prints more than one edition a day (again, check the masthead on the first page to see if an edition is given).

For inclusive page numbers, check the pagination system of the newspaper carefully. If the newspaper doesn't have sections or if it numbers continuously through the edition, you'll need only the page number(s) after the date (e.g., 8 Oct. 1990: 38). If the newspaper includes the section number with the page number(s), the appropriate section-number combination can follow the date (e.g., 8 Oct. 1990: A12–A13). But if the section designator is not combined with the page number(s), then show the section designator between the date and the page number(s) (e.g., 8 Oct. 1990, sec. 3: 12).

```
Carey, Kelly. "What's Become of the Gulags?" Star-Herald
     [St. Louis, MO] 8 Oct. 1990, early morning ed.:
     A12-A13.
Fedor, Alison. "Burdensharing for the Persian Gulf
     Crisis." Washington Post 29 Sep. 1990: A4.
```

Author Unknown

Whatever the type of periodical, if no author is given, begin with the article's title. The format for the rest of the entry, of course, depends on the type of periodical in which the article appears; the sample below is for a monthly magazine.

```
"Prehistoric Skywatchers Charted the Heavens." Ancient
     History May 1989: 53-67.
```

Editorial

Begin with the author if named, otherwise with the editorial's title, and follow the title with "Editorial." The rest of the entry depends on the source; our sample uses a daily newspaper.

```
"Is Washington a 'District of Colombia'?" Editorial.
     Washington Post 17 Sep. 1989: A15.
```

Letter to the Editor

Since letters to editors can appear in any type of periodical, the portion after the title depends on the type of publication in which the letter appears. We show a journal (with continuous pagination).

```
Im, Lee. Letter. Journal of Antiquity 15 (1990): 276.
```

Review

Reviews may be signed or unsigned and titled or untitled, and they may appear in any type of periodical. For a signed review, use the name(s) of the reviewer(s), the review title (if there is one), and then "Rev. of. . . ." For an unsigned review, give the title (if there is one); if not, begin with "Rev. of. . . ." The first entry below shows a signed and titled review in a monthly magazine; the second sample is for an unsigned, untitled review in a daily newspaper.

```
Black, Donna B. "Styles and Whistles." Rev. of Formatting
     With Word 4.0, by Holly Allen. Computers at Home
     Oct. 1990: 32-45.
Rev. of Singapore Tales, by Lee Chin. Austin Gazette
     12 Dec. 1988, sec. 4: 13.
```

ENTRIES FOR OTHER SOURCES

General Form: Other Sources

This mixed group of reference types lacks a "standard form." Still, the general idea for documentation entries applies: (1) person(s) or group responsible for the piece of material you're documenting; (2) the title(s); (3) amplifying information, to help identify or describe the work precisely; (4) publishing information, or similar information that will help someone find the work; and (5) identification of the portion you are citing.

Sample Entries: Other Sources

If you can't find a sample that fits your needs exactly, adapt entries or create a format, but keep the general guidelines in mind.

Speech

Use the speech title, if known; when it isn't, use in its place a designator such as Address, Keynote speech, or Lecture (titles, as below, go in quotation marks, of course, but the descriptive designators would be used without quotation marks).

```
Binder, Calvin. "Community Action Groups Combat
     Neighborhood Drug Trafficking." Conference of Law
     Enforcement Officers. Cincinnati, 10 Sep. 1990.
```

Class Handout or Lecture

Show class, place, and date; as appropriate and available, give speaker and title.

```
"Recognizing and Correcting Passive Voice." English 101
     handout. Wolfram State College, 1990.
Unruh, Michael. Math 210 lecture. Miami U, 17 Oct. 1990.
```

Reference Work

Entries for items in standard reference works require less information than do basic entries for books. For a signed encyclopedia article (the first entry below), give the author, article title, encyclopedia title, and edition. For an unsigned article, begin with the article title. If citations are for encyclopedias or dictionaries that alphabetize articles, volume and page references are unnecessary. Of course, if the encyclopedia has separate major divisions, each of which has articles in alphabetical order, include the division title with the encyclopedia title (e.g., *Encyclopaedia Britannica: Macropaedia*). For other standard reference works, such as one of the *Who's Who* series, give only the edition, if applicable, and publication year after the title (e.g., 12th ed. 1982–83). However, treat an article in a less common reference work as a piece in a book collection (see "Part of a Collection," page 264), and give full publication information.

Adams, Raymond. "Istanbul." <u>Funk & Wagnalls New
        Encyclopedia</u>. 1989 ed.
"Stonehenge." <u>Encyclopedia Americana</u>. 1988 ed.

Computer Software

For commercially produced computer software, begin with the writer of the program, if available; if not, begin with the title. Show the version number (for example Vers. 1.2). Label with the term "Computer software" and give as a minimum the distributor and publication year. Optional information may be added at the end of the entry—such as the computer for which the program is designed, the operating system, and the type of medium the program is recorded on (cartridge, cassette, or disk).

<u>Filefolder Data Base Management</u>. Vers. 1.2. Computer
        software. Scienobyte, 1990. Macintosh, disk.

Material From a Computer or Information Service

Material from a computer service (such as DIALOG, Mead, or BRS) or an information service (such as ERIC or NTIS) is like other printed material, but after the publishing information you need to add a reference to the service, giving its name and the accession or order number for the material you're citing. Thus, most of the sample entry below corresponds to a document that is part of a series, while the end of the entry refers to the information service.

Wahlberg, Doris J. <u>The Effect of Mass Testing on
        Curriculum</u>. Classroom Education Techniques, No. 12.
        Syracuse: Syracuse UP, 1984. ERIC ED 043 372.

Unpublished Thesis or Dissertation

When a thesis or dissertation has been published, treat it as a book. However, if you use an unpublished form, show the type of work, the institution for which it was prepared, and the year it was accepted. Note that the title appears in quotation marks because the work is unpublished.

Keifer, Jesse Monroe. "Communist Command Economies and
        Environmental Destruction in Eastern Europe." Diss.
        U of Nebraska, 1989.

Unpublished Letter

Treat a published letter as a part of a book collection or as a letter in a periodical. The first entry below shows the format for a letter you yourself have received. The second illustrates an unpublished letter in an archive.

Acton, Anthony Norton. Letter to the author. 11 Dec. 1990.
Dean, George B. Letter to Robert James Webb. 17 Mar.
        1866. Robert James Webb Collection. Hurley Museum
        Library. Huntington, SC.

Interview

To document an interview you have conducted, begin with the name of the person interviewed, show the type of interview (personal or telephone), and give the date it was held.

```
Nelson, Barbara. Personal interview. 22 Jun. 1990.
```

Film, Filmstrip, Slide Program, or Videocassette

For a film usually you'll begin with the title, followed by the director, distributor, and year released. Other information (stars, writers, etc.) is optional but should be included if it bears on how you discuss the film in your paper; put this information as amplification after the director. However, if your paper deals with the work of a particular individual connected with the film, begin with that person. For a filmstrip, slide program, or videocassette, show the type of medium after the title and then follow the format for a film citation.

```
Braving Winter. Dir. Julia Kowalski. Panorama, 1989.
Installing Memory Chips in a Macintosh Plus.
     Videocassette. Dir. Jill Vantine. Video Concepts,
     1990.
```

Radio or Television Program

As a minimum, give the program title, the network that aired it, the local station and city for the broadcast that you viewed or heard, and the broadcast date. An episode title, if available, can be shown in quotation marks preceding the program title (as in our sample), and a series title, with no special markings, can be shown after the program title. Other information may be added for amplification, and if your paper deals with the work of a particular person connected with the broadcast, begin the entry with that individual's name.

```
"Hotline." Weekend Newsline. ABC. WCAM, Cincinnati.
     22 Sep. 1990.
```

Record or Tape

Begin the entry with the person you want to emphasize (speaker, author, composer, producer, etc.); then give the title and follow it with "Audiotape" if your source is a tape rather than a record. Show the artist(s) (along with any appropriate amplification), manufacturer, identification number, and release year.

```
Gatti, Carlo. Cats of Venice. Audiotape. Read by Veronica
     Erno. Recorded Books, 89172, 1989.
```

Legal Citation

Complex legal citations are beyond the scope of this volume. Consult the Harvard Law Review Association's *A Uniform System of Citation* for help. The sample entries below are for federal statutory material; both use section references rather than page references. Use similar entries for state constitutions and statutes.

```
5 US Code. Sec 522a. 1974.
US Const. Art. 3, sec. 1.
```

Citations for law cases show the names of first plaintiff and first defendant, the volume of the report being cited, the name of the report, the page of the report, the name of the court where the case was decided, and the year decided.

```
Jefferson v. Sommers. 153 AS 613. Ind. Ct. App. 1978.
```

SPECIAL RULES FOR TITLES

Capitalization

Do use capital letters for the *first letters* of the following types of words in titles:

- each important word in the title (see below for "unimportant" words)
- the first word in a title (e.g., "*A* House on Tatum Hill")
- the first word after a colon that joins a title and a subtitle (e.g., "Faulkner's 'Delta Autumn': *The* Fall of Idealism")
- parts of compound words that would be capitalized if they appeared by themselves (e.g., "School Declares *All-O*ut War on Misspelling")

Don't use capital letters for the following "unimportant" words:

- the articles *a, an,* and *the*
- short prepositions such as *at, by, for, in, of, on, to, up*
- the conjunctions *and, as, but, if, nor, or, for, so, yet*
- the second element of a compound numeral (e.g., "Twenty-*f*ive Years of Tyranny")

Neither Quotation Marks nor Underlining

Don't use either quotation marks or underlining (or italics) for the following:

- the Bible, the books of the Bible, and other sacred works such as the Talmud or the Koran
- legal references (such as acts, laws, and court cases)
- extratextual material in a book (such as the Introduction or Foreword)

Underlining

Printers usually use italics, but in typing you use underlining (or italics if your typing system, such as a word processor, has this capability) for certain types of titles. Underline the title of works published separately—such as novels and poems that are entire books or pamphlets—and the titles of periodicals (magazines, journals, and newspapers). Also underline the titles of movies and radio or television programs.

Quotation Marks

Use quotation marks to enclose titles of works published as parts of other works—such as short stories, most poems, and essays. Also, enclose titles of speeches and class lectures in quotation marks.

If, however, a work that has been published separately appears as part of a larger work—such as a novel as part of an anthology—underline the title. For example, underline Voltaire's *Candide* even when it is a part of an anthology entitled *Great Works of World Literature.*

Mixed Quotation Marks and Underlining

You have to adapt the rules somewhat when one title appears within another. The following samples illustrate the markings for the four possible combinations of titles with quotation marks and titles with underlining (or italics):

- "Faulkner's 'Delta Autumn': The Fall of Idealism" (a short-story title within an essay title: each title without the other would have double quotation marks, but here the title within a title has single quotation marks)
- Faulkner's "Delta Autumn" and the Myth of the Wilderness (a short-story title within a book title: each title has its normal markings)
- "Laertes as Foil in *Hamlet*" (a play title within an essay title: each title has its normal markings)
- Shakespeare's "Hamlet": Action Versus Contemplation (a play title within a book title: the title within a title, which by itself would be underlined, here has double quotation marks)

SPECIAL RULES FOR PUBLISHERS' NAMES

Shortening

Follow these rules in shortening publishers' names for your Works Cited entries:

- Omit the articles *a, and,* and *the.*
- Omit business designators such as *Co., Inc.,* or *Ltd.*
- Omit labels such as *Books, Press,* or *Publishers. Note:* University presses create an exception. Since both universities and their presses may publish independently, use *P* for *Press* when the publisher is a university press (thus, *Indiana U* is distinct from *Indiana UP*).
- If the publisher's name includes the name of one person, use only the last name (*Alfred A. Knopf, Inc.* becomes *Knopf*).
- If the name includes several people, use only the first name (*Holt, Rinehart and Winston* becomes *Holt*).

- Use the following standard abbreviations: *UP* for University Press; *GPO* for Government Printing Office; *HMSO* for Her (His) Majesty's Stationery Office; *MLA* for The Modern Language Association of America; *NAL* for The New American Library; *NCTE* for the National Council of Teachers of English; and *NEA* for The National Education Association.

Imprints

When the title page or copyright page of a book shows a publisher's special imprint, combine the imprint with a shortened version of the publisher's name: for example, a Sentry Edition published by Houghton Mifflin Company becomes Sentry-Houghton; a Mentor Book published by The New American Library becomes Mentor-NAL.

SPECIAL RULES FOR INCLUSIVE PAGE NUMBERS

When you indicate inclusive page references, often you can shorten the second number. Up to 100, show all digits (e.g., 3–4, 54–55). Thereafter, reduce the second number of a set to two digits (e.g., 253–54, 304–05, 2614–15) *unless* the hundred or thousand changes (e.g., 499–501, 2998–3002).

EXERCISE

Prepare a Works Cited page to include entries for the works below.

1. A journal article entitled "Successful Drug Abuse Prevention Programs in Industry." This article, by Daniel P. Pansall, appeared on pages 313 through 334 of volume 7, the summer 1990 issue, of the *Journal of American Industry,* a journal that paginates continuously throughout a volume.

2. An editorial entitled "What About Drug *Prevention* in the Workplace?" This unsigned editorial appeared on page A14 of the *Denver Post* on 14 November 1990.

3. A book by Lily Mahal entitled *Employee Rights* and subtitled *Personnel Management in Industry.* This book was published in 1988 by the University of Tennessee (at Knoxville).

4. Another book by Lily Mahal, this one called *What Employees Need To Know About Their Employers.* The book was published by Shirlington Press, of New York City, in 1990.

5. An article entitled "Who's Watching the Authorities?" This article, by Scott Palmer, appeared on pages 62 to 74 of issue 10, October 1990, of *Business World.* This magazine is published monthly.

6. *Personnel Management,* a two-volume work by Arthur N. Larson. Both volumes were published in 1989 by Burning Tree Press of Arlington, Virginia.

7. An article on pages 37 to 44 of the 21 September 1990 issue of *American Industry News,* a weekly magazine. No author was given for the article, which was entitled "Drug Testing Program Proposal Enrages Employees at Mississippi Plant."

8. An article entitled "Drugs and Workers," which appeared on pages 216 through 234 of a collection of essays entitled *What Businesses Can Do* and subtitled *Drug Abuse Prevention, Testing, and Rehabilitation.* The article was written by William Nicholson. Barbara N. McIntyre edited the collection of essays, which was published in 1989 by Schocken Books, Inc., of New York.

9. A book by the Association of American Businesses entitled *Guidelines on Drug Testing for Industry,* published in 1990 in Washington, DC, by the Association of American Businesses.

Improving Your Punctuation and Expression

279

Part Six

Punctuation

There's more to good writing than just getting commas and apostrophes in the right places—yet those commas and apostrophes are important, too.

We don't try to cover everything about punctuation in this part of the book—just those rules we think will be especially helpful for you.

Chapter 26

Definitions

Why begin studying punctuation with a review of grammar? If you understand the terms in this chapter, learning to punctuate a sentence will be easy, for punctuation is not really very mysterious. In fact, once you understand these terms, you probably will be surprised just how easy punctuation can be.

The catch (and, of course, there is a catch) is that you must work hard to understand them.

A Pep Talk

Skimming this chapter once, or even reading it once through carefully, will not suffice. You have to memorize a few terms. So please learn this material well, because all of it is essential in later chapters.

---

1. Clause. *A clause is a group of words containing a subject (S) and a verb (V).*

$$\text{S} \quad \text{V}$$

Clause: Sharon ran in the New York marathon.

Sometimes people are fooled into believing a group of words is a clause simply because it contains something that looks like a verb:

Not a clause: Running in a marathon.

The above group of words cannot be a clause for two reasons: (1) it has no subject; (2) it has no verb. Words that end in *-ing* and seem like verbs are really *verbals*. Just remember that an *-ing* word can never function by itself as a verb, and you will stay out of trouble. To be a verb, the *-ing* word must have a helper:

Rosemary is running along the beach. (The word *is* is a helping verb.)

Because we have added a subject and a helping verb to the *-ing* word, we now have a clause.

Clauses are either *independent* or *dependent*.

2. Independent clause (IC). *An independent clause is a clause that makes a complete statement and therefore may stand alone as a sentence.*

Independent clauses: The monkey is brown.

The automobile runs smoothly.

Marilyn knows her.

(You) Close the door.

3. Dependent clause (DC). *A dependent clause is a clause that makes an incomplete statement and therefore may not stand alone as a sentence.*

Dependent clauses: *Although* the monkey is brown . . .

If the automobile runs smoothly . . .

. . . *whom* Marilyn knows.

After you close the door . . .

Dependent Clause

Notice that a dependent clause is not a sentence by itself. That is why it is dependent—it depends on an independent clause to make a complete, or even an intelligible, statement. By itself, a dependent clause does not make any sense.

This definition and the one above on independent clauses—though fairly standard, of course—may not satisfy you. Fortunately, we can offer another definition that works almost all the time (and the exceptions you don't need to worry about). A *dependent clause* almost always contains a subordinating conjunction or a relative pronoun (both covered later in this chapter; we've italicized them in the examples of dependent clauses above so you can see where they are. The subordinating conjunctions and relative pronouns are like red flags signaling dependent clauses. You can recognize an *independent clause,* then, because it's a clause not containing a subordinating conjunction or a relative pronoun.

4. Sentence. *A sentence is a group of words containing at least one independent clause.*

Sentences (independent clauses are underlined once):

Marilyn knows her.

Although Marilyn knows her, she does not know Marilyn.

After you close the door, Susan will turn on the record player, and Sally will get the potato chips.

5. Phrase (P). *A phrase is a group of two or more related words not containing both a subject and a verb.*

Phrases: in the submarine

running along the beach (remember, *-ing* words are not verbs)

6. Subordinating conjunction (SC). *A subordinating conjunction is a kind of word that begins a* dependent *clause.*

You should memorize the italicized words (which are quite common) in the list of subordinating conjunctions below.

after	how	though
although	*if*	unless
as	in order that	until
as if	inasmuch as	*when*
as long as	provided	whenever
as much as	provided that	where
as though	*since*	wherever
because	so that	whether
before	than	while

Here are some examples of subordinating conjunctions beginning dependent clauses (the dependent clauses are underlined twice):

SC

Because your horse is properly registered, it may run in the race.

SC

The race will be canceled <u>if the rain falls.</u>

SC

Sign up for the trip to Memphis <u>while vacancies still exist.</u>

7. Relative pronoun (RP). *A relative pronoun is a kind of word that marks a* dependent *clause.*

However, unlike a subordinating conjunction, it does not always come at the beginning of the dependent clause, although it usually does. You should memorize these five common relative pronouns:

who, whose, whom, which, that

Here are some examples of relative pronouns used in dependent clauses (the dependent clauses are underlined twice):

RP

The woman <u>who runs the bank</u> is registering her horse.

RP

The man <u>whose car lights are on</u> is in the grocery store.

RP

The woman <u>whom I met</u> is in the broker's office.

V

The schedule <u>with which I was familiar</u> is now obsolete.

RP

The schedule <u>that I knew</u> is now obsolete.

Sometimes, unfortunately, these same five words can function as words other than relative pronouns, in which case they *do not* mark dependent clauses:

Not relative pronouns: *Who* is that masked man?

Whose golf club is this?

Whom do you wish to see?

Which car is yours?

That car is mine.

As a general rule, unless they are part of a question, the four words in our list that begin with *w* (*who, whose, whom,* and *which*) are relative pronouns. The other word, *that,* is trickier, but we can generally say that unless it is pointing out something, it is a relative pronoun. In the sentence "That car is mine," *that* points out a car, so it is not a relative pronoun.

GENERALLY, THESE QUESTIONS ARE ANSWERED BY ADVERBS: HOW, WHEN, WHERE, WHY, : TO WHAT EXTENT

CA'S don't necessarily answer this

8. **Conjunctive adverb (CA).** *A conjunctive adverb is a kind of word that marks an* independent *clause.*

Many students make punctuation errors because they confuse subordinating conjunctions (which mark dependent clauses) with conjunctive adverbs (which mark independent clauses). You should memorize the italicized words (which are quite common) in the list of conjunctive adverbs below:

accordingly	*however*	next
as a result	indeed	otherwise
consequently	in fact	second
first	instead	still
for example	likewise	*therefore*
for instance	meanwhile	thus
furthermore	moreover	unfortunately
hence	*nevertheless*	

Transition Words

You may remember seeing some of these words in Chapter 5, "Coherence." A conjunctive adverb serves as a *transition,* showing the relationship between the independent clause it is in and the independent clause that preceded it.

A conjunctive adverb may not seem to mark an independent clause, but it does. The following examples are perfectly correct as sentences because they are independent clauses:

CA
Therefore, I am the winner.

CA
However, the car is red.

Often a conjunctive adverb begins the second independent clause in a sentence because that clause is closely related in meaning to the first independent clause:

CA
I finished in first place; therefore, I am the winner.

CA
You thought your new car would be blue; however, the car is metallic brown.

Sometimes a conjunctive adverb will appear in the middle or even at the end of a clause (that clause, of course, is still independent):

CA
I finished in first place; I am, therefore, the winner.

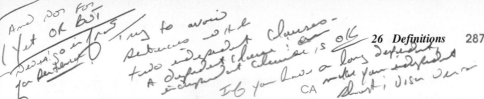

I finished in first place; I am the winner, therefore.

9. Coordinating conjunction (CC). *A coordinating conjunction is a word that joins two or more units that are grammatically alike.*

You should learn these seven coordinating conjunctions:

and, but, or, nor, for, so, yet

A helpful learning aid is that the coordinating conjunctions are all two or three letters long.

A coordinating conjunction can do the following:

                           CC

Join two or more words: Billy and Mary

                           CC

Join two or more phrases: in the car and beside the horse

                                                 CC

Join two or more dependent clauses: after the dance was over but before the party began

Join two or more independent clauses: He won the Philadelphia marathon,
                                                     CC
                                                  for he had been practicing several months.

Remember: Unlike subordinating conjunctions, relative pronouns, and conjunctive adverbs, the coordinating conjunction is not a marker for either an independent clause or a dependent clause. It simply joins two or more like items.

EXERCISES

In the sentences below, underline the independent clauses once and the dependent clauses twice. Then label all subordinating conjunctions (SC), relative pronouns (RP), conjunctive adverbs (CA), and coordinating conjunctions (CC).

1. Humphrey Bogart was Lauren Bacall's first husband.
2. Which Shakespeare play is your favorite?
3. When you go out, mail the rent check.
4. Although it has no nutritional value, fiber still affects nutrition, so high-fiber diets are worth considering.

5. Insoluble fibers reduce constipation, and soluble fibers help to produce a sense of fullness.

6. Because they provoke a sense of fullness or satisfaction and because they function as natural laxatives, fiber-rich foods are encouraged in weight reduction plans.

7. Sunshine is dangerous for unprotected skin; this does not mean that exposure to the sun is unacceptable, however.

8. Sir Walter Raleigh discovered and named Virginia.

9. Jackie Gleason and Art Carney made famous the characters Ralph Kramden and Ed Norton; Kramden was a bus driver, while Norton was a sewer worker.

10. Brisk walking may be all that is needed for a sound exercise program; this should be, however, a period dedicated to walking as an exercise.

11. In tiddlywinks the piece that you flip into the cup is the wink.

12. What are your plans for the summer?

13. Many people believe that they should continue playing sports even though they hurt; nevertheless, pain is a natural warning that they should heed.

14. Mammals have self-regulating body temperature, hair, and, in the females, glands to produce milk.

15. Herman kept the stereo very loud until his father threatened to cut off the power plug.

16. Emotions do affect health, and hard-driving, aggressive people appear to be prone to heart attacks.

17. Excitable, hurried people have an increased risk of heart problems; they can, however, reduce the risk by modifying their approach to life.

18. The dandelion's name comes from the French for "tooth of the lion."

19. In *The Mouse That Roared* the country of Grand Fenwick declares war on the United States so that the country can receive aid after losing the war.

20. "Low impact" aerobics involves reduced stress: nevertheless, it still includes impact.

21. Because he brought liberal reforms to the Soviet Union, Mikhail Gorbachev upset many old party bosses.

22. Remember to send the application before Monday.

23. William Styron's *The Confessions of Nat Turner* is about a black preacher who leads a slave revolt.

24. The Treaty of Versailles ended World War I.

25. James Michener won the 1948 Pulitzer Prize for *Tales of the South Pacific,* which is a collection of related short stories.

Chapter 27

Sentence Fragment

[handwritten: Preposition : IN ON —]
[handwritten: Prepositional Phrase — follows]
[handwritten: A preposition]

A sentence fragment is an error involving punctuation.

> **Sentence fragment (Frag).** *A sentence fragment is a group of words punctuated like a sentence but not containing an independent clause.*

Because it lacks an independent clause, a sentence fragment is just a piece of a sentence. Here are some examples:

Sentence fragments: Running along the beach.

Even though the movie won an Oscar.

See? These so-called sentences are really frauds: they begin with a capital letter and end with a period, but they don't contain an independent clause.

Usually a sentence fragment is very closely related to the sentence that preceded it. The two examples above might have appeared in the following contexts:

Sentence fragments: I finally found that stray mutt. Running along the beach.

Marie absolutely refused to go to the theater. Even though the movie had won an Oscar.

To correct a sentence fragment, either connect it to an independent clause or add a subject and a verb to convert it to an independent clause.

Fragments connected to independent clauses:

I finally found that stray mutt running along the beach.

Marie absolutely refused to go to the theater even though the movie had won an Oscar.

Fragments converted to independent clauses:

I finally found that stray mutt. He was running along the beach.

Marie absolutely refused to go to the theater. The movie had won an Oscar.

Of the two types of changes above, most readers would prefer the connection of the fragment to an independent clause. That solution provides smoother writing, avoiding the choppiness resulting from converting each fragment to its own independent clause. More important, however, the first solution increases coherence: connecting the fragment to an independent clause links the thought of the fragment to the thought of the independent clause.

Are fragments always wrong? No, of course not. Fragments are common in speech and appear in all types of writing. You'll find examples in this book because the writing was designed to communicate to you directly, as if the authors were speaking to you. Because fragments break the conventional pattern of writing, they can create a useful effect. For example, the second "sentence" of this paragraph—really a fragment—communicates the desired thought more directly and simply than would this sentence combination: "Are fragments always wrong? No, of course fragments are not always wrong." And because the fragment answers the question in the first sentence, there is no loss of coherence.

Cautions

- Fragments are never acceptable if they destroy coherence.
- Be aware of your probable readers. Some may never find fragments acceptable.
- Use fragments sparingly for good effect.

EXERCISES

A. Correct the fragments in each of the following sentence-fragment combinations in two ways:

1. The Canary Islands appear in legends. Seen as the highest peaks of the lost continent of Atlantis.

2. Milk is heavier than cream. Although many people guess the opposite.

3. Commonplace reading material in American barbershops once was the *National Police Gazette*. Printed on pink paper.

B. For each "sentence" below, indicate whether it is a complete sentence or only a fragment:

1. Turning white in winter.

2. Vichyssoise, sounding like an old European dish, having been invented for an American restaurant opening in 1910.

3. Seeds separated from the cotton in a cotton gin.

4. A fragment providing an incomplete thought.

5. Siberia's Lake Baikal is the deepest lake in the world.

6. A man with his hands covering his ears in Munch's famous painting *The Scream.*

7. In 1950 a "giant" television screen of 12 inches was introduced.

8. Are any peanuts left?

9. Because Harry Truman had bowling lanes installed in the White House.

10. We're almost there.

11. The mummified body of Francisco Pizarro residing in Lima, Peru.

12. So that astronaut John Glenn could see them, residents of Perth, Australia, turned on their lights.

13. After becoming popular on American college campuses in 1937, benzedrine, also known as pep pills.

14. You'll do.

15. Men being more prone than women to color blindness.

16. Amelia Earhart, called "Lady Lindy."

17. Named such because it sleeps at night.

18. A symbol used in calculating the area of a circle.

19. Most of the state's population residing on Oahu.

20. Turkey, named for what was thought to be its country of origin, although that wasn't true.

C. Correct the following sentence fragments:

1. In Naples, Italy, foreigners joke that traffic signals are only "recommendations." Because local drivers so often ignore traffic lights.

2. A manhole cover from the ancient Roman sewer system today is a tourist attraction. The reason being that the drainage hole is the mouth of a man's face and is supposed to bite the hand of anyone who tells a lie.

3. The manhole cover is named *Bocca della Verità,* or "Mouth of Truth." Because of the story about biting the hands of liars.

4. Rome's famous and emblematic "She Wolf" statue being actually from the Etruscans, with the figures of Romulus and Remus added in a later time.

5. The archaeological sites of Pompeii and Herculaneum never fail to fascinate visitors. Although the best of the artifacts are in a museum in downtown Naples rather than at the sites.

6. In Italian cities it is not unusual to see stray cats eating spaghetti. That being an inexpensive leftover that is readily available as cat food.

Chapter 28

Comma Splice and Fused Sentence

Comma splices and fused sentences are sentences that are punctuated incorrectly.

1. Comma splice (CS). *A comma splice occurs when two independent clauses are joined by only a comma.*

In other words, it is two independent clauses "spliced" together with only a comma. Using the abbreviation IC for independent clause, we can express the comma splice as follows:

Comma splice: IC,IC

Here are some comma splice errors:

Wrong: We hiked for three days, we were very tired.

Wrong: The television is too loud, the picture is fuzzy.

Correcting Comma Splices

There are five ways to correct a comma splice.

1. Change the comma to a period and capitalize the next word. (IC. IC.)
   Correct: We hiked for three days. We were very tired.

2. Change the comma to a semicolon. (IC;IC.)
   Correct: We hiked for three days; we were very tired.

3. Change the comma to a semicolon and add a conjunctive adverb. (IC;CA,IC.)

Correct: We hiked for three days; hence, we were very tired.

4.   Add a coordinating conjunction before the second independent clause. (IC,CC IC.)

Correct: We hiked for three days, so we were very tired.

5.   Change one independent clause to a dependent clause. (DC,IC.)

Correct: Because we hiked for three days, we were very tired.

A very common form of comma splice occurs when only a comma precedes a conjunctive adverb at the beginning of the second independent clause in a sentence.

Wrong: Mount Rainier is beautiful, however, it is also forbidding.

The best way to correct this kind of comma splice is to change the first comma to a semicolon. (IC;CA,IC.)

Correct: Mount Rainier is beautiful; however, it is also forbidding.

Another form of comma splice occurs when two independent clauses are separated by a dependent clause but the strongest mark of punctuation is still only a comma.

Wrong: The artist is selling the portrait, because he does not have enough money, he has run out of paint.

How would you correct the above sentence? Does the writer mean that the artist is selling the portrait because he does not have enough money? Or does the writer mean the artist has run out of paint because he does not have enough money? Here is one instance in which correct punctuation is important to meaning. One of several ways to correct the sentence is to place a period on the appropriate side of the dependent clause, depending on the meaning you wish to express. (IC DC.IC.) or (IC.DC,IC.)

Correct: The artist is selling the portrait because he does not have enough money. He has run out of paint.

Correct: The artist is selling the portrait. Because he does not have enough money, he has run out of paint.

2. Fused sentence (FS). *A fused sentence occurs when two independent clauses are joined without punctuation or a coordinating conjunction.*

In other words, a fused sentence is a comma splice without the comma.

Fused sentence: IC IC.

Here are some fused sentence errors:

Wrong: We hiked for three days we were very tired.

Wrong: The television is too loud the picture is fuzzy.

Correcting Fused Sentences

Correct a fused sentence with essentially the same methods you used to correct a comma splice:

1. Add a period after the first independent clause and capitalize the next word. (IC. IC.)

   Correct: The television is too loud. The picture is fuzzy.

2. Add a semicolon after the first independent clause. (IC;IC.)

   Correct: The television is too loud; the picture is fuzzy.

3. Add a semicolon and a conjunctive adverb after the first independent clause. (IC;CA,IC.)

   Correct: The television is too loud; furthermore, the picture is fuzzy.

4. Add a comma and a coordinating conjunction after the first independent clause. (IC,CC IC.)

   Correct: The television is too loud, and the picture is fuzzy.

5. Change one independent clause to a dependent clause. (DC,IC.)

   Correct: Whenever the television is too loud, the picture is fuzzy.

EXERCISES

A. Correct the following comma splice in five different ways: *Lonesome Dove* won the Pulitzer Prize for fiction in 1986, the judges recognized that Larry McMurtry wrote much more than a cowboy tale.

B. Correct the following fused sentence in five different ways: McMurtry received critical attention for *The Last Picture Show* and *Terms of Endearment* both of these were made into very successful movies.

C. For each sentence below, write *CS* if the sentence has a comma splice, *FS* if it is a fused sentence, or *Correct* if it is correct.

1. _____ Larry McMurtry also wrote *Horseman, Pass By* it was filmed as *Hud*.

2. _____ McMurtry has written that he thought *Horseman, Pass By* would be a memorable title, but he found that even his friends had trouble getting the title right.

3. _____ Because *Horseman, Pass By* seemed to be too literary Paramount Studios wanted to change the title *Hud* was the final compromise.

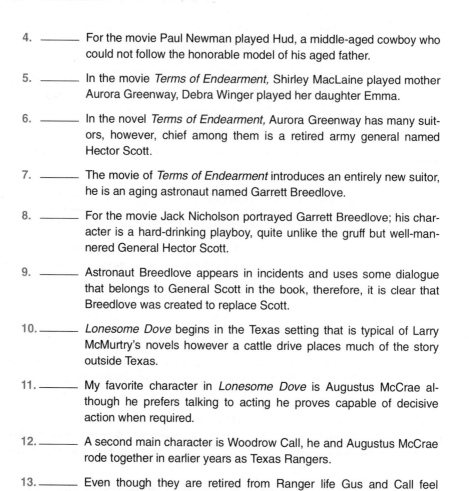

4. _____ For the movie Paul Newman played Hud, a middle-aged cowboy who could not follow the honorable model of his aged father.

5. _____ In the movie *Terms of Endearment,* Shirley MacLaine played mother Aurora Greenway, Debra Winger played her daughter Emma.

6. _____ In the novel *Terms of Endearment,* Aurora Greenway has many suitors, however, chief among them is a retired army general named Hector Scott.

7. _____ The movie of *Terms of Endearment* introduces an entirely new suitor, he is an aging astronaut named Garrett Breedlove.

8. _____ For the movie Jack Nicholson portrayed Garrett Breedlove; his character is a hard-drinking playboy, quite unlike the gruff but well-mannered General Hector Scott.

9. _____ Astronaut Breedlove appears in incidents and uses some dialogue that belongs to General Scott in the book, therefore, it is clear that Breedlove was created to replace Scott.

10. _____ *Lonesome Dove* begins in the Texas setting that is typical of Larry McMurtry's novels however a cattle drive places much of the story outside Texas.

11. _____ My favorite character in *Lonesome Dove* is Augustus McCrae although he prefers talking to acting he proves capable of decisive action when required.

12. _____ A second main character is Woodrow Call, he and Augustus McCrae rode together in earlier years as Texas Rangers.

13. _____ Even though they are retired from Ranger life Gus and Call feel compelled to uphold law much as they did in their Texas Ranger days.

14. _____ Gus and Call delay the start of their cattle drive until they can be joined by Jake Spoon, although he also had been a Ranger, Jake's difficulty with ethics proves his undoing.

15. _____ Larry McMurtry's novels often feature a boy who must learn the ways of the world in *Lonesome Dove* that character is a boy named Newt.

16. _____ Because it could not be an epic of the American West without a good-hearted barmaid of loose virtue, *Lonesome Dove* includes Lorena, she actually has little interest in pursuing her trade.

17. _____ Lorena's chief interest is getting to San Francisco, where she believes life will be better, because men offer passage west, much of Lorena's life is spent accompanying them.

18. _____ Most of the cowboys Gus and Call hire for their cattle drive are boys from neighboring ranches; however, the most unlikely cowboys on the

drive are Allen and Sean O'Brien, two Irish tenderfeet they pick up lost in Mexico.

19. _____ Two interesting minor characters in *Lonesome Dove* are a pair of blue pigs that apparently will eat almost anything they are devouring a rattlesnake when the story opens.

20. _____ *The Last Picture Show* features two boys entering manhood in a small Texas town in the 1950s, in *Texasville,* however, the same characters and town reappear in the 1980s.

21. _____ Although *Texasville* repeats primary characters from *The Last Picture Show,* critics have complained that the *Texasville* characters have little in common with their counterparts from the earlier novel.

22. _____ The passing of thirty years between the time settings of the two novels causes significant differences in the situations of the main characters, nevertheless, both *Texasville* and *The Last Picture Show* deal with similar themes.

23. _____ In *The Last Picture Show* Sonny Crawford and Duane Moore are coming of age, while they are struggling with middle age in *Texasville.*

24. _____ In a series of essays published as *In a Narrow Grave: Essays on Texas,* Larry McMurtry discusses the passing away of the ideals of the Old West, clearly many of his novels deal with the same theme.

25. _____ Although *Horseman, Pass By, The Last Picture Show,* and *Texasville* focus on the loss of the Old West, *Lonesome Dove*—which shows the passing—celebrates the older ways, perhaps that celebration explains the appeal of *Lonesome Dove.*

D. Choose three sentences with comma splices and three fused sentences from exercise C and rewrite them.

Chapter 29

Comma

This chapter presents the nine most important uses of the comma (,).

1. Use a comma after every item in a series except the last item.

Example: The ethics of contemporary surgery are often a problem for the patient, the doctor, and the patient's family.

You probably already knew to put a comma after the first item (*patient* in this case), but why do you need one after the next-to-last item (*doctor*)? Consider this example:

Example: The ethics of contemporary surgery are often a problem for the patient, the doctor and the hospital board, and the patient's family.

Commas tell your readers that you are moving to the next item in a series. When you omit a comma, you're telling them you're still in that same item—a compound item—so they won't have to reread your sentence.

2. Use a comma before a coordinating conjunction that joins two independent clauses. (IC,CC IC.)

and, nor, for, but, yet

Examples: I never liked parsnips, but my mother made me eat them.

She thought they were great, and she thought they would make

me grow taller.

Note: Do not confuse a coordinating conjunction that joins two verbs with a coordinating conjunction that joins two independent clauses.

S   V   CC   V

The parsnips tasted awful and looked like paste.

The coordinating conjunction above is not preceded by a comma because it connects only the two verbs *tasted* and *looked.*

3. Use a comma after a dependent clause that begins a sentence. (DC,IC.)

DC   IC

Examples: Although Harriet tried as hard as she could, she could not

win even a fun-run.

DC   IC

Because she couldn't run fast enough, she couldn't have the free

T-shirt we awarded to the first 200 runners to cross the finish line.

4. Use a comma after a long phrase that begins a sentence. (Long phrase, IC.)

The word *long* is rather vague, of course, but usually you will wish to place a comma after an introductory phrase of three or more words.

Long phrase

Examples: Even after a grueling night of writing, I didn't get the paper entirely finished.

Long phrase

Running to my next class, I tried to think of an excuse to give my professor.

5. Use commas to set off any word, phrase, or clause that interrupts the flow of the sentence.

In other words, if you could set off a word or group of words with parentheses but do not wish to, then set off that word or group of words with commas.

Examples: My excuse, wild as it was, didn't sound convincing.
The class, together with the professor, turned their heads as I plowed into the classroom.
John, who has the seat next to mine, laughed at me as I sat down.
The professor ignored me as he finished the course, "Freshman English for Nonconformists."

Notice that interrupters in the middle of sentences have commas on *both* sides.

[handwritten margin note, top: Two independent Clauses not joined by a Coordinating Conjunction — and combined using a ;.]

[handwritten margin note: Veteran writers don't get this one. M.M.]

6. Use commas to set off nonrestrictive clauses.

This rule is actually an expansion of rule 5, because all nonrestrictive clauses are interrupters. You may wonder, though, just what restrictive and nonrestrictive clauses are.

A *restrictive clause* is essential to defining whatever it modifies. In the following example, let's assume you have several brothers:

My brother *who is wearing a red motorcycle helmet* is meaner than I am.

The restrictive clause ("who is wearing a red motorcycle helmet") is essential because it tells us which of your several brothers is meaner than you are. It *restricts* the word *brother* from any one of your brothers to the one wearing the helmet. If you left out the restrictive clause, we would not know which brother you meant. You probably noticed that these restrictive clauses are not interrupters and, therefore, are not set off with commas.

A *nonrestrictive clause* is not essential in defining whatever it modifies. Since it is not essential, you could omit it and everybody would still know who (or what) you are talking about. Now let's assume that you have only one brother:

My brother, *who is wearing a red motorcycle helmet,* is meaner than I am.

Because you have only one brother, you could omit the nonrestrictive clause and still make sense. The word modified—*brother*—is not *limited* in any way by the clause; it is only described in more detail. In other words, without the clause we still know which brother you're talking about. Set off these nonrestrictive clauses with commas.

7. Use a comma after a conjunctive adverb unless it is the last word in the sentence. (CA,IC.) or (IC;CA,IC.)

[handwritten margin note: You will not comma out]

This rule applies no matter where the conjunctive adverb appears within the sentence.

[handwritten margin note: Use which only when Clause is restrictive]

[handwritten margin note: If you're being a while — See if a that would be better — the See if you could do without THAT.]

```
                                    IC
         ┌────────────────────────────────┐  CA  ┌──────┐
Examples:  The beautiful young princess kissed the frog. However, his lily
                                    IC
         ┌────────────────────────────────┐
         pad started sinking when she stepped on it.
                                    IC
         ┌────────────────────────────────┐  CA  ┌──────┐
         The beautiful young princess kissed the frog; however, his lily
                                    IC
         ┌────────────────────────────────┐
         pad started sinking when she stepped on it.
                                    IC
         ┌──────────────────────────────┐ ┌─
         The beautiful young princess kissed the frog; his lily pad,
            CA                         IC
         ┌────────────────────────────────┐
         however, started sinking when she stepped on it.
```

Note: If, as in the last example, the conjunctive adverb is in the middle of the independent clause, it will have commas on *both* sides of it.

8. Use a comma between coordinate adjectives unless they are joined by "and."

Coordinate adjectives are sets of adjectives that independently modify a noun.

Example: The bulldog is noted for its wrinkled, flattened face.

Both *wrinkled* and *flattened* modify *face* independently. That is not the case with cumulative adjectives. When an adjective's modification is cumulative, it modifies not only the noun but also the whole adjective-noun phrase it precedes.

Example: Alicia wore a red felt hat.

Here *red* modifies not just *hat* but the phrase *felt hat.* Notice that no comma is used with cumulative adjectives.

Coordinate and Cumulative Adjectives

Distinguishing between coordinate and cumulative adjectives isn't always simple. However, because of the independence of coordinate adjectives, you can check for two characteristics that help identify them.

- Coordinate adjectives are reversible, whereas cumulative adjectives aren't. That is, *flattened, wrinkled face* works as well as *wrinkled, flattened face.* On the other hand, *felt red hat* just sounds foolish.
- *And* fits naturally between coordinate adjectives, but not between cumulative adjectives. Thus, you could write *wrinkled and flattened face* but not *red and felt hat.*

Of course, modifier chains can include both coordinate and cumulative adjectives.

Example: The stands were full for the homecoming game even though it was a cold, rainy autumn day.

Cold and *rainy* are coordinate and are separated by a comma. However, both modify *autumn day* rather than just *day,* so there is no comma after *rainy.*

9. Use a comma to set off words in direct address.

Words in direct address normally are names but can be phrases used in place of names.

Examples: Kristina, have you washed the dishes?
Where are you going now, little sister?
You look charming, Alicia, wearing that red felt hat.

Notice that the word in direct address in the last example has commas on *both* sides because it occurs in the middle of the sentence.

EXERCISES

A. For each pair of sentences below, answer the accompanying questions.

   1. Which of the following implies that there were more topics but the Secretary of State covered only the three high-interest ones?

     a. The Secretary of State briefed the President on the three topics which were of extremely high interest.

     b. The Secretary of State briefed the President on the three topics, which were of extremely high interest.

   2. Which sentence indicates that there will be no questions at all (because the Research Department has prepared well)? Which sentence implies that the board members are likely to attack some of the Research Department's initiatives?

     a. The board members are not likely to question the Research Department's initiatives, which are generally well prepared.

     b. The board members are not likely to question the Research Department's initiatives which are generally well prepared.

   3. Which sentence implies that there was at least one version of the competency test before the one mandated in 1986?

     a. The high school competency test, which was mandated in 1986, has changed the way teachers do their jobs.

     b. The high school competency test which was mandated in 1986 has changed the way teachers do their jobs.

B. In the following sentences, add commas where necessary.

   1. Juan do you know which part Peter Lorre played in *Casablanca*?

   2. Alligators have broad short snouts but crocodiles have longer more pointed snouts.

   3. My little brother brought home two large hairy stray dogs and asked if he could keep them.

   4. As a result Sir Walter Raleigh was buried with a pipe and tobacco.

   5. Authorities say that truckers who drive unsafe rigs cause most of the accidents on the Beltway. (Punctuate to imply that all truckers drive unsafe equipment.)

   6. Authorities say that truckers who drive unsafe rigs cause most of the accidents on the Beltway. (Punctuate to imply that some truckers have safe rigs.)

   7. *Pâté de foie gras* hard as it is to say sounds more appetizing than goose liver.

8. No matter how rushed, don't miss the *David* in Florence.

9. Although they aren't the best known, and certainly aren't designed for quick reference, the Blue Guide tour books offer the best in-depth coverage of European cities.

10. The six possible murder weapons in *Clue* are a candlestick, a knife, a lead pipe, a revolver, a rope and a wrench.

11. Enrico thought he had impressed the charming elegant woman but that was before he tripped and spilled red wine on her gown.

12. The board has requested therefore that all tenants wait until morning before putting their garbage bags outside.

13. Lee Harvey Oswald who was accused of shooting John F. Kennedy was himself shot only two days after the assassination.

14. Even though he ruled Bavaria for only twenty-two years Ludwig II was responsible for constructing three magnificent castles today among the most visited spots in southern Germany.

15. Ludwig II of Bavaria built the castles of Neuschwanstein Linderhof and Herrenchiemsee.

16. Was Goya Spanish or Italian Rosalie?

17. Tourists who show proper respect are welcome in the churches of Italy. (Punctuate to imply that not all tourists show proper respect.)

18. Tourists who show proper respect are welcome in the churches of Italy. (Punctuate to imply that all tourists show proper respect.)

19. Although he made his name in music with *Cats Evita* and *Starlight Express* Andrew Lloyd Webber changed style dramatically in 1984 with *Requiem* a work in very traditional style.

20. Rated at 550 times the sweetness of sugar saccharin was the basis of the diet food industry for years.

21. Simone was dressed for success in a dark gray wool suit; however she hadn't noticed the ink splotch on her blouse.

22. Named for a Cuban city a daiquiri is composed of rum lime and sugar.

23. I visited Rome four times over a three-year period yet I was never able to see Trajan's Column because it was covered by scaffolding and drapes; however I was able to see a copy of it in London's Victoria and Albert Museum.

24. When you look for the airport in Rome Harry you'll have to remember that some highway signs say "Leonardo da Vinci" but others say "Fulmacino."

25. The most widely used seasoning in the world salt is not always the safest seasoning.

26. If you visit Rome don't miss the Trevi Fountain only a few blocks from the Spanish Steps.

27. A number of U.S. presidents have been shot in office; however Ronald Reagan was the first incumbent to survive being shot.

28. Because they didn't understand what being "chief" meant in many Indian tribal organizations Americans often didn't deal with leaders who actually had the type of control the whites believed they had.

29. Of the ruins recovered from the A.D. 79 eruption of Vesuvius Pompeii best shows the religious social and political aspects of Roman life and Herculaneum provides the best sense of living structures.

30. Herculaneum shows well the range of building styles for homes and even has remnants of wood and fabric from A.D. 79.

Chapter 30

Semicolon

The semicolon (;) is stronger than a comma but weaker than a period. This chapter presents the three most important uses of the semicolon.

1. Use a semicolon between two independent clauses closely related in meaning but not joined by a coordinating conjunction. (IC;IC.)

IC   IC

Examples: Lee won some battles; Grant won the war.

IC   IC

The pale sun rose over the frozen land; the arctic fox gazed

quietly at the sky.

2. Use a semicolon between two independent clauses when the second independent clause is joined to the first with a conjunctive adverb. (IC;CA,IC.)

IC

CA

Examples: Auto theft is a major national crime; however, people keep

IC

leaving their cars unlocked.

IC   CA   IC

Most stolen cars are recovered; unfortunately, many have been

vandalized.

Note: If a conjunctive adverb is moved from the beginning of the second independent clause into the middle of it, the conjunctive adverb is then preceded by a comma instead of a semicolon; the semicolon, however, remains between the independent clauses.

```
                              IC
        ┌────────────────────────┐ ┌──       CA       ──────┐
```

Example: Most stolen cars are recovered; many, unfortunately, have been

```
        ┌────────────────┐
```

vandalized.

3. When commas occur within one or more of the items in a series, use semicolons rather than commas to separate the items in the series.

Commas normally separate the items, with the commas clearly indicating where each portion of the series begins and ends. When any portion needs its own commas, however, readers may become confused if commas separate the portions of the series.

Confusing: Key air routes include Lisbon, Portugal, Rome, Italy, Frankfurt, Germany, and Istanbul, Turkey.

Readers with a good sense of world geography probably would understand this sample. However, you can make the readers' job easier by using semicolons to separate the major items in the series.

Better: Key air routes include Lisbon, Portugal; Rome, Italy; Frankfurt, Germany; and Istanbul, Turkey.

This way readers won't have to reread to understand the structure of the series.

EXERCISES

A. In the following sentences, add semicolons and commas where necessary.

1. Rosencrantz and Guildenstern have very minor roles in Shakespeare's *Hamlet* in Tom Stoppard's *Rosencrantz and Guildenstern Are Dead* however they become the chief characters.

2. Some software companies devise complicated programming schemes to prevent copying of their programs nevertheless other companies market software packages to permit users to copy those protected programs.

3. Leon's cousins live in Indianapolis Indiana Omaha Nebraska and Colorado Springs Colorado.

4. General George Patton slapped a private one Paul Bennett because of the outcry that resulted George Patton was forced to apologize publicly.

5. Garrison Keillor has written humorously but also precisely about small towns in America several times as I read about Lake Wobegon I caught myself reaching for an atlas to see where the town is in Minnesota.

6. Ancient Romans liked their dining rooms to open onto a pleasant garden people too poor to afford a real garden sometimes had one painted on the walls of the dining room instead.

7. Romans built walls with rubble core and they found that adding mortar to the rubble strengthened the wall over time this practice brought about the development of concrete.

8. To deal with housing shortages Roman engineers developed an inexpensive rapid-construction building style for which square wooden frames were filled with rough stones and mortar although the Romans didn't consider this type of building permanent one such house at Herculaneum has survived over 1,900 years.

9. As he strode into the village Luis saw old women most dressed all in black old men all wearing the clothes of farm laborers and a few small children.

10. Live television can create embarrassing moments for example many fans of *The Tonight Show* even ones who didn't actually see the show remember Ed Ames for throwing a badly aimed tomahawk.

11. Dolby technology advanced the state of art of tape players by reducing significant levels of background noise compact disc players however went a step further by eliminating almost all background noise.

12. For several years I thought compact disc players were just another electronic toy but I've changed my mind since I heard the clarity of the music they produce.

13. Because playing a compact disc causes no wear on the disc many people believe that compact discs are indestructible in fact manufacturers warn that the disc itself is subject to damage from improper handling.

14. For high school graduation my parents bought me a passport a round-trip airplane ticket to Europe and a Eurorail Pass I spent two months traveling in France Germany and Italy.

15. Humphrey Bogart had important roles in the 1950s including his Oscar-winning part in *The African Queen* but he's admired most for his films of the 1940s: *The Maltese Falcon Casablanca To Have and Have Not* and *The Big Sleep*.

16. Bogart and Lauren Bacall worked together well in *The Big Sleep* however the attraction between the two in *To Have and Have Not* clearly demonstrates why their partnership was so effective.

17. When Kerry prayed at night she was careful to include her three aunts in Hawaii her only uncle a relative stranger she had met only once and who also lived in Hawaii and her grandparents though all four were dead.

18. Michelangelo's *Pietà* is still on display in St. Peter's but it is less visible than it was prior to 1972 today the art treasure sits behind a bulletproof glass wall that was erected after an individual attacked the statue with a hammer.

19. For hundreds of years residents of Rome believed that Peter's tomb lay directly beneath St. Peter's Basilica excavations beneath St. Peter's have provided considerable evidence that this popular belief was true.

20. Because of the media attention they receive, few U.S. presidents today can avoid being criticized for some simple act or comment that meant little at the time Lyndon Johnson learned this when the media saw him pick up a pet beagle by the ears.

Chapter 31

Colon

There are many rules for the colon, several of them relatively obscure. But there is one important rule you should know:

Use a colon after the last independent clause in a sentence to point to some more useful information about what you just said.

Virtually any grammatical unit can then follow the colon:

- a word or phrase
- a series of words or phrases
- a dependent clause
- an independent clause (or sentence)
- even a series of independent clauses or sentences

Examples:

The used car had one large defect: no engine.

The used car had three large defects: no tires, no brakes, no engine.

She sold the car for good reason: because it had no engine.

She sold the car for good reason: it had no engine.

She sold the car for three good reasons: It had no tires. It had no brakes. It had no engine.

When you have one entire sentence after the colon, should you capitalize the first letter of that sentence? There's no real standard: some people do and some people don't. (*Or* There's no real standard: *Some* people do and some people don't.) When you have a *series of sentences* after the colon, though, you should begin each with a capital letter.

The rule in this chapter says to put a colon after an independent clause. There are ways to put colons after only words, phrases, and dependent clauses. However, we suggest you learn and apply the one simple rule we give you: it can do wonderful things for your writing.

You should avoid unnecessary colons, however. If your sentence would read fine with no punctuation at all where you have a colon, simply leave the colon out. Here are some examples of incorrect colons:

He bought: two bicycle tires, a bicycle pump, and a tire repair kit.

The weather radar showed the blizzard was: crossing the Rocky Mountains, heading for Kansas, and building up strength.

EXERCISES

A. Write five sentences using a colon correctly. Follow the colon with these grammatical units (using a different grammatical unit for each of the five sentences you write):

- a word or phrase
- a series of words or phrases
- a dependent clause
- an independent clause (or sentence)
- a series of independent clauses or sentences

B. What different effects do these two sentences have?

She worked all weekend for one reason: money.
She worked all weekend for money.

C. In the following sentences, add colons where appropriate.

1. The leaves fell slowly from the trees the people were even slower raking the leaves.

2. Most places don't let people burn leaves for two good reasons the danger of fire and the pollution to the air.

3. Most places don't let people burn leaves because of the danger of fire and the pollution to the air.

4. The tie was tight around the boxer's neck he preferred being in the gym.

5. The two boxers glared ferociously at one another showing one primal emotion hatred.

6. The two boxers glared ferociously at one another showing the primal emotions of hatred and fear.

7. The rugby shirt had many colors burgundy, green, white, and blue.

8. The rugby shirt had one dominant color blue.

9. The rugby shirts were popular because they were colorful, rugged, and cheap.

10. The rugby shirts were popular for three reasons because they were colorful, because they were rugged, and because they were cheap.

Chapter 32

Dash

Years ago, people considered the dash too informal for most writing other than letters home. Today, though, the dash has come into its own—it's an extremely handy mark if you want to give a slightly more personal feeling to your writing. If you want to close the gap between you and the readers, use dashes. If you want to widen the gap, don't.

We'll discuss two common rules for the dash. Notice that the first rule we discuss is identical to the one we gave you for the colon (but—yes—the dash gives a more personal feeling).

1. Use a dash after the last independent clause in a sentence to point to some more useful information about what you just said.

Virtually any grammatical unit can then follow the dash (though not normally a series of independent clauses):

- a word or phrase
- a series of words or phrases
- a dependent clause
- an independent clause (or sentence)

Examples:

The used car had one large defect—no engine.

The used car had three large defects—no tires, no brakes, no engine.

She sold the car for good reason—because it had no engine.

She sold the car for good reason—it had no engine.

2. Use a dash in the same place you could use parentheses to set off some useful information in the middle of a sentence.

In the following sentences notice these points:

- The dashes add emphasis to the words they set off.
- The parentheses take emphasis away, making the words set off like a whispered aside.
- The commas provide standard emphasis.

With dashes: The store—the one around the corner—was robbed again.

With parentheses: The store (the one around the corner) was robbed again.

With commas: The store, the one around the corner, was robbed again.

Note: A dash is a line that's a little longer than a hyphen. So . . . how should you make a dash on a typewriter? A typewriter has only a hyphen (-) but not a dash (—). There are three ways:

- You can make a dash - which isn't on a typewriter - by using a hyphen with spaces on each side, as in this sentence.
- You can make a dash--this way--with two hyphens in a row (and no space at all on either side).
- Or you can make a dash -- this way -- with two hyphens in a row and a space before and after each set of hyphens.

Your choice.

EXERCISES

A. Write four sentences using a dash correctly. Follow the dash with these grammatical units (using a different grammatical unit for each of the four sentences you write):

- a word or phrase
- a series of words or phrases
- a dependent clause
- an independent clause (or sentence)

B. Write four sentences, with dashes, that have useful information in the middle of the sentence. The topic? Four different places you'd like to visit on a vacation.

C. What different effects do these two sentences have?

She worked all weekend for one reason—money.
She worked all weekend for one reason: money.

D. What different effects do these two sentences have?

The August breeze—surprisingly chilly—made spring seem far away.

The August breeze (surprisingly chilly) made spring seem far away.

E. In the following sentences, add dashes or colons where appropriate.

1. The mirror the one with small cracks running through it said the queen was the fairest in the land.

2. The queen was beautiful on the outside, but that beauty concealed an inner and ugly spirit.

3. The tree had a reminder of summer a single leaf.

4. The leaf looking like a brown scrap was clinging despite a terrific snowstorm.

5. Leaves normally fall during autumn not during winter.

6. The brick house the one with white, peeling paint was the oldest one on the block.

7. The house was really old it was built in 1723.

8. The house preceded one of our nation's key events the Revolutionary War.

9. The slipper tossed around the den by a new puppy was no longer useful.

10. The puppy was no longer very popular, either it had eaten a Gucci slipper.

Chapter 33

Apostrophe

The apostrophe (') is, for very good reason, one of the most neglected marks of punctuation. Unlike other punctuation marks, the apostrophe can usually be omitted without any loss of meaning. Because it is still an accepted convention of our language, however, we should know its two important uses.

1. Use an apostrophe to show possession.

Examples: Sara's silver Honda
the dog's fleas

Note A: To form the possessive, follow these general rules:

(1) If the word does not end in an *s,* add an apostrophe and an *s*:

Base word: carpet

Possessive: carpet's design

(2) If the word ends in an *s,* add only an apostrophe (though adding an apostrophe and an *s* is correct, too):

Base word: dolls

Possessive: three dolls' dresses

Notice that if the word is singular, you simply apply these rules. If the word is to be plural, however, you make the word plural first, and then apply the rules.

Examples: dog (singular)
a dog's fleas (singular possessive)
two dogs (plural)
two dogs' fleas (plural possessive)

Note B: Some words—particularly those expressing units of time—may not seem possessive but still require an apostrophe:

Examples: a day's work
seven minutes' delay
a month's pay

Note C: Do not use an apostrophe to show possession for personal pronouns *(yours, his, hers, its, ours, theirs).*

Wrong: It's shell is broken.

Correct: Its shell is broken.

2. Use an apostrophe to show that letters have been left out of a word.

Examples: *can not* becomes *can't*
do not becomes *don't*
does not becomes *doesn't*
I will becomes *I'll*
let us becomes *let's*
it is becomes *it's*

Note: The word *it's,* by the way, has only two meanings: "it is" or "it has."

EXERCISES

A. Form the singular and plural possessives of these words:

	singular possessive	*plural possessive*
second		
piano		
chairman		
elephant		
train		
week		
terra-cotta		
potato		
scissors		
engine		

B. Add the necessary apostrophes to these sentences:

1. Shelley said its been too long since weve visited my family or hers.

2. Zelda Fitzgeralds life is described in Nancy Mitfords *Zelda*.

3. Lisa didnt know that Mount McKinley is the United States highest mountain.

4. The squirrel collected its seeds into a small pile on the sheds roof.

5. The sound wasnt clear because one of the speakers wires was loose.

6. I dont know whether its true, but Janet claims that her neighbors dog has been howling for three nights.

7. As we slowly climbed the monasterys steps, we looked forward to seeing the chapels mosaic floor.

8. Germanys invasion of Poland in 1939 proved the might of the modern worlds weapons.

9. Lets discuss your companys offer over tomorrows lunch.

10. Its been too long since we visited that hunting cabin of yours.

11. After two days sightseeing in Florence wed seen the Baptistrys famous doors, the Uffizis paintings, and Michelangelos *David* in the Academy Gallery.

12. Enid indicated he wouldnt tolerate a seconds delay in making the stock his.

13. When you check the car to see if its finish was damaged by last nights hail, move the car back to its proper parking place.

14. Jacob stopped at the jewelers shop to see if both girls bracelets were engraved.

15. If that scarf is yours, see that its put away immediately.

Chapter 34

Quotation Marks

This chapter presents the two important uses of quotation marks (" ") and three rules for using other punctuation within quotation marks.

1. Use quotation marks to enclose the exact words written or spoken by someone else.

Example: Irving Knoke stated, "If someone is looking for an easy way to commit suicide, all he needs to do is stick his thumb out on any road."

2. Use quotation marks to enclose the title of a poem, short story, magazine article, or newspaper article.

In other words, use quotation marks to enclose the title of a work that is published as part of another work. Poems and short stories are rarely published separately; rather, they are usually part of a book that includes other poems or stories. Similarly, magazine articles appear as part of a magazine, and newspaper articles appear as part of a newspaper.

Note: The book, magazine, or newspaper title—that is, the title of the larger work containing the poem, short story, or article—should be underlined (or italicized).

Examples: "The Lottery," *Learning Fiction* (a short story in a collection of fiction)

"The Love Song of J. Alfred Prufrock," *Poetry for First Graders* (a poem in a collection of poetry)

"The Problems of Bigamy," *Gentlemen's Weekly Journal* (an article in a magazine)

"Mayor Silvers wins again!" *Cripple Creek News* (an article in a newspaper)

The following rules explain how to use other punctuation with quotation marks:

1. Always place periods and commas inside quotation marks.

Examples: I enjoyed reading "The Lottery."
I just read "The Lottery," a strange story by Shirley Jackson.

2. Always place semicolons and colons outside quotation marks.

Examples: I just read "The Lottery"; it is weird.
There are three really interesting characters in "The Lottery": Mrs. Hutchinson, Old Man Warner, and Mr. Summers.

3. A. Place question marks and exclamation points inside quotation marks if the quotation is a question or an exclamation.

Examples: Tessie Hutchinson yelled, "That's not fair!"
The crowd answered, "Why do you say that, Tessie?"

Note: This rule applies even if the sentence is also a question or an exclamation.

Example: Was the crowd afraid of something when it asked Tessie, "Why do you say that, Tessie?"

B. Place question marks and exclamation points outside quotation marks if the sentence is a question or an exclamation but the quotation is not.

Examples: Who just said, "Steak fries are good"?
I can't believe you said, "Steak fries are better than noodles"!

EXERCISES

A. Add the necessary quotation marks in these sentences. Be careful to place quotation marks clearly inside or outside any other punctuation.

1. I'm particularly fond of three short stories by H. H. Munro, who wrote under the name Saki: Sredni Vashtar, about a boy and his pet ferret; Tobermory, about a cat who talks; and Mrs. Packeltide's Tiger, about a wealthy woman and her tiger skin.

2. In the story Sredni Vashtar, the title character is a polecat-ferret that is being kept by a boy named Conradin.

3. When Conradin's cousin and keeper, Mrs. de Ropp, notices the time Conradin spends at the toolshed, she asks, What are you keeping in that locked hutch?

4. After Mrs. de Ropp looks in the toolshed to find out Conradin's secret, only the ferret leaves the shed; Munro describes the exiting ferret this way: out through

that doorway came a long, low, yellow-and-brown beast, with eyes a-blink at the waning daylight, and dark wet stains around the fur of jaws and throat.

5. Do you know why Mrs. de Ropp's maid says, Whoever will break it to the poor child?

6. The maid also explains, I couldn't for the life of me!

7. In H. H. Munro's Tobermory, the main character is the house cat of Sir Wilfrid and Lady Blemley; a guest at their house party has taught the cat to talk.

8. After looking for Tobermory to give a demonstration, Sir Wilfrid returns to his guests saying this about Tobermory: by Gad! he drawled out in a most horribly natural voice, that he'd come when he dashed well pleased! I nearly jumped out of my skin!

9. Mavis Pellington makes the mistake of asking Tobermory this: What do you think of human intelligence?

10. Tobermory counters, Of whose intelligence in particular?

11. When Mavis makes clear she is asking about her own intelligence, Tobermory replies, Sir Wilfrid protested that you were the most brainless woman of his acquaintance, and that there was a wide distinction between hospitality and the care of the feeble-minded.

12. Why does Major Barfield try to change the subject by asking, How about your carryings-on with the tortoise-shell puss up at the stables, eh?

13. Tobermory causes general panic at the house party when he answers, From a slight observation of your ways since you've been in the house I should imagine you'd find it inconvenient if I were to shift the conversation on to your own little affairs.

14. Can you blame Sir Wilfrid when he announces, We can put some strychnine in the scraps he always gets at dinner-time?

15. Like the story Tobermory, Mrs. Packeltide's Tiger is also a satire about life among the English gentry.

Part Seven

Expression

Your writing style is how you express yourself. Basic to that style are principles of punctuation (such as those you studied in Part Six) and of grammar—both part of the way we communicate with each other in writing.

This section presents some grammar "*do's*" and "*don't's*" to help you deal with expression problems common in the writing of college students. It also demonstrates techniques that will help you advance your style beyond the basics so that you express yourself skillfully.

Chapter 35

Subordination : *The dependent clause*

Anything that you put in a dependent clause is not important
Anything in a phrase is less important
So, always put your best stuff in the independent.

Liberal use of introductory phrases : independent clauses will take care of your transition needs.

You probably know what *in*subordination is, but subordination is something else altogether.

When you first learned to read and write, almost every sentence was an independent clause: "Jane, see Spot." Every idea—small as it was—had exactly the same emphasis as every other idea. Of course, nobody in college writes like that, but too often college students have not progressed far enough from that grade-school style.

Your challenge is to combine related ideas into one sentence, giving them just the right emphasis. To succeed, you must learn *subordination—making less important ideas part of more important ideas.*

We all know that a subordinate is someone who ranks lower than someone else. Parts of a sentence have a rank structure, too.

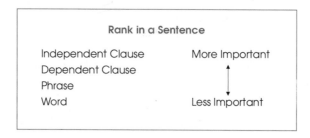

Rank in a Sentence	
Independent Clause	More Important
Dependent Clause	↑
Phrase	↓
Word	Less Important

Ideas expressed in an independent clause naturally seem more important than ideas expressed by only a word. Subordination, then, reduces the emphasis of an idea by lowering its position on the rank structure.

We might subordinate an idea originally in an independent clause by placing it in a dependent clause, a phrase, or—sometimes—even a word. For example:

IC   IC

Original: Art flew to Gila Bend. He arrived on time.

DC   IC

Subordination   Because he flew to Gila Bend, Art arrived on time.
(a dependent clause):

Phrase   IC

Subordination (a phrase):   By flying to Gila Bend, Art arrived on time.

Notice that subordination here has two effects:

- It shows what the writer believes to be the important idea: Art's arriving on time (expressed in the independent clause).
- It shows the relationship between the two ideas: the words *because* in the first revision and *by* in the second act as road signs, telling readers to be ready for a cause-effect relationship. (Because something happened, something else resulted: "Because he flew to Gila Bend, Art arrived on time.") These road signs make the readers' task much easier.

Subordination Beyond the Sentence Level

This chapter focuses on subordination at the sentence level. But subordination also is important elsewhere in the writing process—especially in prewriting when you cluster related ideas and when you develop topic sentences and a thesis statement. As you study the essay and research paper models in the first five parts of this book, you see subordination in an outline form:

- In a one-paragraph essay, related specific support ideas are clustered and then subordinated to a topic sentence idea.
- In a five-paragraph essay, related central paragraphs are clustered and subordinated to a thesis idea.
- In a research paper, related main ideas are clustered and subordinated to the research paper's thesis idea.

The relationships among the ideas vary with the patterns of development. However, for all of these increasingly complex levels of organization, the *effects of subordination* are the same as those within a sentence: *showing what the writer wishes to emphasize as most important and showing relationships among ideas.*

Now let's return to our sentence example. We could have subordinated the second independent clause if we had decided that Art's flying to Gila Bend was more important than the idea that he arrived on time.

```
              IC                    IC
        ┌──────────────┐ ┌──────────────────┐
```
Original: Art flew to Gila Bend. He arrived on time.

```
                    IC                      DC
            ┌────────────────┐ ┌────────────────────────┐
```
Subordination   Art flew to Gila Bend, where he arrived on time.
(a dependent clause):

```
                    IC                  Phrase
            ┌────────────────┐ ┌──────────────────┐
```
Subordination (a phrase):   Art flew to Gila Bend, arriving on time.

When you write, therefore, you have to decide which ideas you wish to emphasize and which you wish to subordinate.

"But," you might protest, "I use subordination all the time." Sure you do—though probably not enough. Let's express some ideas in grade-school style, early college style, and a more sophisticated style.

Degrees of Subordination

Grade-school style	The girl is playing tennis. Her name is Sally. She is a beginner. She is taking lessons. Karen is teaching her. Karen is a professional. Karen teaches at the Andromeda Club. Karen teaches every Tuesday morning.
Early college style	Sally is playing tennis. She is taking beginning lessons from Karen. Karen is a professional, and she teaches at the Andromeda Club every Tuesday morning.
Improved style	Sally is taking beginning tennis lessons from Karen, a professional who teaches at the Andromeda Club every Tuesday morning.

The last revision certainly is easier to read than either of the other versions. Why? Subordination pushes the unimportant ideas to the side of the stage so the viewers can easily see the star, the independent clause.

Apply Subordination During Editing

Here's a final tip to help you with subordination. On a first draft, you're naturally too busy thinking of ideas and how they relate to each other to worry about subordination at the sentence level. When you edit the draft—during the rewriting phase—pay attention to how you piece ideas together *within sentences.* Depending on the time you have available, you may even want to make a trip through your paper, beginning to end, just working on the best way to combine ideas into better sentences. The results will be worth the effort.

Remember, your work while you write makes your readers' work much easier. Subordination lets readers see which main ideas you consider important. And, after you finish school, that's the main reason you will write.

EXERCISES

A. Combine the simple sentences in two different ways, emphasizing a different idea each time.

1. Tonya laughed at his jokes. She was trying to be friendly.

   a. _____

   b. _____

2. Mark Twain wrote during the nineteenth century. He is still a famous author.

   a. _____

   b. _____

3. The conference room door slammed shut. The company president stormed out.

   a. _____

   b. _____

4. Belize is a small country in Central America. Until 1973 it was called British Honduras.

   a. _____

   b. _____

5. The *Hindenburg* was the world's largest airship. It crashed at Lakehurst, New Jersey, in 1937.

   a. _____

   b. _____

B. For each numbered exercise below, combine all the ideas in the simple sentences into one good sentence.

1. Martha played her cassette recorder.
   She played a song.
   The song was by Bob Dylan.
   It was "Hard Rain."
   She played the song eight times in a row.

   _____

   _____

   _____

2. Chen finally reached the mall.
   The mall is near the new baseball stadium.
   He rode buses for three hours.
   He was exhausted.
   He was frustrated.
   He was starved.

   _____

   _____

   _____

3. Ellen Watkins wrote the "Student Manifesto."
   She is a political science major.
   The manifesto demands more open hours for the library and better food at the cafeteria.
   The manifesto was approved by 94 percent of the student body.

   _____

   _____

   _____

4. In the late 1800s huge wagons hauled borax.
   They transported the borax out of Death Valley.
   Death Valley is in California.
   Eighteen mules pulled a wagon.
   Two horses also helped pull a wagon.
   The idea of freight wagons pulled by multiple teams became popular.
   The borax was called "twenty-mule team borax."

   _____

   _____

   _____

5. Theodore Roosevelt refused to shoot a bear.
   Theodore Roosevelt was President at the time.

Clifford Berryman drew a political cartoon about the incident.
The bear in the cartoon was little and cute.
Cuddly stuffed bears became known as "Teddy Bears."

_____

_____

_____

Chapter 36

Sentence Variety

After the preceding chapter, you may suspect that "good" writing consists of one complicated sentence after another. Not so: you'd lose the readers after a couple of pages. On the other hand, how would you like to read sentence after sentence in grade-school or early college style?

Well, then, is the solution a compromise of all medium-length sentences? No, not really. Good writing has a mixture:

- varied sentence lengths
- varied sentence structures

Now, variety just for the sake of variety isn't really the goal. But good sentence variety is often an indication of good coherence—of the smooth flow of ideas from one to another. So if you find yourself writing many short sentences in a row, or beginning many sentences with the subject of the independent clause, ask yourself, "Do my sentence patterns help my ideas flow smoothly? Or do they make my ideas seem fragmented, choppy?"

This chapter will give you some tips on how to vary your sentences to achieve better coherence.

SENTENCE LENGTH

Actually, not very many beginning writers have poor sentence variety from writing only long sentences. The problem is usually a series of short sentences:

The new governor was sworn in today. He is a Democrat. Ten thousand people attended the ceremony. The governor gave a brief inaugural address. The governor promised to end unemployment. He said he would reduce inflation. He also promised to improve the environment. The audience gave him a standing ovation.

Pretty dismal, right? The average sentence length is only six and a quarter words, and all the sentences except the second are either six or seven words long—not overwhelming variety. Let's use the technique of subordination we learned in the last chapter to come up with something better:

> The new Democratic governor was sworn in today. At a ceremony that ten thousand people attended, he gave a brief inaugural address, promising to end unemployment, reduce inflation, and improve the environment. The audience gave him a standing ovation.

This version is certainly much easier to read, mainly because we've eliminated choppiness and subordinated some unimportant ideas. The average sentence is now thirteen words long, within the desirable goal of twelve to twenty words per sentence.

Practical Writing: The Problem of Complex Sentences

Although beginning writers tend toward short, choppy sentences, writers in business, industry, and government sometimes tend the other way. Some even believe that writing long, complex sentences is a mark of their educational competence. They think their superiors *expect* them to write long sentences, and they aim to please.

Here's a sample of the type of writing that results:

> Whether the terrorists style themselves as separatists, anarchists, dissidents, nationalists, Marxist revolutionaries, or religious true believers, what marks them as terrorists is that they direct their violence against noncombatants with the goal of terrorizing a wider audience than the immediate victims, thereby attempting to gain political influence over the larger audience. In one variant of terrorism, organizational terrorism, represented by such groups as the Red Army Faction in Germany, the Red Brigades in Italy, Direct Action in France, and 17 November in Greece, small, tightly knit, politically homogeneous organizations that are incapable of developing popular support for their radical positions resort to terrorism to gain influence. In a second variant of terrorism, that conducted within the context of ethnic separatist or country-wide insurgencies, such as in the Philippines, El Salvador, and Colombia, groups conducting paramilitary or guerrilla operations against the established government turn to attacks on the populace at large to undermine the government's credibility, legitimacy, and public support.

These three sentences, all roughly the same length, average fifty-four words each. You can understand what they say, of course—if you read very carefully.

Yet, successful writers—and the people they work for—today are insisting on something else. They're demanding simpler writing so that busy readers don't have to struggle with the material they need to understand. Sentence averages in the twelve to twenty word range simply communicate more effectively.

SENTENCE STRUCTURE

Let's look again at the bad example that began the discussion on sentence length. Notice how many sentences begin with the subject (and its modifiers) of an independent clause:

The new governor was sworn in today. He is a Democrat. Ten thousand

people attended the ceremony. The governor gave a brief inaugural address.

The governor promised to end unemployment. He said he would reduce

inflation. He also promised to improve the environment. The audience

gave him a standing ovation.

Every sentence begins with the subject of an independent clause. Surely there is a better way to move from sentence to sentence than to begin every one with the subject. Some should begin with dependent clauses, others with phrases, and still others with transitional words. For example, look again at the revision:

The new Democratic governor was sworn in today. *At a ceremony that ten thousand people attended,* he gave a brief inaugural address, promising to end unemployment, reduce inflation, and improve the environment. The audience gave him a standing ovation.

The introduction to the second sentence provides nice relief.

Many sentences, of course, should begin with the subject of an independent clause; still, they should not all look alike. They could end with a dependent clause, they could contain a couple of independent clauses, or they could contain a series of parallel phrases or clauses (see Chapter 37). The sentences in the paragraph you are now reading, for example, all begin with the subject of an independent clause, but after that beginning, their structures vary considerably.

Apply Sentence Variety During Editing

You may think *you* would never begin a lot of sentences all the same way. And surely you'd never string together all short, choppy sentences or long, overly complex ones. Yet, in our first draft many of us write with just those patterns.

We think of an idea and write it down: "subject—verb"; we think of another idea and write it down: "subject—verb"; and so on. Similarly, we become comfortable writing sentences with much the same lengths—short ones or long ones, whichever way we're used to writing. Then, because we don't take the time to rewrite the draft, our sentences look much the same.

Check your last few pages to see if you've fallen into this bad habit.

Good writing is not an automatic process, a flow of uninterrupted inspiration flowing forth onto the page. Good writing results from a painstaking and *very conscious* process.

Don't just hope sentence variety will happen in your writing. After you write a draft, ask yourself these questions:

- Are my sentences different lengths?
- Do my sentences begin in a variety of ways?
- Do the sentences that begin with the subject of an independent clause have a variety of structures?

If the answers are "no," then edit your paper for sentence variety. Be careful, though, not to sacrifice clarity for the sake of variety. And don't create grotesque, unnatural sentences.

Variety is a means to achieve good writing—not the goal itself.

EXERCISES

A. Revise these paragraphs for better sentence variety. In both the original and your revision, circle the subject of the first independent clause in every sentence. Then compute the average number of words in each sentence (count all the words in the paragraph and divide by the number of sentences).

1. Original:

Government agencies, large corporations, and small businesses use computers. They are using them more frequently. They use them to maintain many records. These records include pay statements and inventory records. The danger of computer theft is increasing. Computer theft means changing computer records illegally to transfer to yourself money or something else valuable. Computer-theft losses run into billions of dollars a year. For every computer crime discovered, ten go undetected. The staggering losses occur because computer owners are ignorant. They do not realize their system is vulnerable. They do not use the available protective measures to reduce theft.

Average number of words per sentence: _____

Your revision: _____

_____

_____

_____

_____

_____

_____

_____

_____

_____

_____

Average number of words per sentence:_____

2. Original:

Many people today associate Mickey Spillane only with television commercials for low-calorie beer. Paperback book racks reveal the real Spillane legacy. Mickey Spillane popularized a type of tough detective. For this detective ends justify means. Mike Hammer is the "hero" in Spillane's *I, the Jury.* Hammer seeks revenge for the brutal killing of a close friend. Hammer declares himself judge, jury, and executioner. Then Hammer breaks most ethical and social laws while he pursues his private brand of justice. Hammer's actions in other books are equally immoral. However, the ugliness always occurs as Hammer rights some wrong. For years the marketplace success of Spillane's books has been tremendous. *I, the Jury* was first published in 1947. Authors still routinely reproduce Mike Hammer and his ethic. The questionable honor of spawning modern paperback series belongs to Mickey Spillane. These series include the Avenger, the Revenger, and the Executioner. You are sure to find some of these wherever cheap literature is sold.

Average number of words per sentence:_____

Your revision: _____

_____

_____

_____

_____

_____

_____

_____

_____

_____

_____

Average number of words per sentence: _____

3. Original:
Many U.S. citizens learned a story about George Washington and Betsy Ross. We learned that in 1776 George Washington visited Betsy Ross. He asked her to sew a new flag for the Continental Army. We learned that Betsy showed General Washington how to make a five-pointed star. Washington liked what he saw. Betsy Ross set to work making the Stars and Stripes. Many of us even have visited the Ross house. It is where the event took place. We also know what the resulting flag looked like. There is a famous painting called *The Spirit of '76*. It is by Archibald Willard. It shows two drummers and a fife player. Behind them is the flag we know. We're sure it flew throughout the American Revolution. The flag has thirteen red and white stripes. It has a blue field in the upper left corner. It has thirteen white stars in a circle. The stars have five points. There is an irony to what we know. None of these "facts" is true. Records show that Betsy Ross made flags. She made them for the Pennsylvania Navy. There is no evidence for the Washington-Ross story. In 1870, Betsy's grandson told the tale to the Pennsylvania Historical Society. He said he had heard it from Betsy. The legend found its way into popular history. It also was written down in books. There is no evidence that the flag Willard painted ever existed. In 1777, the Continental Congress passed a resolution about flags. It could have led to the flag in Willard's painting. However, units actually flew a variety of flags. In 1873, Washington received a shipment of flags. They were for the Continental Army. The shipment came near the end of the war. The "history" we've learned about the Stars and Stripes seems to have a lot of romance. It doesn't seem to have a lot of substance.

Average number of words per sentence: _____

Your revision: _____

_____

_____

_____

_____

_____

_____

_____

_____

_____

_____

_____

_____

_____

_____

Average number of words per sentence:_____

B. Revise the three sentences in the box called "Practical Writing: The Problem of Complex Sentences" for better sentence variety. Those three sentences have fifty-one, fifty-five, and fifty-four words, for an average of fifty-four words per sentence. The average number of words per sentence in your revision should fall in the twelve to twenty word range. Although the primary purpose of this exercise is to reduce the average sentence length, be sure your revision also demonstrates a variety of sentence structures.

Your revision: _____

_____

_____

_____

_____

_____

_____

_____

_____

Average number of words per sentence:_____

Chapter 37

Parallelism

Now that you've studied sentence variety, you may be afraid of writing sentences that repeat simple patterns. Don't be. Some ideas work best in sentences that clearly show a pattern. When you analyze an idea, you take pains to discover similarities and differences among its parts. Whether you intend to compare or contrast those elements, you want readers to see how the parts are alike or different. Parallelism is the key.

The principle of parallel construction is simple: *be sure ideas that are similar in content and function look the same.* Parallelism works because the similarity of the appearance of the items shows clearly the pattern of the thought. The principle of parallelism applies most often to the following:

- two or more items in a series (usually with a coordinating conjunction)
- a pair of items with correlative conjunctions—a special type of series and conjunctions we'll explain later in this chapter

ITEMS IN A SERIES

The principle of parallelism requires that all items in a series must be grammatically alike. That is, all words in a series must be the same type of word, all phrases the same type of phrase, and all clauses the same type of clause. Grammatical likeness also applies to sentences in a series: each item in the series must be a *complete* sentence—not a fragment—and, therefore, the same "type" of sentence. However, the structures within these complete sentences can vary, so the patterns within the sentences may appear somewhat different, as we'll see later in this section.

Coordinating Conjunctions With a Series

Two or more in a series within a single sentence normally use a coordinating conjunction (CC)—*and, but, or, nor, for, so,* or *yet*—before the final item.

Thus, the series looks like this:

> item CC item

or this:

> item, item, CC item

A series of complete sentences, however, usually will not include a coordinating conjunction before the final item.

Here are sentences with parallel constructions:

Words in series: I saw John and Mary.

I saw John, Bill, and Mary.

Phrases in series: I see him going to work and coming home.

I plan to eat in a restaurant and to see a movie.

Dependent clauses in series: The phone rang when I reached the motel but

before I unpacked my suitcases.

Independent clauses in series: I liked the parrot, so I bought it for my mother.

Complete sentences in series: She sold the car for three good reasons:

It had no tires. It had no brakes. It had

no engine.

Notice that each item—word, phrase, clause, or sentence—in a series has the same form as the other items in the same series.

A Reminder: Use Commas and Semicolons With Items in a Series

As you saw in Chapters 29 and 30, commas and sometimes semicolons mark the division of items in a series within a sentence. Commas are the most common dividers:

> The ethics of contemporary surgery are often a problem for the patient, the doctor, and the patient's family.

When commas occur within one or more of the items in a series, semicolons mark the divisions between the items:

> Key air routes include Lisbon, Portugal; Rome, Italy; Frankfurt, Germany; and Istanbul, Turkey.

Words in a Series

The words in a series of words seldom present special problems. However, the articles that appear with the series can create a minor parallelism problem.

Articles With Words in a Series

Articles are *a, an,* and *the.* When articles appear with words in a series, be sure the articles fall in one of these two patterns:

article word, word, CC word

article word, *article* word, CC *article* word

Notice the placement of the articles in these sample sentences:

Wrong: I bought food for *the* dog, cat, and *the* horse.

Correct: I bought food for *the* dog, cat, and horse.

Correct: I bought food for *the* dog, *the* cat, and *the* horse.

The correct sentences have either an article before the entire series or an article before every item in the series.

Phrases in a Series

Unlike words in a series, phrases often cause problems. Many times students mix types of phrases. Be sure that *-ing* phrases fit with other *-ing* phrases, *to* phrases with *to* phrases, and so forth.

Wrong: I like *swimming in the pond, cycling down the lane,* and *to ride horses in the pasture.*

Correct: I like *swimming in the pond, cycling down the lane,* and *riding horses in the pasture.*

Correct: I like *to swim in the pond, to cycle down the lane,* and *to ride horses in the pasture.*

Wrong: I plan *to study hard, doing well on my exams,* and *to graduate with honors.*

Correct: I plan *to study hard, to do well on my exams,* and *to graduate with honors.*

Correct: I plan on *studying hard, doing well on my exams,* and *graduating with honors.*

Clauses in a Series

Clauses in a series seldom cause major problems. However, if the series contains dependent clauses, you can help your readers by signaling the beginning of each dependent clause. Consider this sentence:

I expect to be entertained if I'm going to pay $5 to get in a theater and I'm going to sit there for two hours.

What does the *and* join? Does it join the two independent clauses?

item   CC

I expect to be entertained if I'm going to pay $5 to get in a theater and
item

I'm going to sit there for two hours.

Or does it join two dependent clauses?

item   CC

I expect to be entertained if I'm going to pay $5 to get in a theater and
item

I'm going to sit there for two hours.

The intended meaning is probably the second one: the *and* joins two dependent clauses. Readers will see the separation of the items more easily if the writer repeats the word that signals the beginning of the clauses:

item   CC

I expect to be entertained *if* I'm going to pay $5 to get in a theater and

item

if I'm going to sit there for two hours.

Now the meaning is clear. Here's another sample:

> "I can see that you don't like the meal and that you'd rather not be here," she pouted.

Notice that the repetition of *that* (which signals the beginning of dependent clauses) makes the parallel construction clear.

Like Grammatical Units in a Series Within a Sentence

In addition to having like words, like phrases, and like clauses in a series within a sentence, be sure that the items in the series are the same type of grammatical unit. Do not, for instance, mix phrases and clauses in a series, as in this sentence:

item CC item

Wrong: My roommate likes to sleep in bed and when he's in class.

The sentence is awkward because the writer has joined a phrase (*in bed*) with a clause (*when he's in class*). Here's what the writer should have written:

Correct: My roommate likes to sleep when he's in bed and when he's in class.

Now a clause fits with a clause. (Notice also that the sentence repeats *when*, the word that signals the beginning of each dependent clause.)

Complete Sentences in a Series

In the earlier sample of full sentences in a series, all of the sentences are quite short, and their internal structures are exactly alike: "It had no tires. It had no brakes. It had no engine." Clearly, this is a technique you have to apply sparingly. This type of series could provide a punchy variation if it were mixed in with longer sentences. Too much of it, though, could create the type of choppy, repetitive writing you learned to avoid when you studied about sentence variety in the last chapter.

However, complete sentences in a series don't have to be so much alike. Here's another sample, this time with some variation within the sentences.

> My great-grandfather wrote that Abraham Lincoln's appearance at the caucus was striking: Lincoln's beard was short and neatly trimmed. His suit was of a dark cloth that gave him a somber but dignified air and seemed to hang on his lank frame. In his hand he loosely held a black stovepipe hat.

These sentences are of varied lengths: seven, twenty-three, and ten words, respectively. Obviously their internal structures are not exactly alike. Are they parallel? Well, yes, they are. In the simplest sense, they have grammatical similarity, as each is a complete sentence. More important, each provides the same type of information—a quick descriptive example—that answers the same question: How was Lincoln's appearance striking? And even though the structures of the sentences are not exactly alike, their basic idea patterns are similar: his beard was . . . ; his suit was . . . ; his hand held. . . .

Parallelism in Headings and Indented Lists

In Chapter 10 you learned about layout techniques that can make your writing look better. Two of those techniques—headings and indented lists—depend on parallelism.

Here are the headings that were added to the sample paper about the humorous things children do as they grow up:

Learning to Speak
Discovering Objects Aren't Human
Imitating Others Around Them

Notice that the headings are parallel phrases, each the same type of phrase: learning . . . , discovering . . . , imitating. . . .

Parallelism is even more important when you use indented lists. Their purpose is to *emphasize a pattern* of organization, and that is also the reason for using parallel construction. Here's a sample list without parallelism:

Desktop publishing offers our department three benefits:

- product more professional
- Production time will be cut.
- saves money

This list a a jumble of styles that reminds us of the result of brainstorming, where we're interested in jotting down ideas quickly without worrying about how well they communicate. Readers will get the point—if they take the time to apply the organization that the writer has left out. Notice the difference that parallel construction makes in this revision:

> Desktop publishing offers our department three benefits:
>
> - a more professional-looking product
> - reduced production time
> - cost savings

PAIRS OF ITEMS WITH CORRELATIVE CONJUNCTIONS

Correlative conjunctions mate pairs of related items. The rule for parallelism with correlative conjunctions is simple: the grammatical units following each of the correlative conjunctions must be alike.

Correlative Pairs

Common correlative conjunctions are these: *either . . . or; neither . . . nor; not (only) . . . but (also);* and *whether . . . or.*

Items mated by correlative conjunctions (CorC) will look like this:

CorC item CorC item

Here are sentences with such pairs:

CorC   item   CorC   item

I don't like either his appearance or his manners.

CorC   item CorC item

Neither my aunt nor my cousin will speak to me.

Can you find the problem in this sentence?

Wrong: *Either* I go to bed early *or* get up late.

This sentence demonstrates the most common failure to maintain parallelism with correlative conjunctions: *either* precedes the subject of the sentence *(I),* but *or* precedes the second verb *(get).* There are two methods to deal with the problem:

Correct: I *either* go to bed early *or* get up late.

Correct: *Either* I go to bed early *or* I get up late.

The first solution moves *either* so that both correlative conjunctions precede verbs *(go* and *get).* The second solution places *either* and *or* before subjects of clauses *(I* and *I).* In both corrections, the grammatical units following each correlative conjunction are alike.

All of this may seem complicated, but it's not. You wouldn't try to compare apples and automobiles, because they're not alike. Similarly, you can't expect your readers to accept a comparison of items that don't appear to be alike. The principle of parallelism requires only that you make like items *look* alike so readers can see the similarity.

EXERCISES

A. Improve the parallelism in each of the following sentences:

1. I enjoy swimming, cycling and to ride horses.

2. Mr. Stein hooked a walleye, perch, and a trout.

3. Tossed by high waves and with strong winds hammering it, the small boat seemed certain to capsize.

4. When he came home from college, Lorenzo both wanted to eat home-cooked meals and to sleep all day.

5. Even though Marla was tired from jogging five miles and she practiced wind sprints for twenty minutes, she was ready for a night of dancing.

6. Ramon loves backpacking, camping, and especially to climb mountains.

7. The fountain was beautiful as the droplets spread out in the air and were made to sparkle by the sunlight.

8. Greek temples for the god of medicine, Asklepios, were not only places of worship but also of healing.

9. After a test in chemistry and I revised my English paper, I still needed to study for a test in psychology.

10. Rosa skipped the lecture because she didn't have the time, the energy, and she wasn't interested.

11. At Christmas we like to decorate the tree, making special cookies, and singing carols.

12. Not only the students but also those who teach them were upset by the new university policy.

13. I think about Grandmother's farm when I drive in rush-hour traffic or reading about crime in the streets.

14. I'll jog outside if it neither snows nor it rains.

15. The director wanted to film scenes in the forums of ancient Rome and where the streets are narrow and crowded in Naples.

16. Crane's department store is offering a special price on the towels, sheets, and the bedspreads.

17. The tomb of China's emperor Qin Shi Huangdi was protected not only by an army of over 6,000 terra-cotta soldiers but there were real drawn crossbows set to shoot intruders who set off their triggers.

18. Before going onto the stage and she heard the opening applause, Thea was very nervous.

19. Alex went to the party for the food, the entertainment, and to meet people who might become customers.

20. Charles finally told his mother he wanted to go skiing, soak in the hot tub, and always avoid working.

21. Dennis talked to an immigration officer, a bishop, and to his senator about helping.

22. Overheated by the sun and with dehydration, I stopped running at mile seven in the July 4th road race.

23. The Romans constructed their baths by elevating the floors on brick pillars, enclosing the pillars and rooms to control the air circulation, and then installed furnaces to circulate hot air.

24. Edith bought a computer, dot-matrix printer, and a popular word-processing software program.

25. I never feel prepared for final exams, whether I study for weeks in advance or cramming twelve hours the day before the test.

B. In these exercises, revise the indented lists so the items will be parallel.

1. In his war with the Celtic tribes of Gaul in 52 B.C., Julius Caesar encircled the Gauls with a field of hazards:
   * The field facing the Gauls had pits with sharp stakes at the bottom—all covered with brush to hide the traps.
   * A thicket of pointed branches angled toward the Gauls.
   * Two trenches, one filled with water, came after the thicket.
   * A steep wall with towers from which Caesar's soldiers could throw spears.

2. Greek health care centers, called *Asklepieia,* offered a variety of services to the ill and infirm:
   * Facilities for bathing and ritual exercise.
   * There were pavilions in which patients could sleep and be visited by the god of healing, Asklepios.
   * Temples for worship of Asklepios and for handling dogs and snakes, which were associated with Asklepios, also were available.
   * Operating theaters where temple physicians performed surgery.

Chapter 38

Misused Modifiers

Dangling participle! Nothing—not even "split infinitive"—can strike such terror in the heart of an English student. But don't be afraid. Behind the fancy name is a simple concept you'll understand after studying this chapter. You won't learn the differences between dangling participles, dangling gerunds, and dangling infinitives because the differences aren't really important: we'll treat them all more simply as *dangling modifiers*. In addition to the special type of modifier problem, you'll also study *misplaced modifiers*.

What Is a Modifier?

Modifiers are words, phrases, or clauses that limit or provide additional information about other words.

In "I never saw a purple cow," the modifier *purple* limits the discussion from "all cows" to only "purple cows." (As you saw in the discussion of comma usage in Chapter 29, modifiers that limit the definition of other words are restrictive modifiers.)

In "Standing on the bridge, the captain watched his ship move slowly through the channel," the modifier *standing on the bridge* provides additional information about the captain—but it in no way limits the definition. (Modifiers that provide information but do not limit definition are nonrestrictive modifiers.)

This chapter focuses on placement of modifiers within a sentence. Because placement problems can occur with both types of modifiers, restrictive and nonrestrictive, we do not distinguish between them. However,

---

if you study the examples carefully, you'll see that the most common problems are with placing nonrestrictive modifiers. Why? Because a nonrestrictive modifier is less essential to the point of the sentence, a writer is less likely to notice that the modifier is misplaced.

As you've seen in earlier chapters, modifiers allow you to combine several ideas into one sentence. You might write this:

Jonathan ate the doughnut. It was the only doughnut.

However, you save time and space by reducing the second sentence to a modifier:

Jonathan ate the *only* doughnut.

Still, there is a catch: word order in an English sentence often determines meaning; therefore, different word arrangements may yield different meanings. Let's see what happens if we place *only* in every possible position in "Jonathan ate the doughnut."

Only Jonathan ate the doughnut.	(No one else ate it.)
Jonathan *only* ate the doughnut.	(He didn't do anything else to it.)
Jonathan ate *only* the doughnut.	(He ate nothing else.)
Jonathan ate the *only* doughnut.	(There were no other doughnuts.)
Jonathan ate the doughnut *only*.	(He ate nothing else.)

Five combination yield four distinctly different meanings. Play this game with other sentences and such words as *almost, every, just, merely, most, nearly, only, primarily,* and *principally.*

The game's implication is obvious, isn't it? Unless you carefully place the modifiers in your sentences, you may not write what you really mean. Modifiers are terrific savers of time and space in your writing—but they also can obscure or distort your meaning, sometimes making your writing appear ridiculous.

MISPLACED MODIFIERS

Placing a modifier in a sentence requires good judgment and careful editing. No particular place in a sentence is always right for a modifier, but this much is true: *a modifier tends to modify what it is close to.* "Close to" may be before or after the thing modified, so long as the sentence makes sense.

These sentences don't make much sense.

A jeep ran over the soldier *that had muddy tires.*

People stared in amazement *on the sidewalk.*

The accident left *neatly pressed* tire marks on the soldier's shirt.

In these sentences something comes between the modifiers and the things modified. As a result, the modifiers appear to refer to the things they are closest to: *that had muddy tires* seems to modify *soldier; on the sidewalk* seems to refer to *amazement;* and *neatly pressed* appears to modify *tire marks.*

Let's move the modifiers so they modify what they should.

A jeep *that had muddy tires* ran over the soldier.

On the sidewalk, people stared in amazement.

or

People *on the sidewalk* stared in amazement.

The accident left tire marks on the soldier's *neatly pressed* shirt.

Notice that *on the sidewalk* works before or after *people,* whereas *that had muddy tires* works only after *jeep* and *neatly pressed* works only before *shirt.* What matters, then, is that the modifier must be close enough to the thing it modifies to complete the thought logically.

A second type of placement problem occurs when you write strings of modifiers. Consider this example:

A man *with red hair in a green suit* crossed the street.

Both *with red hair* and *in a green suit* should modify *man,* but instead *in a green suit* seems to refer to *hair.*

One solution is to put one modifier before and another after the thing modified:

A *red-haired* man *in a green suit* crossed the street.

or

Wearing a green suit, a man *with red hair* crossed the street.

A second solution is to combine the modifiers with a coordinating conjunction:

A man *with red hair and a green suit* crossed the street.

Again, the exact position of the modifier doesn't matter if the result makes sense.

DANGLING MODIFIERS

Dangling modifiers can occur anywhere in a sentence, but the most common problem is at the beginning. A modifier that *begins* a sentence must refer to something that follows. Because of convention, readers expect an introductory word or phrase modifier to refer to the subject of the sentence.

Walking along the beach, Mary found a sand dollar.

Since we expect the opening phrase *(walking along the beach)* to modify the subject of the sentence *(Mary),* we know that Mary, not the sand dollar, was walking along the beach. But what if the sentence reads this way?

Walking along the beach, a sand dollar was found by Mary.

Again we expect the introductory phrase to modify the subject of the sentence, but sand dollars don't walk. Since the modifier cannot logically modify the subject of the sentence, we say that the modifier "dangles."

The following sentences contain dangling modifiers:

Enthusiastic, the hour seemed to pass quickly.

Finishing the game, the crowd loudly booed the home team.

After examining the data, the steam engine appeared to be the best choice.

To enjoy surfing, the waves must be high.

When only nine, John's mother took him to a circus.

Was the hour enthusiastic? Did the crowd actually finish the game? Did the steam engine examine the data? Can waves enjoy surfing? Do you really believe that John had a mother who was only nine years old? Because the modifiers above have no logical connection to the subjects of the sentences, the modifiers dangle.

You have two options to correct dangling modifiers:

- The first, the most obvious, is to recast the sentence so the subject matches the modifier.

Enthusiastic, we thought the hour passed quickly.

Finishing the game, the home team heard loud booing from the crowd.

After examining the data, we concluded that the steam engine was the best choice.

To enjoy surfing, you need high waves.

When only nine, John went to the circus with his mother.

- The second method is to change the word or phrase modifier into a clause.

Because we were enthusiastic, the hour seemed to pass quickly.

As the game ended, the crowd loudly booed the home team.

After we examined the data, the steam engine appeared to be the best choice.

If you want to enjoy surfing, the waves must be high.

When John was only nine, his mother took him to a circus.

The Bottom Line

You can avoid *both* types of problem modifiers—misplaced as well as dangling—if you keep in mind the essential relationship between modifiers and the things they modify:

> • A modifier tends to modify what it is close to.
> • A modifier should be close to what it must modify.

EXERCISES

A. 1. Write one sentence with a misplaced modifier and one with a dangling modifier.

   a. _____

   _____

   b. _____

   _____

   2. Now correct your sentences.

   a. _____

   _____

   b. _____

   _____

B. The game at the beginning of the chapter isn't just an amusing pastime: it's based on a real and very common type of modifier placement problem in business and technical writing. Here's a sentence—less the modifier *only*—from a business report:

   He has been a member of the party since 1989.

   Now, place *only* in every possible position in the sentence—there are eleven—and evaluate the number of different meanings you generate. How many are there? Which do you think the author meant to write?

C. Rewrite the following sentences to eliminate the modifier problems.

   1. The cat drank the milk with black spots.

   2. Driving through Yellowstone, the bears came right up to the car.

   3. A woman driving a half-ton pickup with a wide-brimmed hat bought the horse that won the show.

   4. Having run the first leg of the race, the baton was passed by Phil to Jack.

   5. Adjusting his large, red nose, the master of ceremonies announced the clown.

   6. The boy holding flowers with a shy smile approached his date.

   7. When cooked, pepper should be sprinkled on the chicken.

8. To ensure they arrive on time, cards should be mailed by the first day of December.

9. Stretching far to the left to catch the badly thrown ball, the runner dashed past the catcher at home plate.

10. The horse jumped the fence with its mane flying in the wind.

11. Having reached the campsite, the tent was erected by the tired campers.

12. After reaching a rolling boil, the cook can skim the fat from the surface of the soup.

13. He was only a child a mother could love.

14. A girl in a raincoat with a Girl Scout uniform was standing outside the super-market selling cookies in the rain.

15. Opening the shutters, the top of the mountain came into view.

16. Bleating piteously, Mary allowed the lamb to follow her to school.

17. The mortician figured that he had very nearly embalmed 1,200 bodies.

18. When completely filled out and checked, the taxpayer should sign the form.

19. The coach told him frequently to run wind sprints.

20. Laurie borrowed an egg from Alice that was rotten.

21. Julio almost seemed disappointed about the appointment.

22. When completely empty, the technician should refill the tank.

23. Who is the woman who told you how to find the studio in the business suit?

24. He put the cowboy hat on his head that he bought in Albuquerque.

25. The president wishes you to notify her if you will attend on the enclosed card.

Chapter 39

Subject-Verb Agreement

One of the most common grammar problems for students is agreement between subjects and verbs. The rule itself is quite simple: *a verb must agree in number with its subject*. If the subject is singular, the verb must be singular; if the subject is plural, the verb must be plural.

Singular and Plural Verbs

Usually the verb itself doesn't cause trouble. In fact, the forms for many singular and plural verbs are identical, so they can't cause a mistake in agreement. Yet, English verbs retain one peculiarity that some students find troublesome.

You know that an *-s* or *-es* ending on a noun makes the noun plural: car, cars; tomato, tomatoes. The same would seem to be true for verbs, but it isn't. An *-s* or *-es* ending on a verb makes the verb singular:

Plural	Singular
They run.	He runs.
They go.	She goes.
They jump.	It jumps.

If you understand this difference between verbs and nouns, verbs are not likely to cause you agreement problems. The problems stem from the subjects of the verbs.

Most errors in agreement occur because of some difficulty related to the subject of a sentence, particularly in

- identifying the subject
- recognizing the subject's number

IDENTIFYING THE SUBJECT

Some agreement problems result from difficulties in finding the subject of a sentence. Two sentence structures make identifying the subject particularly troublesome:

- when the subject is delayed—so it isn't where we expect it to be
- when a phrase comes between the subject and the verb—confusing us about the subject's identity

Delayed Subject

We usually can find the subject if it comes in its ordinary place—just before the verb—but we may have trouble if it follows the verb. Watch for sentences opening with *there* or *here*. These words delay the subject so that it appears after the verb. You'll have to think through such a sentence because you won't know whether the verb should be singular or plural until you get beyond it to the subject.

      V   S
There *are* three *sailboats* at the dock.

      V   S
There *is* the *sailboat* with the sail on upside down.

    V   S
Here *are* the *supplies* you ordered.

    V   S
Here *is* the *box* you wanted first.

Phrase Between Subject and Verb

Sometimes even when the subject comes where we expect it to be, before the verb, it is still hard to identify because of a phrase between the subject and verb. Because of the intervening phrase:

- We may think a word in the phrase is the subject.
- We may think the phrase is part of the subject, making it plural.

Let's look first at an example in which a word in the phrase might seem to be the subject:

                      S   V
Wrong: One of the Coyne *boys have climbed* the water tower.

Here the word *boys* is so close to the verb that the writer thought it was the subject. He was wrong. *Boys* is simply part of a phrase that comes between the subject and the verb. The real subject is *one:*

                 S   V

Correct: *One* of the Coyne boys *has climbed* the water tower.

Now let's look at a phrase that might seem to be part of the subject:

                             S   V

Wrong: *Martha, as well as her sisters, work* in the fields regularly.

As well as her sisters seems to be part of the subject. It seems to be equivalent to *and her sisters.* But it isn't.

Confusing Prepositional Phrases

    The words here are merely prepositions; they begin phrases that have nothing to do with determining the agreement between a subject and its verb:

as well as	including
accompanied by	like
along with	together with
in addition to	with

    How can we find the subject in our example above? Mentally eliminate the entire phrase:

                    S   V

Correct: *Martha* (as well as her sisters) *works* in the fields regularly.

The subject is now clear.

RECOGNIZING THE SUBJECT'S NUMBER

The problems we just looked at occur because the subject isn't where we expect it to be. Sometimes, though, we can find the subject and still not know whether it is singular or plural. These rules will help you:

   • *Two or more subjects joined by* **and** *are almost always plural. The* **and** *joins the items—singular, plural, or mixed—into one plural unit.*

     S   S   V

Charlotte and her *mother drive* the metallic brown dune buggy.

     S   S   V

That *woman* and her *husband look* a lot alike.

• *If **or** or **nor** joins subjects, the verb agrees with whichever subject is closer to the verb.*

```
    S                    S    V
```

Either *Beverly* or my other *aunts have* my thanks.

Here *aunts* is closer to the verb than is *Beverly,* so the verb is plural. What if we reverse the subjects?

```
              S         S    V
```

Either my other *aunts* or *Beverly has* my thanks.

Now *Beverly* is closer, so the verb is singular.

A Tip on Word Order

Does "Either my other aunts or Beverly has my thanks" seem awkward to you? It's technically correct. However, many readers feel uncomfortable when the singular subject (*Beverly* here) of a mixed singular-plural set forces use of a singular verb (*has* in this case). The better choice is to put the plural portion of the set closer to the verb so the verb will be plural.

The rule still applies if both items are singular or if both items are plural. If both are singular, naturally a singular subject will be next to the verb, so the verb is singular. Likewise, if both subjects are plural, a plural subject will be next to the verb, so the verb is plural.

• *Some, all, most, part, half (and other fractions) may be either singular or plural, depending on the phrase that follows them.*

You probably think we're crazy because we told you in the first part of the chapter not to let a phrase between the subject and the verb influence subject-verb agreement. Well, here is an exception to that rule.

Many times the words in the previous list are followed by a phrase beginning with *of* ("All *of* the jurors . . . ," "Some *of* the tea . . ."). If the main word in the *of*-phrase is plural, then the verb should be plural. However, if the main word is singular or just can't be counted (we wouldn't say "one *milk*" or "thirteen *tea,*" for example), then the verb should be singular.

```
 S              V
```

Some of the grapes *are* still on the table. (*Grapes* is plural, so the verb is plural.)

```
 S                 V
```

Some of the milk *is dripping* on the floor. *(Milk* cannot be counted, so the verb is singular.)

- *Relative pronouns (***who, whose, whom, which, *and* that***) *may be singular or plural, depending on the word they refer to.*

Usually the relative pronoun refers to the word just before it:

                             S   V

Jeannette is one of the children *who love* to read. (*Who* is a pronoun replacing *children.* Not just one child but all the children love to read.)

Again, here comes an exception. What if Jeannette is the only one in the group who loves to read? Then the pronoun *who* refers to the word *one,* not the word *children:*

                                S   V

Jeannette is the only one of the children *who loves* to read.

The exception, then, is that in the phrase *the only one . . . who/that,* the relative pronoun refers to the word *one,* so the verb must be singular (after all, what can be more singular than *one?*).

- *A collective noun as subject requires a singular verb when the group acts as a unit but a plural verb when the members of the group act as separate persons or things.*

A collective noun names a group: *audience, class, committee, family, jury, orchestra, team,* and so forth. The key is to determine whether the parts of the group are acting as a single body or as separate entities (that are doing the same thing).

     S   V

The *jury has been sequestered.* (The members of the collective group have been separated from the public as a single body, so the verb is singular.)

     S V

The *jury are* unable to agree on a verdict. (Clearly, the members of the collective group are acting as separate individuals—since they can not agree as a unit—so the verb is plural.)

EXERCISES

A. Use one of the following verbs when completing this exercise:

Singular verbs: *throws, goes, misses, takes*
Plural verbs: *throw, go, miss, take*

Do not use other forms of these verbs (such as *threw, had thrown,* or the like).

1. a. Write a sentence that has the subject following the verb. Use a singular verb.

      _____

  b. Now use a plural verb.

      _____

2. Write a sentence with a singular subject and the phrase *as well as (fill in a word)* between the subject and the verb.

_____

3. Write a sentence that has two subjects joined by *and.*

_____

4. a. Write a sentence with two plural subjects joined by *or.*

_____

   b. Write a sentence with two singular subjects joined by *or.*

_____

   c. Write a sentence with a singular and a plural subject joined by *or.*

_____

   d. Rewrite sentence *c* but reverse the order of the subjects.

_____

5. Write a sentence with *all* as the subject and a phrase beginning with of between it and the verb.

_____

6. Write a sentence that contains a relative pronoun as a subject and draw an arrow to the word it refers to.

_____

7. a. Write a sentence with a collective noun as the subject and with a singular verb.

_____

   b. Write another sentence with the same collective noun as the subject and with a plural verb.

_____

B. Circle the correct verb in each set of choices below.

1. Here (is, are) the cap you lost in the park.

2. Laura together with her friends (is, are) playing Old Maid.

3. One of the boys or Annette (is, are) coming by later for the package.

4. The team (is, are) cleaning out the lockers now that the season is over.

5. Carlos is the only one of the swimmers who (has, have) a chance to win a medal.

6. Neither the boxer nor his trainers (wants, want) him to go back into the ring.

7. Jenny is the only one of the children who (likes, like) the licorice gumdrops.

8. There (was, were), according to Senator Stevens, at least one reason to question the President's nominee.

9. A chorus of hoots and jeers (was, were) heard throughout the field house.

10. Ignorance is one of the major failures that (causes, cause) crime.

11. Do you think the boys and Martha (realizes, realize) the mistake?

12. The brand of computer that man is buying for his children (carries, carry) a ninety-day warranty.

13. The committee (has, have) decided to decorate the gym in blue and yellow.

14. Baci is one of those dogs that (likes, like) everybody.

15. Neither the bird nor the bee (has, have) to be told about people.

16. As a result, there (is, are) bloodshed and chaos.

17. Several members of my mother's graduating class (is, are) starting a scholarship fund.

18. The crowd (was, were) very quiet as Congressman Billings spoke.

19. Those books, including that first edition of Faulkner's The Sound and the Fury, (is, are) worth more than you and I can imagine.

20. Each of the clerks (complains, complain) about the smoke in the office.

21. Economics (is, are) a difficult subject because there (is, are) so many factors to consider.

22. The family (is, are) not likely to agree on how to divide Aunt Julia's property.

23. All of the ice (has, have) melted.

24. Two possibilities to solve the crisis (has, have) been proposed, but so far neither (has, have) been taken seriously.

25. Some of the committee (is, are) waiting for the President's nominee to explain his finances.

26. There (is, are) only the piano and one bed left to move.

27. Part of the logs (has, have) fallen off the pile.

28. The first two sections of the report (was, were) uninspiring.

29. The rest of the report, however, along with the drawings and photographs, (was, were) worth reading.

30. A third of the cookies (is, are) to go in a package for Lenny.

Chapter 40

Pronoun Agreement

This chapter deals with another agreement problem—agreement between pronouns and the things they refer to.

Pronouns and Antecedents

Pronouns replace nouns or other pronouns in sentences. A pronoun must have something to refer to—called the *antecedent* of the pronoun. Look for the antecedent for *his* in this sentence:

The boy found his dog.

Clearly, *his* refers to *boy,* so *boy* is the antecedent for *his.*

The grammar rule that students often find troublesome is this: *A pronoun must agree in number with its antecedent.* If the antecedent is singular, the pronoun must be singular; if the antecedent is plural, the pronoun must be plural.

Because the pronoun's number depends on the antecedent, our attention should be on problem antecedents. When the antecedent is simple, making the pronoun agree is a simple task. You wouldn't write this:

The *boys* looked for *his* books. (Assume all the boys are missing books.)

Boys is a plural antecedent, so you'd write this:

The *boys* looked for *their* books.

Yet, special problems do arise with two types of antecedents:

- indefinite pronoun antecedents
- compound antecedents

INDEFINITE PRONOUN ANTECEDENTS

The biggest headache connected with pronoun agreement occurs when the antecedent is an indefinite pronoun like *everyone* or *nobody*. We needn't be concerned here with all indefinite pronouns, but we must look at one problem group.

Singular Indefinite Pronouns

The following indefinite pronouns are singular and always require singular pronoun references:

each	everyone	everybody
either	someone	somebody
neither	anyone	anybody
another	no one	nobody
one		

The words formed from *-one* (like *everyone*) and from *-body* (like *everybody*) often seem to be plural, but they're not. Try thinking of them as if they had the word *single* in the middle, like this: *every-single-one* or *every-single-body*. Now they seem to be singular, which they really are.

An unusual mental block is associated with the indefinite pronouns above. Few people would write this:

Everyone *have* a coat.

Have just doesn't sound right following *everyone*. And for good reason. *Have* is plural, but *everyone* is singular.

Yet, often the same people who recognize *everyone* as a singular subject have trouble recognizing *everyone* as a singular antecedent. Far too often they write this:

Everyone *has their* coat.

Has, of course, is correct: the singular verb agrees with the singular subject. But plural *their* cannot refer to singular *everyone*. As illogical as this problem seems, it is still common.

Study these samples:

Wrong: Everyone wore *their* coat.

Correct: Everyone wore *his* coat.

Wrong: Nobody looked at *their* books.

Correct: Nobody looked at *his* books.

Avoiding Sexist References

You may be uneasy with the "correct" revisions above: often the *everyone* you are talking about refers to a mixed group of men and women, so *his* may seem inappropriate. You're right, of course.

Usage is changing, though in formal English the conventional use of *his* to refer to both sexes is still common. On the other extreme, some writers— particularly advertisers—are matching *their* with indefinite pronouns like *everyone*. Unfortunately, that solution would return us to the illogical agreement issue we just discussed.

So what's the solution? Well, fortunately there are a number of ways to avoid the sexist tone that comes from using only masculine pronouns— without having to match plural pronouns with singular antecedents.

Here are four techniques to avoid sexist pronoun references:

- You can use *his or her,* as in these sentences:

    No one can read his or her assignment.

    Everybody brought his or her book instead.

This technique works well for occasional references, but it will grow awkward and tiresome, attracting attention to itself, if you use it frequently.

- You can alternate between *his* or *her,* so readers can perceive a balance in your treatment of the sexes.

    No one can read his assignment.

    Everyone wore her coat.

Set together like this, the sentences seem silly, don't they? This technique is useful only in long works, where the writer can use masculine references in some passages and feminine references in others—but not close together. (For instance, this is a technique we've employed occasionally in this textbook.)

- You can avoid the problem altogether by omitting the pronouns whenever possible.

    Instead of this: Everyone wore his coat.

    Better: Everyone wore a coat.

    Instead of this: Each of the voters cast her ballot.

> Better: Each of the voters cast a ballot.
>
> • You also can avoid the problem by changing both antecedents and pronoun references to plural forms.
>
> Instead of this: Everyone wore his coat.
>
> Better: All wore their coats.
>
> Instead of this: Each of the voters cast her ballot.
>
> Better: All of the voters cast their ballots.
>
> For most writing, the last two methods are the techniques of choice. Considerate writers will avoid implying that the world has only masculine members (by avoiding such statements as "man's best friend is his dog"). They also will avoid implying that specific groups (such as teachers, lawyers, nurses, vice presidents, and so forth) have members of only one sex. A significant part of avoiding such gender-specific language is avoiding sexist pronoun references.

Similar problems occur with words like *each, either, neither, another,* and *one.* Usually, however, these pronouns are followed by a phrase beginning with *of* and ending with a plural noun, like these:

Each of the girls . . .

Either of the students . . .

Don't be fooled. The singular indefinite pronoun, not the word in the *of*-phrase, is the antecedent for a pronoun in the rest of the sentence.

Wrong: Each of the girls gave me *their* money.

Correct: Each of the girls gave me *her* money.

The pronoun refers to *each,* not to *girls.*

Wrong: Either of the students may bring *their* books.

Correct: Either of the students may bring *his or her* books.

His or her refers to *either,* not to *students.*

Better: Either of the students may bring the books.

COMPOUND ANTECEDENTS

Compound antecedents may be joined with *and, or,* or *nor.* And the antecedents themselves may be all singular, all plural, or a mixture of singular and plural. The rules for agreement depend on the various combinations of these factors.

• *Two or more antecedents joined by* **and** *require a plural pronoun.*

It makes no difference whether the antecedents are singular, plural, or mixed: the *and* makes the compound antecedent plural.

John and the other boy found *their* seats.

John and the other boys found *their* seats.

• *Plural antecedents joined by* **or** *or* **nor** *require a plural pronoun.*

Either the boys or the girls will clean *their* rooms first.

Neither the boys nor the girls want to clean *their* rooms.

• *Singular pronouns joined by* **or** *or* **nor** *require a singular pronoun.*

Either the dog or the cat will get *its* food first.

Neither the dog nor the cat will eat *its* food.

• *When* **or** *or* **nor** *joins a singular antecedent and a plural antecedent, the pronoun agrees with whichever antecedent it is closer to.*

Neither Freddy nor the other boys like *their* jobs. (The pronoun *their* agrees with *boys.*)

Neither the other boys nor Freddy likes *his* job. (*His* agrees with *Freddy.*)

A Reminder About Word Order and Agreement

"Neither the other boys nor Freddy likes his job" is technically correct, but it may seem awkward. The problem—as well as the solution—is the same as you saw with subject-verb agreement in the last chapter. The better choice is to put the plural portion of a singular-plural subject/antecedent set closer to both the verb and the pronoun reference: "Neither Freddy nor the other boys like their jobs."

EXERCISES

A. Circle the correct pronoun in each set of choices below.

1. Neither Albert nor Carlos could get (his, their) car started after the snow Thursday.

2. Each car that needs a new license must have (its, their) exhaust inspected.

3. Another of the men handed in (his, their) resignation today.

4. If anyone asks for me, tell (him, her, him or her, them) I'll be back in an hour.

5. Political action groups differ from political parties in (its, their) funding and purpose.

6. Janet and Ed spent (his, her, his or her, their) vacation in North Carolina again this year.

7. If Teresita or her sisters find the mistake, (she, they) will want to correct it.

8. Somebody will see (himself, herself, himself or herself, themselves) as the hero.

9. The jury is returning to the courtroom to announce (its, their) verdict.

10. Either the waiter or the waitress will seat you in (his, her, his or her, their) section.

11. One of the women pulled out (her, their) credit card to pay for the dinner.

12. Members of the steering committee will try to earn support for (his, her, his or her, their) positions.

13. Everybody said (he, she, he or she, they) enjoyed the new Vietnamese restaurant.

14. No one could believe it when Michele and her son arrived without (his, her, his or her, their) tickets.

15. Nancy and Edgar found (his, her, his or her, their) seats in the field house.

B. Correct errors in pronoun agreement in the following sentences.

1. Neither of the children can tie their shoes.

2. When our tour group arrived in London, I found my luggage, but neither Jerry nor Dennis could find their suitcases.

3. After Martin and Lars lay in the sun all day, each had badly burned their arms and legs.

4. Each of the women knew their assignments.

5. Everyone wants to get what is due him.

6. Neither Sue Ellen nor her aunt could find their gloves.

7. Economy and service may have been the garage's ideals in the beginning, but it won't do as the slogan today.

8. The Chamber of Commerce is seeking workers for their festival next Friday.

9. Myrna and Tina each knew her lines but neither knew their stand-in part.

10. Warfare and hunger savaged the people, but no one seemed able to stop it.

C. Revise the following sentences to eliminate the gender-specific language.

1. A successful businessman knows he has to work long hours.

2. One of the nurses tried to use her influence to convince the hospital management to modify the visitation rules.

3. Each soldier must have his pack ready for inspection tomorrow.

4. Everyone hopes he will win the lottery.

5. No vice president in the company will be willing to give up his personal parking place.

6. Each of the team members will replay the game in his mind tonight.

7. Can everyone finish his work on schedule?

8. The pilot is responsible for ensuring that his aircraft is serviceable before takeoff.

9. Each musician knows how to care for her instrument.

10. Every actor knew his lines.

Chapter 41

Passive Voice

Do you ever find yourself struggling with a passage you're reading even though you know all the words? Does the phrasing seem wordy and sort of backwards? Perhaps the passage is loaded with passive voice. Like most readers, you've come to expect sentences in the active voice, although you may not know what active and passive voice are.

Active and Passive Voice

"Voice" is a grammatical term for a particular form of a verb; it refers specifically to the relationship between the subject of a sentence and the *action* of the verb.

The natural order of the English sentence—actor-action-acted upon— requires *active voice,* as in the following:

Adam   *ate*   the *apple*.
(actor)   (action)   (acted upon)

The subject of the sentence is the actor, the one doing the eating.

Passive voice reverses this normal, expected order. The subject is no longer the actor; the new subject is acted upon, as in this *passive voice* sentence:

The *apple*   *was eaten*   by *Adam*.
(acted upon)   (action)   (actor)

Notice that the actor now appears after the verb, in a "by" prepositional phrase.

However, a passive voice sentence may not even name the actor, as in this version:

The *apple*   *was eaten.*
(acted upon)   (action)

The subject still is acted upon, but we no longer know the identity of the actor.

Comparing even the simple active and passive sentences above allows us to see some of the disadvantages of the passive voice:

- A passive construction is *more wordy* than an active one.
- Because it reverses the normal order of an action, passive voice is *indirect.*
- As its name implies, a "passive" verb *lacks the vigor* inherent in an active verb.
- And if the writer doesn't include the actor, the passive construction *may be vague.*

Passive Voice in Business and Technical Writing

Passive voice is one of the less desirable features of "bureaucratic writing" or "governmentese." Moreover, some business writers, particularly in technical fields, have developed the notion that eliminating the actor from a sentence—which often results in passive voice—will make their writing more objective. Don't be fooled. Passive constructions have a function, as we'll see later in this chapter, but usually the passive voice does more harm than good.

Why? In addition to the disadvantages of passive voice listed above, *passive constructions generate other awkward writing.* For example, if you look back at the exercises for modifiers in Chapter 38, you'll find a high incidence of passive voice attached to misplaced modifiers. Moreover, wordy sentences, such as ones beginning with *It is* and *There are* also often include passive voice.

Professional editors know to look for certain wording patterns when they attack an awkward passage. They know that addressing one or two easily recognizable structures is a quick way to get at the rest of the problems in a complex passage. Of course, passive voice is chief among those structures.

Let's look at an awkward piece of bureaucratic writing and see how an editor would work with it:

> There has been very little effort made by overextended police forces to attempt interdiction of drug shipments and processing laboratory destruction operations.
>
> The beginning of the sentence combines a passive construction (*has been . . . effort made by . . . forces*) with a *There are* type of opening. Revising to eliminate the passive construction fixes both voice and wordiness problems:
>
> > *Overextended police forces have done little* to attempt interdiction of drug shipments and processing laboratory destruction operations.
>
> Now the editor can focus on the wordiness and lack of parallelism in the rest of the sentence:
>
> > Overextended police forces have done little *to interdict drug shipments and destroy processing laboratories.*
>
> The revision is simpler and certainly more clear. Of course, an editor might begin revising at the end of the sentence. Yet, editors learn to attack the simple problems in a sentence first, and revising passive voice is an easy place to begin once you know how to recognize passive voice and deal with it.

RECOGNIZING PASSIVE VOICE

Identifying passive voice is really quite simple. Only a passive sentence will receive "yes" answers in all of the following tests:

- *Is the subject of the sentence acted upon?*

In our sample sentence, *apple,* the subject of the sentence, is acted upon (eaten) by Adam.

- *Does the sentence use a form of the verb* to be *followed by the kind of main verb that almost always ends in -ed or -en?*

The simple forms of *to be* are these: *is, am, are, was,* and *were.* Compound forms of *to be* use *be, being,* or *been* (for example, *will be, is being, has been*). Thus, passive verbs look like these: *is divided, was beaten,* and *will have been destroyed.* In our sample passive sentence, *was eaten* is the passive verb form.

- *If the actor appears in the sentence, is the actor in the prepositional phrase* by someone or something? *Or if the actor doesn't appear in the sentence, does the* sense *of the sentence imply* by someone or something?

"The apple was eaten by Adam" ends with *by Adam,* whereas "The apple was eaten" implies *by someone.*

Passive Voice and Past Tense

Don't confuse passive voice and past tense. They sound alike, but there is no essential connection between them. Both active and passive verb forms can appear in any number of tenses, as this sample shows:

Tense	Active Voice	Passive Voice
present	takes	is being taken
past	took	was taken
future	will take	will be taken

USING PASSIVE VOICE

You may have decided by now that the passive voice was created (by someone) merely to entrap you. Not so. In fact, passive constructions have legitimate uses:

- *Passive voice is useful when the object of the action is more important than the actor.*

Residents of Sandstone, Nevada, are afraid that a lethal gas manufactured in nearby Cactus Flower may someday poison them. They fear, for example, that the *lethal gas may be released* by a defective valve or a worn gasket.

The emphasis in the last sentence is clearly on the lethal gas. That is, the context of the passage makes the gas more important than the parts that might allow a leak. Only passive voice will allow the object of the action (lethal gas) to gain emphasis by appearing first in the sentence.

- *Because passive voice can hide the actor, it is useful when the actor is obvious, unimportant, or uncertain.*

For example, if we did not know who dropped a canister of gas, we might write this:

When a canister *was dropped,* a lethal gas enveloped the laboratory workers.

Passive Voice and Evasiveness

A strong warning is necessary here. Passive voice makes it all too easy for a writer to omit the "by" part of a thought; this evasiveness in particular is a mark of "bureaucratic writing." Imagine being told this:

Leave your application in the box. If you *are found* acceptable, you *will be notified.*

"By whom?" you want to demand. Omissions of the responsible individuals in statements like this frustrate and irritate readers.

Deciding when passive voice is a good choice requires some thought. You can stretch the justifications for its use to cover most sentences if you try hard enough. Therefore, keep in mind this general rule: *write with the active voice unless you have an excellent reason for using the passive.*

ACTIVATING THE PASSIVE

Far too often writers use passive voice because they can't think how to write the sentence in the active voice; in such cases, the passive is more accidental than intentional. You can prevent this lack of control in your own writing by learning the following three methods to convert passive voice into active:

- *Reverse the object and the subject.*

  Passive: An example *is shown* in Figure 3.

  Active: Figure 3 *shows* an example.

- *Delete the main verb, leaving the sentence with a form of* **to be** *as the only verb.*

  Passive: Your cousin *is seen* as the best candidate.

  Active: Your cousin *is* the best candidate.

- *Change the verb.*

  Passive: Jonathan *was given* a new book.

  Active: Jonathan *received* a new book.

If you learn to recognize the passive voice and determine to avoid the passive whenever you can, these three methods will provide you the tools you need to write simple, direct, and vigorous active sentences.

EXERCISES

A. Rewrite the following sentences to eliminate the passive voice. When necessary, supply the actors.

1. The mail carrier's leg was chewed by a small gray dog.

2. When the first stage of the building has been finished, the second stage may begin.

3. The second choice is viewed as the best option.

4. The bomb was left in the office building by a short, dark-haired man with a thin mustache.

5. A dark residue is left on the cleaning rag.

6. The greatest area coverage is offered by open-wire lines.

7. The processing plants are located in the north.

8. About 17,000 people are employed in research institutes.

9. The group is made up of several factions and fronts.

10. The State of the Union address will be delivered by the President tomorrow.

11. The pencil shaft is made of wood.

12. For once the rapist was caught before he could rape again.

13. Once the machine is started, you must not stop it.

14. If the hook is placed inside the eye, the door is secure.

15. Carbon dioxide is the most commonly used lasing medium in gas lasers.

16. Cracks in the foundation were not considered serious until the building collapsed.

17. Hundreds of balloons were released by children at the festival.

18. The Special Olympics were cancelled in our town when funds were not raised by the sponsors.

19. If the package is delivered in time, we will have the materials that are needed to begin work.

20. We regret to inform you that your medical records have been lost.

21. Opposition to the tax increase was voiced by a crowd of irate citizens.

22. If you are seen as best for the job, you will be notified tomorrow.

23. The news that a politician has been indicted by a federal grand jury no longer surprises us.

24. The end of the semester was welcomed by students and professors alike.

25. Four serious accidents have been caused at that corner by drunk drivers.

B. Each of the following sentences contains a number of writing problems that need to be corrected. Those problems include at least one passive construction per sentence. Revise the passive voice first and then see what else you can do to improve the sentences.

1. The plan was designed to expand the country's agricultural base with priority being placed on the coffee-growing and the forestry segments of the economy.

2. Until an indigenous capability to produce high-technology components is attained, the nation's electronics industry will remain backward in technology.

3. The organization of the supply system is deficient in great measure because it has been severely affected by corruption in the government and also in the industries as well.

4. The use of the same pistol in each attack may be the method used by the gang in order to authenticate its responsibilities for attacks to the authorities.

5. Nontraditional machining processes can be differentiated from traditional cutting and grinding processes because the nontraditional machining processes are characterized by higher power consumption and lower material removal rates than conventional machining methods.

Chapter 42

Word Choice

The French have a phrase that could be the title of this chapter. The phrase is *le mot juste,* and it means—roughly—"the right word." *Le mot juste* is often the difference between an A paper and a merely ordinary C paper—not just one good word, of course, but a lot of them. This chapter covers some basic and advanced techniques for finding those good words.

BASIC TECHNIQUES

Use Precise Words

What is a good word? Is it something really impressive, a big word that proves how educated we are? No, usually it's a word we all know. Unfortunately, even though it's a common word, we don't use it very often because we choose an even more common word instead. *See* is one of those more general words we might slap down in a rough draft. But think of all the more precise synonyms that might work better: *glimpse, gaze, stare, peer, spot,* and *witness.*

Let's take a longer example. Suppose you are reading a paragraph and run across these words:

The man walked into the room.

The words are so general they could fit into a number of strikingly different contexts:

The policeman, hidden behind a parked car, watched as *the man walked into the room.*

or

The Capitol guard smiled as *the man walked into the room.*

or

The class quieted somewhat as *the man walked into the room.*

or

The patients gasped as *the man walked into the room.*

"What a great clause!" you say. "I can use it anywhere." It's a lousy clause—you can use it anywhere. All the words are general, the kind of words that pop into your mind in a second.

Let's think a second longer and try to make the words more exact. Here are some possibilities:

man: thief, senator, English teacher, Dr. Rodney

walked: sneaked, hurried, sauntered, reeled

room: motel room, antechamber, classroom, office

Now let's rewrite that all-purpose clause using more specific words:

The policeman, hidden behind a parked car, watched as *the thief sneaked into my motel room.*

or

The Capitol guard smiled as the *senator hurried into the antechamber.*

or

The class quieted somewhat as *the English teacher sauntered into the classroom.*

or

The patients gasped as *Dr. Rodney reeled into his office.*

Each clause is better—and certainly more interesting—because the writer took the time to come up with just the right words. Try it yourself. Look for the dull, general words in your own writing and make them more specific. This technique is one of the best ways to improve your writing dramatically.

Beware of Peculiar Words

Don't become so obsessed with the idea of seeking different words that you choose them just because they're unusual. *Perambulate,* for example, means "to walk through," so we could write this:

The senator perambulated the antechamber.

Readers probably will notice the peculiarity of *perambulated* rather than its preciseness. Your goal is to get the right words—not just the unusual ones.

Use Modifiers

The second basic technique, in addition to using the right word, is to use modifiers. Sometimes nouns and verbs don't tell the whole story. To be really precise, you need to add some adjectives and adverbs. Let's work with one of the sentences we improved in the last section:

> The policeman, hidden behind a parked car, watched as the thief sneaked into my motel room.

From the clause we revised (*the thief sneaked into my motel room*), we can modify *thief, sneaked,* and *motel room.* Here are just a few possibilities:

We don't want to overload the sentence with modifiers, so let's just modify *thief* and *sneaked:*

> The policeman, hidden behind a parked car, watched as the furtive thief sneaked noiselessly into my motel room.

We've come a long way from "The man walked into the room," haven't we?

Beware of Piling On

If you watch football, you've seen teams penalized for "piling on"—when players jump onto a pile of tacklers and the ball carrier after the referee has blown the play dead.

Similarly, you need to beware of piling on modifier after modifier. You have to restrain your use of modifiers to what is relevant to accomplish your purpose—and no more. Only the writer and her mother could love this sentence:

> The diminutive, chunky, azure-eyed, eighteen-month-old baby boy toddled to his rocking horse.

ADVANCED TECHNIQUES

Use Comparisons

If you really want to get your readers' attention, use a comparison. It may be the most memorable part of your theme. Remember when we said transitions are like road signs? And when we said the blueprint for your paper is like the architect's design for the structure he plans to build? These and other comparisons really help your readers understand an idea.

Only one problem with comparisons: they're hard to think of, particularly good comparisons. We all can think of bad ones. The familiar phrases that come to mind almost automatically are clichés, and they are as bad as original comparisons are good. Consider this sentence:

> Although he was *blind as a bat,* Herman remained *cool as a cucumber* when he entered the arena.

See how clichés attract the wrong kind of attention to themselves? Hearing a cliché is like hearing a comedian go through the same routine time after time. After a while, nobody listens.

A good rule is that if you have heard a comparison before, don't use it. But do use original comparisons. Be daring. Try one in your next theme.

Replace General Ideas With Specific Samples

Here's something else to try in your next theme: when you want to use a general word that stands for an entire class of items—like *toys* or *vehicles* or *books*—use just one item from that class instead. Let the specific stand for the general.

Take this sentence:

> Inflation means that most Americans can hardly afford to eat, but some congressmen don't seem to care how much *food* costs.

Let's make the sentence a little more interesting by replacing the word *food* (an entire class of items) with *a loaf of bread* (one item from that class):

> Inflation means that most Americans can hardly afford to eat, but some congressmen don't seem to care how much *a loaf of bread* costs.

Here's another example:

> As a photographer she is limited. She may be able to take pictures of *nature,* but she can't take good pictures of people.

We can make the second sentence more interesting by changing the word *nature* to something more specific:

> As a photographer she is limited. She may be able to take pictures of *trees,* but she can't take good pictures of people.

See how the detail instead of the generality makes the sentence livelier?

Most college students don't use either of the advanced techniques in this section. Most of them don't get A's either. If you want to learn how to write an A paper, you might start by occasionally using a comparison or a specific word instead of a general one.

EXERCISES

A. Rewrite the following sentences two different ways, replacing the underlined general words with more precise words.

Example: The <u>official</u> <u>talked</u> to the <u>man</u>.
   a. The <u>district attorney</u> <u>grilled</u> the <u>arsonist</u>.
   b. The <u>manager</u> <u>congratulated</u> the <u>pitcher</u>.

1. The <u>animal</u> <u>ate</u> the <u>food</u>.

   a. _____

   b. _____

2. The <u>audience</u> <u>liked</u> the <u>show</u>.

   a. _____

   b. _____

3. The <u>group</u> <u>disliked</u> the <u>publication</u>.

   a. _____

   b. _____

4. The <u>worker</u> dropped the <u>tool</u>.

   a. _____

   b. _____

5. The <u>scientist</u> <u>talked about</u> her <u>invention</u>.

   a. _____

   b. _____

B. In each sentence below write a modifier in the blank. Make the modifier as colorful and specific as you can. Try to fit it into the context.

Example: The _____ policeman arrested the mayor.

Words like *short* and *young* may not help much. On the other hand, try these choices:

The *rookie* policeman arrested the mayor.

                    or

The *bitter* policeman arrested the mayor.

1. The _____ tiger stalked the gazelle.

2. The _____ woman flinched when the balloon popped.

3. The drunk staggered _____ through the museum.

4. The children were _____ when they toured the exhibition.

5. The gardener was surprised to find such a/an _____ worm on the end of her shovel.

6. My first year in college is a/an _____ experience.

7. The crowd shouted _____ as the diplomat's limousine passed by.

8. Seventeen of us piled into the _____ van.

9. The _____ author was really angry about the mistake in the first printing.

10. As the _____ safecracker gently touched the dial, the telephone suddenly rang.

C. We use comparisons every day, but too many of them are clichés, like "nervous as a cat on a hot tin roof" or "scared as a rabbit." For this exercise write one original comparison on any topic. (If you have trouble thinking of a topic, consider blind dates, a hobby, a famous person.)

_____

_____

_____

_____

D. List three chichés other than the ones we've used as examples. (Remember, clichés are bad. Avoid them like the plague.)

1. _____

2. _____

3. _____

E. Improve the sentences below by changing each italicized generalization to something more specific.

Example: Small movie houses that show film classics are going out of business. After all, who wants to pay *good money* to see *an old movie*?

Revision: Small movie houses that show film classics are going out of business. After all, who wants to pay *five dollars* to see *Humphrey Bogart*?

1. Television critics claim that viewers today are attracted to mindless programs, spending most of their time watching *situation comedies* and *sports*.

situation comedies: _____

sports: _____

2. Social critics claim that *many women's magazines* even today still depict women *in demeaning ways.*

   many women's magazines: _____

   in demeaning ways: _____

3. *A study* reported that *high-school students* could not identify where *some places are.*

   A study: _____

   high-school students: _____

   some places are: _____

4. *Moving* through the crowd, we constantly bumped into a *variety of people.*

   Moving: _____

   variety of people: _____

5. If you listen to radio today, all you hear is *music* and *people talking.*

   music: _____

   people talking: _____

Appendix

Theme Format

Incredible as it may seem, English instructors are just like you and me (well—maybe a little more like me). Like you, they're human and have their little eccentricities. For example, they think that if students have done a good job writing their themes, they'll also want to make them as neat as possible. Silly idea—or is it?

That idea also has its corollary: the student who writes a theme at the last minute probably doesn't take—doesn't even *have*—the time to make it neat.

The moral is clear: be neat so that your instructors think they're looking at an A paper before they've read even the first word. Here are some guidelines, although your instructors may wish to make some changes to suit individual preferences.

- *Handwriting or typing?* Look at the two sample papers that follow. Which one would you rather read? If you can type at all, then do so. The early papers are short enough that typing them shouldn't take very long. If you don't type, use either black or blue ink. Other colors are hard to read.

- *Typing or word processing?* Should you use a typewriter or a computer with a word processing program? The answer is easy: If you have a word processor, by all means use it. It has several overwhelming advantages over the typewriter:

  - You can make corrections easily. That means you're far more likely to engage seriously in the revising process.
  - With many programs, you can use a spelling checker. That means you'll not only correct words you've misspelled but correct typos, too. By helping with the technicalities, the word processor frees you to think about the larger, more important matters of writing. Be careful, though, because spelling checkers can't catch all errors—especially when your typo results in a legitimate word.

- Most important from our point of view, the word processor helps you get words on paper easily in the first place—especially if you can compose at the keyboard. People who have become comfortable with this method know that it is one of the primary benefits of the word processor, and often they refuse to write any other way.

- *Proofreading*   Do it—*always*, but especially if you type, and even if you use a spelling checker with a word processor. Otherwise, you might be surprised by what your magic fingers did the night before.

- *Paper*   If you type, use standard-sized (8-½ by 11 inch) typing paper. For a standard typewriter, the erasable kind is especially good because you can make corrections easily. However, most instructors don't like to receive work on erasable paper because it's hard to write on. You can overcome this problem by typing on erasable paper and then making a photocopy to hand in. Do not use thin "onionskin" paper.

  For a word processor, erasing isn't required, so stick to a reasonably heavy bond paper (20-lb. paper, a good weight, is readily available in both separate sheets and continuous form, for tractor-feed printers).

  If you don't type or use a word processor, find a standard-sized tablet or pad of high-quality, lined theme paper. Don't use ordinary notebook paper (or paper torn from a spiral notebook) unless your instructor approves.

- *Corrections*   On a short assignment (like the one-paragraph essay), avoid handing in a paper with obvious corrections. If, however, you're torn between making a correction at the last minute or handing in a neat paper, of course make the correction. What good is a neat error?

- *Spacing*   If you're typing, double-space except where format requirements call for different spacing. If you're writing by hand, write on every other line.

- *Margins*   Allow an inch on the top, left, right, and bottom. On page one, begin the identification block (see below) one inch from the top of the page, quadruple-space (double-spaced twice) to find the line for the title, and then quadruple-space again to find where to begin the first line of your paper. (The comments on the pages facing the sample research paper in Chapter 19 discuss format requirements for students who need to follow MLA page layout guidance.)

- *Page numbers*   Don't number the first page, but do count it as page one. For other pages, use Arabic numerals (2, 3, 4, etc.) and put the number in the upper right-hand corner, ½ inch from the top of the page and in line with the right margin. (Chapter 19 shows the MLA format, which uses a somewhat different pagination style for the research paper.)

- *Identification*   Put your name, your instructor's name, the course number, and the date in the upper left-hand corner of page one, one inch from the top of the page. Your instructor may direct you to put this information on a title page for your research paper.

- *Fastening the paper*   Unless your instructor directs you to put your paper in a binder, use a stapler to fasten pages together. Paper clips are fine in theory, but in a stack of themes they tend to clip themselves onto other themes.

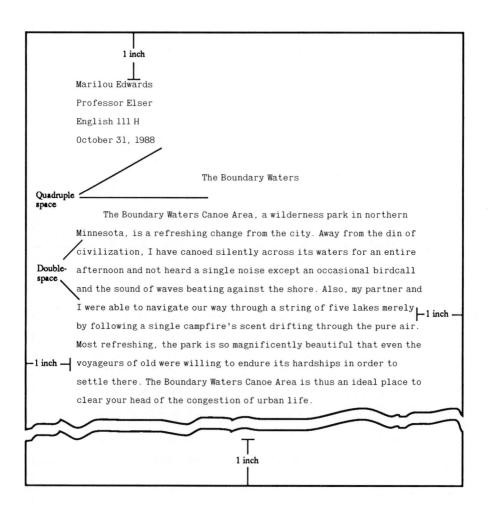

1 inch

Marilou Edwards

Professor Elser

English 111 H

October 31, 1988

The Boundary Waters

Quadruple space

The Boundary Waters Canoe Area, a wilderness park in northern Minnesota, is a refreshing change from the city. Away from the din of civilization, I have canoed silently across its waters for an entire **Double- space** afternoon and not heard a single noise except an occasional birdcall and the sound of waves beating against the shore. Also, my partner and I were able to navigate our way through a string of five lakes merely by following a single campfire's scent drifting through the pure air. Most refreshing, the park is so magnificently beautiful that even the voyageurs of old were willing to endure its hardships in order to settle there. The Boundary Waters Canoe Area is thus an ideal place to clear your head of the congestion of urban life.

1 inch

1 inch

1 inch

Marilou Edwards
English 111 H
Professor Elser
October 31, 1988

The Boundary Waters

The Boundary Waters Canoe Area, a wilderness park in northern Minnesota, is a refreshing change from the city. Away from the din of civilization, I have canoed silently across its waters for an entire afternoon and not heard a single noise except an occasional bird call and the sound of the waves beating against the shore. Also, my partner and I were able to navigate our way through a string of five lakes merely by following a single campfire's scent drifting through the pure air. Most refreshing, the park is so magnificently beautiful that even the voyageurs of old were willing to endure its hardships in order to settle there. The Boundary Waters Canoe Area is thus an ideal place to clear your head of the congestion of urban life.

Index